THE ESSENTIAL
SAN JUAN
ISLANDS
G U I D E

2nd Edition

NOW WITH 1999 LODGING UPDATES,
INCLUDING WEB PAGE AND
E-MAIL ADDRESSES
(See pages 273 – 280)

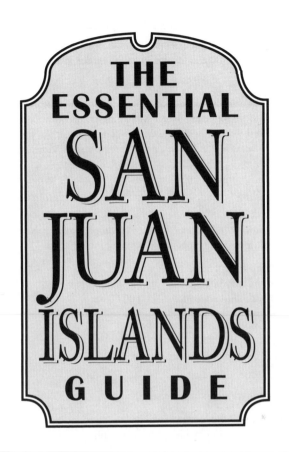

THE ESSENTIAL SAN JUAN ISLANDS GUIDE

2nd Edition

Marge & Ted Mueller

© 1996 by Marge and Ted Mueller

First edition, May 1994
Second edition, March 1996
Second printing, second edition, March 1997

JASI
P.O. Box 313
Medina, Washington 98039
(206) 454-3490

Printed in the United States of America

Cover and book design by Marge Mueller
Production and typesetting by Gray Mouse Graphics

All photos by the authors except as noted

Cover photos: *top ,* The formal garden at Roche Harbor Resort; *center,* A Washington State ferry near Lopez Island; *bottom,* Friday Harbor. Back cover photo: Kayaks on Orcas Island.
Frontispiece: The lighthouse at Lime Kiln State Park on San Juan Island

Mueller, Marge
     Essential San Juan Islands guide / Marge & Ted Mueller. -- 2nd ed.
        p. cm.
     Includes index.
     ISBN 1-881409-15-5
     1. San Juan Islands (Wash.)--Guidebooks. I. Mueller, Ted.
II. Title
F897.S2M77 1996
917.97'74--dc20   96-14422
                                    CIP

Contents

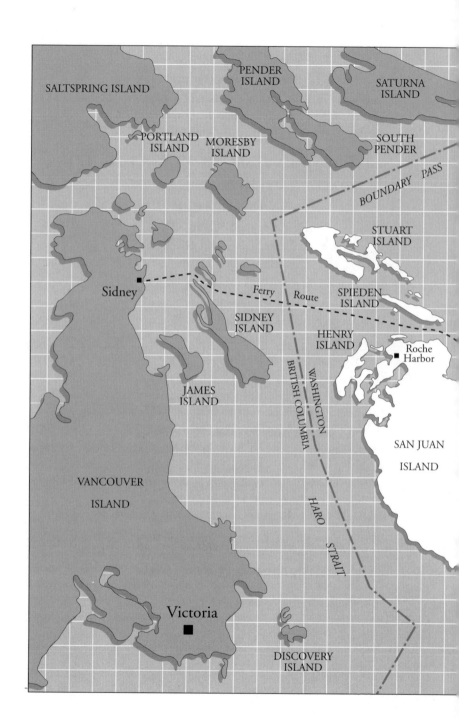

SALTSPRING ISLAND

PENDER ISLAND

SATURNA ISLAND

PORTLAND ISLAND

MORESBY ISLAND

SOUTH PENDER

BOUNDARY PASS

STUART ISLAND

Sidney

Ferry Route

SPIEDEN ISLAND

SIDNEY ISLAND

HENRY ISLAND

Roche Harbor

BRITISH COLUMBIA

WASHINGTON

JAMES ISLAND

VANCOUVER ISLAND

SAN JUAN ISLAND

HARO STRAIT

Victoria

DISCOVERY ISLAND

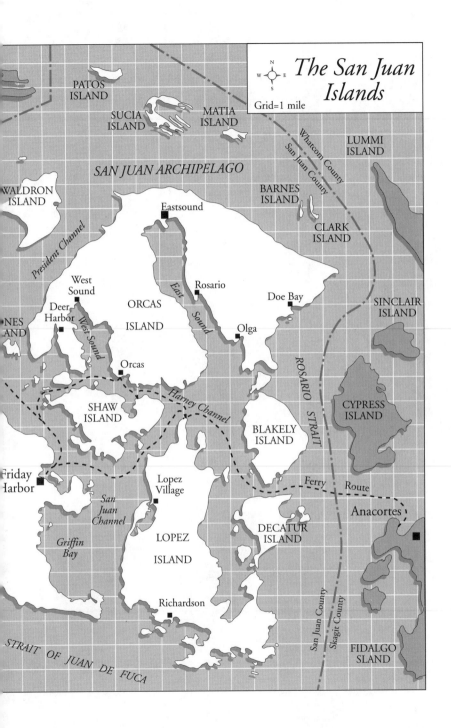

PATOS
ISLAND

SUCIA
ISLAND

MATIA
ISLAND

The San Juan Islands

N
W E
S

Grid=1 mile

LUMMI
ISLAND

SAN JUAN ARCHIPELAGO

Whatcom County
San Juan County

WALDRON
ISLAND

BARNES
ISLAND

CLARK
ISLAND

Eastsound

President Channel

West
Sound

Deer
Harbor

ORCAS

ISLAND

East Sound

Rosario

Doe Bay

Olga

SINCLAIR
ISLAND

NES
AND

West Sound

Orcas

ROSARIO STRAIT

CYPRESS
ISLAND

SHAW
ISLAND

Harney Channel

BLAKELY
ISLAND

Friday
Harbor

Lopez
Village

*San
Juan
Channel*

*Griffin
Bay*

LOPEZ

ISLAND

Ferry Route

Anacortes

DECATUR
ISLAND

Richardson

San Juan County
Skagit County

FIDALGO
SLAND

STRAIT OF JUAN DE FUCA

9

Preface

ISLAND. FANTASY ISLAND, Treasure Island, Gilligan's Island. Just the word "island" conjures up visions of romantic getaways, vacation retreats, or childhood escapes. The San Juans are just such a mystical destination—remote, unknown, mysterious. There's no denying they'd be far less alluring if they were plunked down in the middle of eastern Washington, or even California, with a freeway leading into their heart.

The very remoteness of the islands, their mystery, poses a number of logistical problems. Unless you are willing to place your fate (and your hard earned two-week vacation) in the hands of the gods, you still get caught up in the mundane: Where do I stay? Where do I eat? What's there to do? And even the most practical question of all: How do I get there?

Fifteen years ago we wrote a book called *The San Juan Islands, Afoot and Afloat*. It was—and still is—a bestseller, presently in its third edition. That book covers all the public parks, public nooks and crannies, and recreational possibilities in the San Juans. However, over the years we have received countless inquiries from people wanting the general commercial information that you need if you're not planning to be mostly self-sufficient in the San Juans.

This book gives you the tourist facts necessary to make use of any of the services the islands provide. It contains detailed information on resorts, motels, hotels, and bed and breakfast inns; lists of boat tours and charter services; transportation options; keen places to shop; and restaurant descriptions. Along with these you'll find mention of the various festivals, fairs, and other events that occur in the islands year-round. Public and private campgrounds and parks are included here, as well as youth camps.

It is our hope that this book, a companion volume to our first one, will help you plan your trip to the San Juans and add to your enjoyment of these endlessly enchanting islands.

—*Marge and Ted Mueller*

Opposite: *Cyclists leave the ferry at Shaw Island.*

Friday Harbor on San Juan Island

Introduction

THE STATE OF WASHINGTON curves inward at its far northwest corner, thrust back nearly 100 miles by a watery arm of the Pacific Ocean. Within this coastal embrace lie the San Juan Islands—a cluster of several hundred rocks, reefs, and by-gosh good-sized islands that are year-round home for around 10,000 people. To this remote destination flock several hundred thousand visitors each year.

What draws these people, and why do many return year-after-year, like pilgrims to their personal Mecca? Recreation certainly is one answer. Nearly every type of boating flourishes here—sailing, cruising, kayaking, canoeing—as well as other water-related pleasures such as fishing, clam digging, crabbing, scuba diving, and beachcombing. Camping, picnicking, hiking, bicycling, horse riding, sightseeing, birdwatching, wildlife viewing...the recreation list goes on and on.

The unparalleled beauty of rocky shores, forest-draped hills, pastoral valleys, caressing mists, and rose-tinged sunsets brings those who seek nourishment for their souls. Tranquillity draws others to shoreside resorts where the soft lap of waves and cries of sea birds replace jarring telephone rings and computer beeps. The pace is clearly slowed, even in the islands' few small villages, where at the height of the tourist season a dog can snooze undisturbed on a sunny sidewalk, and the major excitement is the coming and going of the ferry.

STEP UP & TAKE A BOW, SAN JUAN ISLANDS

As far as basic statistics go, the San Juan archipelago covers an area some 25 by 30 miles. Of its several hundred islands, islets, rocks, and reefs (some of which disappear at high tide), fewer than 200 are named, and of these, only a handful have the size and potable water necessary to make them habitable.

Through the island group thread the Washington State ferries, nosing into landings at the four major islands: Lopez, Shaw, Orcas, and San Juan. San Juan and Orcas islands are just a bit under 60 square miles of land each, Lopez is about half that size, and Shaw is a scant 7¾ square miles. Roads run the length of the ferry-served islands, and circle their edges, but you'll find no four-lane highways here, and not a single traffic light. Villages on San Juan, Orcas, and Lopez have restaurants, lodging, and shops. Your car will get you around any of these places, but a bicycle or moped will serve as well, if you're of the athletic bent.

The San Juans were once heavily agricultural, providing grain and fruit to Washington markets. However, irrigation of huge areas of arid land in the eastern part of the state made it impossible for this tiny corner to compete; today most locally grown produce is sold right here on the islands, and tourism has replaced farming as the economic mainstay.

A good reason for the islands' popularity is their balmy weather. The massive bulk of Vancouver Island and the Olympic Mountains to the west frequently cause storms and cold weather to be shunted north or south. The sun shines an average of nearly 250 days a year, and the average annual rainfall is only 29 inches; Friday Harbor residents can be basking in sunshine when Seattleites are popping up umbrellas. Temperatures range in the 70s during the day in summer, rarely rising to the 80s. Summer evenings may occasionally call for a light sweater. Spring arrives early, and fall lingers late; these may well be the best times of all to visit the islands, as the heavy crush of tourists is gone. Residents are even more friendly and relaxed off-season, and ferries are uncrowded.

Year-round residents are ordinary folk—farmers, shopkeepers, fishermen, doctors, and lawyers. There are a lot of resident retirees who see the casual pace and mild climate as the ideal antidote to years in the rat race. You'll also find a good many artists, craftspersons, and authors who nurture their creative muse in the tranquil islands. Ernest Gann, who wrote books such as *The High and the Mighty,* lived here until his recent death. You'll find these islanders uncommonly friendly, although their patience may be tested by the summer onslaught of tourists.

WILD THINGS

The variety of wildlife is a remarkable feature of the San Juan Islands. There's ample wildlife to excite the most ardent binocular-wielding nature lover. Often you'll see seals and sea lions on reefs and rocky shores, and otters in quiet coves. Deer frequently appear at dusk in orchards, meadows, and parks, and if you don't take care of your campsite groceries you are almost assured of being visited by raccoons.

Throughout the islands you'll see the likenesses of orca whales on T-shirts, coffee mugs, mailboxes, and postcards everywhere—you'll think they are the local logo. If you're lucky, you'll even see live ones! Three resident orca family groups, known as "pods," totaling about 80 individuals, have been identified in Puget Sound waters. Orcas (sometimes called killer whales) are most frequently seen in the San Juans, making the area a destination for wildlife watchers. The Whale Hotline, operated by the Whale Museum in Friday Harbor, tracks the movements of the pods for research purposes. Tour boat operators utilize this information to give their clients a reasonable chance of seeing these magnificent mammals. Dolphins, minke whales, and gray whales also may be sighted.

The islands are a mecca for bird lovers. Around 300 different species of birds have been identified in the San Juans. Because the archipelago lies on the Pacific Flyway, hundreds of thousands of migratory birds pass through

Whale watching excursions for orcas, such as these shown in President Channel, are popular in the San Juans.

here annually, and some species use the offshore islands as breeding and nesting sites. To protect these sea birds, 84 of the rocks, reefs, and islands have been designated as the San Juan Islands National Wildlife Refuge. Glaucous-winged gulls, cormorants, pigeon guillemots, and rhinoceros auklets are among the predominant species.

Land-based birds include spectacular bald eagles; some 50 pairs are year-round residents, nesting in tall snags throughout the islands. They represent about one-third of the total number of breeding pairs in the entire country, outside of Alaska. Golden eagles and osprey are also seen, and some nest here as well. Other birds of prey include hawks, harriers, owls, and even vultures.

Beaches, marshes, thickets, and meadows host even more birds, ranging from great blue herons to wrens and wild turkeys. Wild turkeys? Yes. They were introduced in the San Juans some years ago, and have thrived; visitors are sometimes startled to spot them foraging along the roadside.

Sea life is yet another highlight of the islands. It is so abundant and so unique that all of the shores and the entire seabed of the San Juan archipelago, along with nearby Cypress Island, have been designated as a marine biological sanctuary. The University of Washington's laboratories at Friday Harbor are dedicated to studying this habitat. The taking or killing of any marine life, except for food use, is strictly prohibited.

Scuba divers and beachcombers congregate here to view this vast natural aquarium. Rocky undersea walls and tidepools are plastered with rainbow-hued anemones, sea stars, and all manner of curious creatures. Old pilings collect barnacles and tube worms that extend delicate tentacles to capture free-floating plankton. Clams, abalone, mussels, shrimp, sea urchins, and—the gourmet's favorite—Dungeness crab attract modern-day foragers who come with buckets, shovels, and trap-like "pots" in quest of food for the dinner table.

Eager anglers drop lines from boats at reefs, shoals, and current-swept points for salmon and bottomfish that feed on the rich habitat. Commercial fishing (primarily for salmon) was once an economic mainstay of the San Juans; however, largely due to depleted runs, the industry is now much reduced. Sport fishing, fortunately, remains some of the best to be found in the state, and for many visitors it is the prime reason for coming here. Numerous fishing charters operate out of San Juan harbors or nearby mainland ones.

You'll Want to Know...

OUR GOAL IN WRITING this book, which provides information on San Juan facilities, is to help visitors plan their visit to the islands, and more fully enjoy their stay once they arrive. We have not attempted to give a "rating" to any business listed. We recognize that different people are looking for different things in lodgings, restaurants, charters, tours, or even shopping; therefore we try primarily to give a complete, accurate picture so readers can best choose what suits their needs.

Because of the islands' remoteness, reaching them takes a little planning. Most visitors opt for the Washington State ferry. Others pilot their own boats or charter them off-island. Some people drop in via airplane, enjoying the scenic view en route. Several airlines have regularly scheduled runs with small planes, and charters are also available. Various transportation options are covered in other chapters of this book.

In this book most facilities are grouped by island, although some off-island listings and general categories of information are listed. We have tried to include establishments that would be of interest to visitors to the islands.

Any business community has a range of turnovers. Sadly, this is especially true of the San Juans, which is dependent on the seasonal vagaries of the tourist industry. Because of this, although we have made every effort to include current information, some of the businesses researched may not be operating by the time this book reaches bookstores, and new ones may have sprung up. Accommodations tend to be relatively stable, and long-established restaurants that have solved the problem of off-season survival, will still be there.

HOURS & SEASONS

In our descriptions of businesses we have not included specific hours or seasons for most of the businesses because they often change radically from season to season, and can even vary by the weather or personal needs of the owner. In most cases stores are open daily from 10 A.M. to 5 or 6 P.M. from July through September. For restaurants, we have indicated which meals are served, although this, too, can change by season. Before planning to dine at a favorite restaurant or visit a particular shop, it is wise to call to check their current hours.

In April, May, and June businesses are just beginning to gear up for the tourist season, and in October they gear down; some will be open only on weekends, or their hours will be shortened. From Thanksgiving through the end of February a lot of restaurants and stores shut their doors completely; however, if you are visiting during that time, you won't have any difficulty finding lodging, and there are always enough businesses and restaurants open providing service to the year-round residents that you'll be able to meet your basic needs.

If you're looking for a real away-from-it-all vacation, off-season is the time to go. You'll be able to write the Great American Novel or relax to near-oblivion as the islands settle into a cocoon-like state, waiting for spring and their beautiful "butterfly" stage.

Rates & Prices (& Taxes)

Any time of year, but especially in summer, you will find prices for many goods and services range a bit higher in the San Juans than on the mainland. Because little is produced locally, virtually everything on the islands, from toilet paper to tractors, must be brought in by boat or small plane, adding to their cost.

In this book we do not include prices or rates for individual businesses such as boat charters or restaurants because these change from season to season and year to year. Additionally, most businesses have a range of fees, depending on the client's needs. We have included general price ranges where we felt readers would want this information to help them make plans. A phone call to any of the listings will give you their current rates, as well as any added information you may want.

A general range of prices is indicated for restaurants:

$	Inexpensive	Most dinner entrées under $8
$$	Moderate	Most dinner entrées $8 to $15
$$$	Expensive	Most dinner entrées $15 and up

Non-Washington residents will want to know that the state sales tax is 7.2 percent. There is an additional 0.4 percent county tax in the San Juans.

Sales tax is not levied on food purchased in grocery stores, or on prescription drugs. It is levied on the following:

> Beer, wine, soft drinks sold in grocery stores
> Non-food grocery items such as soap and toilet tissue
> Goods such as clothing, non-prescription drugs, sundries, newspapers
> Food and beverages served in restaurants (or even at the corner latté stand)
> Lodging

Any applicable taxes are already included in the price of:

> Packaged hard liquor purchased in a state-owned liquor store
> Entertainment (boat tours, theater tickets)
> Fuel (including marine fuel)
> Ferry fares
> Boat charters
> Airplane fares or charters
> Boat moorage

LODGING

Island lodgings usually have a range of accommodations and facilities, and an accompanying variety of prices. We have indicated the low to high range of facilities. Prices quoted are summer rates, double occupancy, unless otherwise indicated, and are subject to change. Some establishments have hide-a-beds available for additional occupants at a very reasonable charge. Off-season rates generally are lower by 10 or 20 percent, or the second day will be offered at a significant reduction.

A few lodgings are within walking distance of the ferry. Many of those that are farther away will pick you up at the ferry, the airport, or even your marina. If you need transportation, inquire when you make your reservation. Lopez, Orcas, and San Juan islands have taxi services. A few facilities have rental cars or bicycles available for your use on the island.

Both Orcas Island and San Juan Island have bed and breakfast associations that maintain a hotline in the summer. If you are unable to find lodging, or arrive and find the space you've reserved is not suitable for your needs, they will try to find a spot for you. They are dedicated to helping innkeepers deliver the best possible service in the highest quality inns. Be aware that there are times when absolutely everything is filled.

Lopez Island does not maintain a hotline, but general information on

Tower House Bed and Breakfast is one of the many charming inns on San Juan Island.

lodging can be obtained from the Chamber of Commerce. The numbers are:

Bed and Breakfast Association of San Juan Island
P.O. Box 3016; Friday Harbor, WA 98250; phone – (360) 378-3030;
web: http://www.pacificrim.net/~bydesign/bb.html

Orcas Island Chamber of Commerce Innkeeper's Hotline
Phone – (360) 376-8888

Lopez Island Chamber of Commerce
Phone – (360) 468-3663

In addition, a phone tree offers a wealth of information about San Juan Island. By working your way through the directory you can find current information about such things as accommodations, restaurants, and activities. To reach it, call (360) 378-TREE (378-8733).

WEDDINGS & HONEYMOONS IN THE SAN JUANS

What spot could be more romantic for either a wedding or honeymoon than the gorgeous San Juans? Wedding guests will especially enjoy it, as they can combine your festivities with a personal weekend getaway. Book well in advance and inform your guests, so those planning to stay over can get lodging reservations.

Numerous restaurants have banquet rooms, special facilities, and catering for bridal parties. In addition, there are catering companies that specialize in weddings and group gatherings. If you have a spirit of adventure, consider an unconventional nuptial spot—the top of Mount Constitution, Lime Kiln State Park (maybe whales will cavort offshore), or a charter boat. Before planning a wedding in any public spot, be sure to check with the proper authorities regarding any restrictions.

Most San Juan lodgings will do weddings, although you will need to plan well in advance, as they tend to be heavily booked with regular customers during the summer. Some have catering facilities on hand; others can suggest local sources. The skilled staffs at both Rosario Resort and Roche Harbor Resort will assist you in planning a memorable wedding at their facilities. Lodgings that are especially popular for weddings are the Mariella Inn on San Juan Island, and Chestnut Hill Inn on Orcas Island, with its romantic little chapel nearby.

Some Northwest couples have their wedding on the mainland, and then escape to one of the island's exquisite bed and breakfast inns or resorts for romantic seclusion. Several lodgings have honeymoon suites and offer special packages.

In Friday Harbor, the friendly personnel at the San Juan Info Center on the second deck at Friday's Marketplace, next to the ferry landing will assist you in planning and arranging your activities in the San Juans. They have current information and contacts for all types of recreational and tourist activities—camping, transportation rentals, boat charters, kayaking, hiking, restaurants, whale watch tours, art galleries, and more. You can contact them at:

San Juan Info Center
P.O. Box 2809; Friday Harbor, WA 98250; phone – (360) 378-8887

ABOUT PETS

For some people, pets are an integral part of their family, and pets accompany them on car or boat trips. If you bring Bowser to the San Juans, be forewarned that by county ordinance dogs must be confined or kept on a leash in rural areas. The meeting of city dogs with country cows or sheep has at times had very tragic results—generally for the livestock. By law, any unlicensed dog roaming free in rural areas may be shot.

Also, some accommodations do not allow pets. If you wish to stay the weekend in a lovely B&B, or go on one of the wildlife cruises, several boarding kennels offer excellent animal care. Consider one of the following rather than miss a wonderful opportunity:

Animal Inn
497 Boyce Road; Friday Harbor, WA 98250; phone – (360) 378-4735

Eastsound Kennels
Route 1, Box 78H; Eastsound, WA 98245; phone – (360) 376-2410

Kensington Kennels
1811-E Roche Harbor Road; Friday Harbor, WA 98250;
phone – (360) 378-5432

Meg's Home and Animal Care
P.O. Box 1493; Friday Harbor, WA 98250; phone – (360) 378-4917

Sunnyhill Kennels and Cattery
601 Summit Park Road; Anacortes, WA 98221; phone 293-3434

SHOPPING

This book focuses on stores that will be of the most interest to visitors. We have noted businesses that are open only at limited times, although hours may vary from summer to winter for all stores. Shops are listed alphabetically, by island. For ease in locating a particular shopping category, consult the index for facilities by type.

As any shop-o-holic knows, the joy of browsing through stores is in finding that unique "something" that you might not find elsewhere, happening on an especially good buy, or celebrating your visit with an item that embodies the particular character of the spot. Beyond the usual souvenir T-shirts, post cards, and salt and pepper shakers there are specialty items that draw shoppers to the islands.

Fine art and crafts. Many artists make their home in the islands. Look for top-notch paintings, limited edition art prints, gallery photographs, stained glass, pottery, porcelain, sculpture, wood crafts, metalwork, furniture, handmade musical instruments, and jewelry. You may discover unusual items such as baskets woven from dried kelp and chairs fashioned from driftwood, or unique media such as papier-mâché. Many artists rely on local shops to sell their goods, although some artist's studios are open for retail business year-round, or at least during summer months. San Juan Island has an artists' studio open house annually, where you may purchase work directly from the artists.

Friday's Marketplace on San Juan Island has numerous interesting shops.

Fiber arts. Sheep, llamas, and alpacas are raised on the San Juans, and yarn spun from their wool finds its way into local studios and shops. However, because the islands' source is not adequate or varied enough to support

NORTHWEST FLAVOR

I f you're from Connecticut or Chattanooga, what do you shop for that embodies the islands or the Pacific Northwest? Wind kites (flag-like wind socks adapted from Japanese fish kites) are usually fashioned from brightly colored nylon, and are very popular. You'll find them representing nearly everything from ladybugs and pansies to dragons or rainbows. Boaters love to tie them on their rigging to trail colorfully in the wind. They also look great on a patio or in a child's room.

Seagulls, seashells, starfish, and other nautical gewgaws are in abundance. They may not hold much fascination if you already live in a seacoast city, but if you're from the Midwest they'll certainly be a nice remembrance of your trip. The most special treasures from the ocean are glass ball fishing floats, sometimes still carrying vestiges of rope netting. These floats can range from several inches to a couple of feet in diameter. At one time Japanese fishermen used these to support their nets; the balls frequently turned up on Washington beaches. Because they are no longer in use, it is extremely rare to find them on the shore, but you may see them in some stores. Imitations are also for sale; they're nice to buy as a souvenir, but don't be misled by thinking they're the real thing.

Anything with an orca whale is popular, but it can't be just any whale, it's got to be one of those majestic black and white mammals. With the advent of the "Free Willy" movies (which, by the way, were filmed here in the San Juans and nearby British Columbia), there's more orca motif paraphernalia than ever before, especially for kids. San Juan Islanders' like to call these whales their own, even though they roam throughout most of the northern hemisphere.

You'll find salmon-decor items everywhere, and in everything from pillows to pot holders to women's purses and men's ties. The perfect item for the fish lover!

And finally, anything with a ferryboat motif attracts buyers. Christmas tree ornaments, posters, pot holders, and children's toy ferries are a few of the renditions for sale in shops throughout the islands.

the prolific work of local fiber artists, raw materials are also imported. You'll find tapestries, rugs, soft sculpture, and unique "wearable art." If you're a knitter or weaver, you'll revel in stores that are cornucopias filled with feather-soft skeins of yarn.

Northwest Indian art. Early Northwest Indian culture developed a unique, exceptionally powerful art style, utilizing natural and symbolic forms blended in a complex imagery. Totem poles are the most commonly recognized representatives of this art. Small versions of totem poles can be found for sale; however, you'll also discover wonderful carved boxes, masks, sculptures, paintings, and prints utilizing Northwest Indian art forms. Some of the art found in shops is done by tribal members, other pieces are by non-Indians with a good knowledge of the art form. Some modern artists incorporate Northwest Indian motifs in contemporary paintings or sculptures. There are also "knock-offs," although even an inexpensive foreign-made totem pole makes an interesting souvenir. If you're looking for a collector's item, we recommend you have a knowledge of the art, and in addition look for a certificate of authenticity.

Antiques. The inveterate antiquer will love poking into corners of the several shops on the islands. You may find a broader selection on the mainland, but there are some excellent buys here—besides you'll have the fun of a trip down nostalgia lane.

Food and drink. Numerous "cottage industry" food producers thrive on the islands. Look in gift shops and grocery stores for local brands of island-grown jellies and preserves. There's a local brand of coffee (not grown here, of course, but locally roasted). An excellent mini-brewery and two local wineries have their fans. Fresh and dried herbs and herb-flavored vinegars come from local herb farms. Several tartar sauces, salsas, and other condiments are locally made with loving care. Any of these items make an excellent souvenir to take back home—and an excellent reason to return.

Lopez Village, Eastsound, and Friday Harbor all have Saturday farmers' markets in the summer, where you can buy locally-grown produce, garden plants, cut flowers, and fresh-baked goods, as well as the work of local artisans. You never know exactly what you'll find, because the selection varies. It's a terrific way to sample the bounty of the islands, as well as to chat with the people who produce it. The location of the market may change from year to year, but you'll usually find it near the center of town.

Seafood. Salmon, Dungeness crab, clams, mussels, oysters, shrimp, abalone—there's no denying these are locally "grown." In Friday Harbor you

YOU'LL WANT TO KNOW...

can buy fresh salmon right at the docks, and fresh steamed crab, clams, and shrimp are usually available as well. If you're not from the Northwest and have never had local Dungeness crab, don't miss it. It's the best crab in the world.

You'll find fresh seafood in the grocery stores, too. Local people know top quality seafood, and no merchant would consider offering anything but the best. Some stores will pack it in ice or dry ice and ship it for you, guaranteeing that it will arrive fresh. You'll also find locally smoked or canned seafood—another excellent gift.

Books. Statistics say that Northwesterners read more books per capita than any place else in the US (must be those gray winter days). They also write a lot of them. Island bookstores carry an extensive selection of those of local interest, or by local authors. You'll find gorgeous volumes of photography picturing local scenery.

TENNIS & GOLF

If you want to make tennis part of your vacation, you should stay at Rosario on Orcas Island or Roche Harbor on San Juan Island. Both resorts have courts for the use of their guests.

An excellent public tennis court is on Orcas Island at Buck Park, on the north side of the Orcas Island High School. To reach it, drive north out of Eastsound on either Lover's Lane or North Beach Road and turn east on Mount Baker Road. You'll find the tennis court in about a mile, on the south side of the road. The facility is used by the high school, so it may be busy during the time school is in session. A path for jogging and bicycling runs along the side of the road.

On San Juan Island the excellent courts at Friday Harbor High School, at 45 Blair Avenue are available for public use.

Public golf courses on the three major islands are:

Lopez Island Golf Club
Airport Road; Lopez Island, WA 98261; phone – (360) 468-2679

This 9-hole, par 33 golf course sits on the southwest side of Lopez Island, near the airport. The 40-acre public facility enjoys a pastoral setting. Hawks nest nearby, and deer sometimes roam the fairways.

Because the course is lightly played, you don't need reservations. Only the tee boxes and greens are irrigated; by late summer the fairways can become very dry. The clubhouse, which is open from March to October, has golfing supplies, as well as rental clubs and pullcarts. Off-season green fees are paid on an "honor system."

How to get there: Drive south from Lopez Landing and in 2 miles turn west on Fisherman Bay Road. Continue to Lopez Village and follow the road as it curves south around Fisherman Bay. At 7¼ miles from the ferry landing, head west on Airport Road. The entrance road is reached in another half mile. If you reach the airport, you've gone too far.

Orcas Island Golf Course
Route 1, Box 85; Eastsound, WA 98245; phone – (360) 376-4400;
fax – (360) 376-4404

Orcas Island's 9-hole, par 36 course gets very busy in the summer months, so make reservations in advance. Off-season there is no problem getting playing time. Several holes cross a hilltop and some ponds to make the course interesting, as well as a real physical test. An alternate 9-holes makes an enjoyable 18-hole challenge.

The clubhouse has a pro shop, lounge, and scenery-encompassing patio. You can rent either power or pull golf carts.

How to get there: From Orcas Landing head north on Horseshoe Highway. The course lies on the west side of the road, 6 miles from the landing.

San Juan Golf and Country Club
2261 Golf Course Road; Friday Harbor, WA 98250; phone – (360) 378-2254

Great golfing and a superb marine view too! This 9-hole, par 35 course is the best, most popular in the San Juans. Its 6,508 yards make it the longest 9-hole venue in Washington. The particularly delightful course boasts well-kept greens, beautiful flowers, and an overlook of Griffin Bay. Advanced reservations are suggested for weekends during the summer.

The pro shop stocks a complete range of golfers' needs, including rentals. The bar and restaurant are open from May through September. A celebrity tournament is held here every year in early June. *See* Events and Attractions *in the chapter on San Juan Island.*

How to get there: From Spring Street in Friday Harbor turn south on Argyle. Follow this road as it turns west and then south. In 2 miles, as Argyle bends west again, Golf Course Road heads straight south to the clubhouse.

San Juan Camps

San Juan Islands are a destination for vacationing families and adults. However, you may not know that they have wonderful summer camps, too. All the islands' youth camps offer an exciting gamut of outdoor fun ranging from swimming, hiking, and horseback riding to photography and theater arts. Kids will discover they can have a blast without the benefit of electronic gadgets. Older campers have opportunities for out-of-camp trips to remote islands; one camp offers a mountain climb to the top of Mount Baker. Many kids return year after year, working up in the programs, and eventually becoming counselors.

All youth camps offer the basic staples of camping and camaraderie, and are well-supervised by counselors, instructors, and other staff. Private camps are more expensive than the YMCA camp, but they provide more personal instruction, and smaller staff-to-camper ratio. Transportation from nearby cities is generally available; specific information is available from the respective camps, which are described in the chapters on specific islands.

US Customs

For Canadian neighbors or other visitors from foreign ports, San Juan Island has a customs office. Check-in points for boaters are at Friday Harbor and Roche Harbor. Airport check-in is at the Friday Harbor Airport. For information, call:

Anacortes: (360) 293-2331
Friday Harbor and Roche Harbor: (360) 378-2080
Sidney: (604) 363-6644/45

The US has specific restrictions on importing certain food or agricultural products, and on the amounts of alcoholic beverages and tobacco products that may be imported. Check with the customs service for current rules. Pets must have current certificates of rabies vaccination.

Persons arriving in the San Juan Islands from Canada via the Washington State Ferry must clear US Customs before debarking at Friday Harbor. Those continuing east to Anacortes without leaving the vessel in Friday Harbor clear customs at Anacortes.

Privately owned or chartered foreign boats, or US boats returning from a visit to Canada, must clear US customs prior to docking, anchoring, or touching another boat within US waters. The boat's skipper must report to customs at a port of entry immediately upon arrival; no one else may leave the boat until clearance is granted. US customs offices operate during normal business hours at Roche Harbor and Friday Harbor; they also handle customs check-ins for visiting yachts via phone, 24 hours a day, from marinas at Roche Harbor and Friday Harbor.

If checking in by telephone, you must be able to provide the following information:

• Vessel identification number. This is the documentation number for documented vessels, or the user fee decal number issued by the home port province.

• Vessel name and length.

• Names, addresses, citizenship, and birth dates of all passengers. Passports or visas may be required.

• If you're returning to the US from a visit to Canada, you must also have available the clearance number issued to you when you entered Canada.

• An estimated date of departure, if returning to Canada.

Once you've completed an arrival report, and clearance is granted, you must record the clearance number in the ship's log and retain it there for a minimum of one year. Pleasure boats over 30 feet in length entering the US must pay an annual processing fee of $25 on or before the first entry into the US each year. A non-transferable decal is issued to the boat upon payment of the fee.

Boaters who have previously cleared customs in the area are sent a PIN (personal identification number) for future arrivals. Boaters with these numbers can clear customs by calling a 24-hour number, (800) 562-5943, prior to departure, en route, or immediately upon arrival in Puget Sound.

A Washington State ferry threads through Wasp Channel. Photo by Bob and Ira Spring.

GETTING THERE

Ferryboats, Planes, Buses & Bicycles

THEY COME HAULING KAYAKS, canoes, trailers, bicycles, mopeds, suitcases, backpacks, camping gear, and kids. The vacationing throngs descend on the San Juans every year. The Washington State ferry system records over 1.5 million riders to the islands yearly. Of that, the majority are visitors, bent on enjoying this vacationland for a day, or week, or even the summer. Washington State's ferry system is the largest and finest of its kind in the nation. For many, especially those who are not already familiar with it, the ferry ride is nearly as great an adventure as the ultimate destination. It is, indeed, one of the best (and definitely cheapest) ways to tour the islands.

Ferries to the San Juans originate in the city of Anacortes (on the mainland, 86 miles north of Seattle), and travel to the four largest islands: Lopez, Shaw, Orcas, and San Juan. Anacortes is reached by driving I-5 north from Seattle or south from Vancouver, B.C. or Bellingham. Just north of Mount Vernon take exit 230/Highway 20 West and head west to Anacortes. The ferry terminal is on the far west side of town, four miles from the city center; watch for signs that direct you there.

A number of different ferry boats operate on the San Juan runs, and their sizes vary. Most are three-deck ships ranging between 250 and 400 feet in length and holding 75 to 160 vehicles. The largest accommodates several thousand passengers.

Facilities for physically disabled passengers are available on all ferries that make San Juan runs, with the exception of the inter-island ferry. A small elevator operates between the car deck and observation levels. If you are physically disabled, or are traveling with a disabled person, and want to be able to leave your car to go to the observation deck, inform the attendant when you purchase your ticket. The crew will see that your vehicle is parked near the elevator, and that there is room to unload a wheelchair. If traveling without a car, wheelchairs can easily negotiate the overhead passenger ramp that links the terminal and boat at Anacortes. You will need to take the elevator down to the car deck to leave the boat at any of the island landings.

READING THE FERRY SCHEDULE

Three types of ferry runs operate to and within the islands: a regular domestic, an international, and an inter-island. Schedules change every three months, and from year to year. During times of very heavy traffic extra sailings may be added that will not appear on the schedule.

Regular domestic runs originate in Anacortes and travel to Lopez, Shaw, Orcas, and San Juan islands. These boats leave Anacortes approximately 16 times a day in summer, 12 times in winter. The trip to Lopez Island takes about 45 minutes, and Friday Harbor is reached in approximately 1 hour and 15 minutes. However, not all boats go to every island, so check carefully that the ferry you are planning to be on will take you to your destination.

International runs also originate in Anacortes, but end in Sidney, BC, on Vancouver Island near Victoria. This boat runs twice a day in summer, once a day in winter. The one-way trip lasts three hours. Car space can be reserved on this ferry in summer for those traveling to Sidney; therefore, in summer it can be the most difficult run in which to get vehicle space to the islands. If you travel eastbound on a boat that originated in Sidney, you will be subject to customs inspection when you disembark at Anacortes. This is necessary because this boat and some of its passengers cross the Canadian border, even though you did not leave the US.

Inter-island runs travel between the four ferry-served islands, but are never scheduled to go to a mainland destination. These boats can be taken to connect to ferry runs that do not stop at some of the islands. For example,

From the decks of the Washington State ferry visitors can view islands, waterways, and even wildlife.

if you are on Orcas and want to catch the 1:45 P.M. eastbound boat that leaves Friday Harbor, but does not stop at Orcas, you can take the 10:20 A.M. inter-island run that will put you in Friday Harbor at 11:40 A.M., in time to get in line for the eastbound ferry. It's a bit of a hassle, but it can work alright if you are desperate.

The boats on the inter-island runs are smaller than those on other runs and hold fewer cars and passengers. The inter-island route between Orcas Island and Friday Harbor is the most splendid of all the runs. This route is normally not taken by the regular ferry runs. It is here, in tight little Wasp Passage, that the ferry threads its way through "the rockpile" of smaller islands. Some of these islets are privately owned and have quaint cabins and elegant homes, some are marine state parks. As the westbound ferry hangs a left to the south, Yellow Island, one of the preserves held by The Nature Conservancy is in view off the starboard (right) rail.

BOARDING THE FERRY

Because the ferries make stops at the different islands, you will be told to park your car in lanes at the ferry landing according to your destination. This strategy facilitates unloading at each island. *It is important that you follow the parking directions of the ferry crew.*

In the height of summer, catching a ferry can be stressful due to the heavy volume. Plan ahead, go prepared, and you'll enjoy the trip much more. In summer, if you're driving your car, expect to wait in the ferry line whether you are going to the islands or leaving them. On sunny weekends in July and August you may wait…and wait…and wait—it can be several hours, so arrive at least an hour early. Bring something to read, games for the kids, a pillow for a nap, or lunch. Once properly parked you will not have to move your car until the boat is ready to load, so you can leave it to browse nearby shops or grab a quick snack at a cafe. If a ferry employee is around, you would be wise to check how long the wait will be. If you order food at a nearby restaurant, tell your server what ferry you will be catching, and they will try to expedite your order. Above all, stay near enough to watch for approaching ferries and to hear loudspeaker announcements. You should be in your car at least 20 minutes before scheduled departure time. If you are not there when boarding time arrives, traffic will be detoured around your vehicle, you will incur the silent (or not-so-silent) scorn of fellow passengers, and you will be fined and your car towed.

Once on board, you may leave the car deck to go to the observation levels (we recommend you take your camera along). Seats inside and on outside decks provide perfect views of the ever-changing scene as the ship slides past picturesque islands. Early morning and late afternoon provide drifting mists and dramatic lighting. You may spot bald eagles perched in tall tree snags on nearby islands. You may even sight whales; if the captain knows they are in the vicinity, he will usually slow the boat. Sandwiches and beverages are available from a small restaurant on the upper level, and from vending machines. A loudspeaker will announce when it is time to return to the car deck.

When driving vehicles off the ferry, follow the crew's directions. At any of the intermediate stops (Lopez, Shaw, or Orcas) it may be necessary to back vehicles off or on. At Orcas Landing or Shaw this procedure is relatively easy; however, at Lopez a steep uphill incline can make it complicated for those trying to back up with trailers.

Finally, unless you really will need your vehicle for transportation on the islands, consider leaving it at Anacortes. Vehicles can be left at large parking lots adjoining the ferry terminal; however, in summer there is a charge for parking there. A free, 100-car Park-and-Ride lot, serviced by shuttle busses to the terminal, is in downtown Anacortes. Busses run hourly from 6:55 A.M. to 8:55 P.M.

If you walk on board you will not need to worry about long ferry waits, with the possible exception of the fourth weekend in July when the Jazz Festival occurs. Although there is no regular bus service on Lopez or San Juan islands, several hotels are within walking distance of the Friday Harbor or Orcas ferry landings, and most other hotels and resorts will pick you up at the ferry terminal. Other transportation options are described later in this chapter.

Fares. At press time, round-trip ferry fares for vehicle under 20 feet and driver were: Lopez: $12.30 ($14.75 peak season); Shaw/Orcas: $14.70 ($17.65 peak season); Friday Harbor: $16.80 ($20.30 peak season). Passengers, whether walk-on or in car, pay $4.95 to all destinations; children under 11 and senior citizens pay half fare; children under five are free. There is an added charge for trailers and overlong RVs; the fee varies according to length. There may be slight annual increases. Motorcycles are charged a lower rate than autos. There is a charge of $2.75 for bicycles walked on; however there is no tariff for boats that are car-topped or bicycles that are mounted on vehicles.

Because it is assumed nearly everyone will be making a round trip, tolls are collected only on westbound runs, except for the international sailing. If you stop at one island and then later continue west, you'll pay an additional toll.

Washington State Ferries
Colman Dock/Pier 52; 801 Alaskan Way; Seattle, WA 98104-1487
Administrative offices: (206) 464-7800
24-hour schedule information: (800)-84-FERRY
Seattle: (206) 464-6400
Sidney, BC: (604) 381-1551 or (604) 656-1531
Friday Harbor: (360) 378-4777
Orcas Island: (360) 376-2134
Lopez Island: (360) 468-2252
Shaw Island: (360) 468-2142
Anacortes: (360) 293-8166
TDD relay services for the hearing impaired: (800)-833-6388;
    Seattle: (206) 587-5500

SAFETY CONCERNS

• Because of the potential hazard, smoking on the car deck is strictly prohibited, even in cars; the passenger decks have designated smoking areas.
• Cans of gasoline are not permitted on the ferry; propane tanks on

campers must be shut off and sealed with a red tag procured from the toll booth before boarding.

• Animals must be confined to cars or kept on leashes on the car deck. With the exception of animals assisting disabled persons, any animals in the terminal waiting area or on the passenger decks must be confined to cages.

• Finally, do not use your cellular phone during loading.

For schedules, fares, or other information, contact the Washington State Department of Transportation at the following address or phone numbers:

PRIVATE PASSENGER FERRY SERVICE

The following private ferries operate in the San Juans:

Island Transport Ferry Service, Inc.
Skyline Marina; 1900 Skyline Way; Anacortes, WA 98221; phone – (360) 293-6060

A high speed "Taxicat" passenger service links Skyline Marina to the San Juans. The company's six-passenger catamaran will deliver you to any of the San Juan islands, either to a dock or directly onto a beach.

San Juan Island Shuttle Express
355 Harris Avenue, Suite 105; Bellingham, WA 98225; phone – (360) 671-1137

The *Squito* is a small passenger ferry, operated by San Juan Island Shuttle Express, that runs between Squalicum Harbor in Bellingham, Obstruction Pass on Orcas Island, and Friday Harbor on San Juan Island during summer months. It makes the westbound trip in the morning, and the eastbound return leg in the late afternoon.

At Friday Harbor, time is allocated between the eastbound and westbound trips so passengers can spend the afternoon sightseeing in the town. At an additional charge, option travelers may stay aboard for a three-hour whale watch cruise.

Bicycles and kayaks are welcome on the boat, and group rates for transportation are available for parties of six or more. Overnight accommodation packages in Bellingham can also be arranged.

AIR SERVICES

●

Charter or rent planes for touring the islands, or catch a scheduled flight from nearby cities. San Juan, Orcas, and Lopez islands all have small airports; you can usually arrange transportation from the airport to your island destination. Some air services fly seaplanes that spirit you to more remote destinations. A few of the smaller islands have private landing strips built and maintained by the residents for their use. Wheeled aircraft can land at the public air strips on the major islands or at private strips built for residents of several smaller islands. Seaplanes provide versatility for reaching remote spots.

Several companies provide regularly scheduled flights to the San Juan Islands. They also offer charters, sightseeing flights, and freight services for air cargo—including oversize freight and perishable goods.

Virtually any company in the Pacific Northwest that charters planes will fly you or your cargo to the San Juans or take you on sightseeing flights. Some are listed below. You'll find many more listed in phone books of cities such as Seattle, Tacoma, Bellingham, Oak Harbor, and Olympia, as well as in Victoria and Vancouver, British Columbia.

SCHEDULED AIR LINES

●

Harbor Airlines, Inc.
1140 Monroe Landing Road; Oak Harbor, WA 98277;
phone – (800) 359-3220; Oak Harbor: (360) 675-6666;
Friday Harbor: (360) 378-6900; Seattle: (206) 340-0342

This airline, based in nearby Oak Harbor, on Whidbey Island, has daily scheduled flights on multi-engine aircraft between Friday Harbor on San Juan Island and SeaTac International Airport, Oak Harbor on Whidbey Island, and Olympia. You can also arrange charter flights.

Kenmore Air
950 Westlake Avenue North; Seattle, WA 98109
or 6321 NE 175th; Kenmore, WA 98155;
phone – (800) 543-9595; Seattle: (206) 486-1257; fax – (206) 486-5471

Kenmore Air schedules four daily seaplane flights from Lake Union in downtown Seattle. Destinations include Friday Harbor and Roche Harbor on San Juan Island, Rosario Resort and West Sound Marina on Orcas Island, and Islands Marine Center (Fisherman Bay) on Lopez Island. Schedules vary seasonally. On any flights, seats unsold two hours prior to departure are available at a reduced rate for scenic round-trip excursions from Seattle. The airline will make other stops in the San Juan Islands for two or more persons, and charter service is available. Overnight lodging packages with various San Juan hotels are offered.

West Isle Air
400 Airport Road; Anacortes, WA 98221
or Friday Harbor Airport; Friday Harbor, WA 98250
or Eastsound Airport; Eastsound, WA 98245
or Lopez Airport; Lopez Island, WA 98261;
phone – (800) 874-4434; Anacortes: 293-4691; Friday Harbor: (360) 378-2440; Eastsound: (360) 376-4176

West Isle Air offers four daily round-trip flights between Seattle's Boeing Field and Friday Harbor, with connections to Lopez, Blakely, Decatur, and Stuart Islands, and Roche Harbor on Orcas Island. In Seattle, van service is available between Boeing Field and SeaTac International Airport. There are five daily round-trip flights between Anacortes and Eastsound, and five daily inter-island flights between Friday Harbor, Lopez, and Orcas. Four additional round-trip flights link the three island locations to Bellingham, where you'll find connections to Alaska Airlines, Horizon Air, Empire Airlines, and United Express. Schedules vary seasonally and on weekends. Rental cars are available at Bellingham, Anacortes, Eastsound, and Friday Harbor airports. Single and multi-engine charter flights are available to other airstrips in the San Juans.

AIR CHARTERS & SCENIC FLIGHTS
◆

Air Adventure
P.O. Box 1747; Schoen Lane; Eastsound, WA 98245; phone – (360) 376-5113

Vacation on Orcas and learn to fly! For tourists planning an extended summer stay on the island, Air Adventure offers a specially tailored eight-week pilot training course leading to a private license. The company also provides chartered scenic flights, aerial photography, and private carriage contracts.

Aeronautical Services, Inc.
501 Airport Circle; Friday Harbor, WA 98250;
phone – (800) 345-9867; Friday Harbor: (360) 378-2640;
Eastsound: (360) 376-5730

This company provides charter and daily air freight services between Mount Vernon, Seattle, Eastsound, Friday Harbor, Lopez, and Canadian locations. Charter flights accommodate up to nine passengers. Sightseeing flights are also available.

Aviation Northwest
2052 Airport Way; Bellingham, WA 98226; phone – (360) 733-3727

Aviation Northwest charters flights out of the Bellingham airport to Eastsound on Orcas Island, Lopez Island, and Friday Harbor and Roche Harbor on San Juan Island, as well as to SeaTac International Airport and other northwest Washington and BC locations. Special overview flights feature a tour of the San Juan Islands, a flight over the San Juans to Victoria, BC, and a scenic North Cascades flight. Up to three passengers can join a scenic sky tour and split the hourly aircraft charter rate.

Island Air
P.O. Box 2149; 600 South Franklin Drive, Friday Harbor, WA 98250;
phone – (360) 378-2376; fax – (360) 378-3199

Island Air offers both scenic flights in the San Juan Islands and charter flights anywhere within the US and Canada. The service has four beautifully maintained aircraft: two single-engine planes can carry three passengers each, one larger single-engine craft can carry five passengers, and a twin-engine that can carry four passengers. Call for rates and scheduling.

Magic Air Tours
P.O. Box 223; Eastsound, WA 98245; phone – (360) 376-2733

Shades of the Red Baron! An open cockpit TravelAir biplane makes scenic tours out of Eastsound Airport on Orcas Island, providing travelers a unique way of becoming acquainted with the many islands and channels of the San Juans. Don't just stand there, hand me my goggles and scarf!

Regal Air
Paine Field; Everett, WA; phone – (206) 743-9123

Regal Air offers charter flights to airstrips in the San Juans, as well as scenic and photographic flights.

Sound Flight
Renton Airport; Renton, WA; phone – (800) 825-0722 or (206) 255-6500

Charter seaplane flights from Renton, on the south end of Lake Washington, will take you to any island in the San Juans and British Columbia. Cessna 206's can carry up to four passengers, the larger Beavers accommodate six persons. A wheeled Cessna 182 can carry up to three passengers to those islands that have landing strips.

BUS SERVICES
◆

Scheduled bus service is the answer for visitors who are looking for connecting transportation between major airports and the ferry. Some travel companies also offer bus tours of the islands. For information, contact your local travel agent.

Airporter Shuttle
P.O. Box 5625; Bellingham, WA 98227; phone – (800) 235-5247;
US and Canada; (800) 448-8443; Washington: (360) 679-0600

Scheduled shuttle service between Bellingham, Mount Vernon, Marysville, and SeaTac International Airport connects in Mount Vernon with a shuttle to Anacortes and Oak Harbor. The shuttles operate every two hours, seven times a day. On Saturdays, and from mid-January to mid-April, there are only five runs. Reservations recommended.

Trips departing from Oak Harbor stop at Skyline Marina, the San Juan Ferry terminal, downtown Anacortes, the Farmhouse Inn, and Mount Vernon. If you make advance reservations, runs from Mount Vernon will stop at the Farmhouse Inn, Skyline Marina, or the Naval Air Station Whidbey in Oak Harbor. Special fare schedules apply for seniors, military, and children. Special charters and tours may be arranged.

BICYCLES & MOPEDS

The following firm rents bicycles at the Anacortes ferry terminal. Several other companies that rent both bicycles and mopeds on the islands are listed under "On-Island Transportation" in the chapters on specific islands.

Ship Harbor Bicycle Rental
5316 Ferry Terminal Road; Anacortes, WA 98221; phone – (800) 852-8568; Canada: (800) 235-8568; (360) 293-5177

Ship Harbor Inn, overlooking the ferry terminal in Anacortes, provides bicycle rentals. Either add rental bikes to your car, or leave your car on the mainland and make the entire trip by bike. The folks at the Inn will be delighted to help you plan your trip and provide maps and tourist information. Parking is available at the ferry terminal, although there may be a charge. Free parking and shuttle bus service is available in downtown Anacortes.

TWO-WHEEL COURTESY & SAFETY

Bicycles or mopeds are wonderful (and very popular) ways to see the islands. However, because the roads are often narrow and winding, persons who choose either of these modes of transportation should make sure they do not endanger themselves, impede the pleasure of other visitors, or rankle the residents. Bicycles and mopeds are unloaded from the ferry first. Hot on their heels follow the four-wheel vehicles. At both Lopez and Orcas there is a long uphill pull from the ferry landing, and laboring cyclists can cause traffic to back up. When cycling in the San Juan Islands, please observe the following rules of safety and courtesy:

- Ride in small groups of three to four, and space groups widely apart.
- Stay well to the right side of the road and ride single-file to allow cars an opportunity to pass.
- Make stops on the straight-of-way, rather than on a bend in the road or the crest of a hill, where it is difficult for motorists to see you.
- When stopping to rest, move completely off the road.
- Do not trespass; camp only in designated sites.
- Do not litter.

A sailboat tests the wind.

BOATING

Tours, Cruises, Charters & Marinas

ALTHOUGH THE MAJORITY OF VISITORS to the San Juans arrive by ferry, Northwest boaters know well the accessibility of the islands from any of the mainland ports. The trip doesn't require a yacht—even small boats and kayaks with experienced paddlers can make the trek from Anacortes or Victoria in good weather. The table below shows the distance by water to Friday Harbor from nearby ports and landmarks in Washington and British Columbia.

Distances to Friday Harbor by water (in nautical miles)			
Anacortes, WA	18	Port Angeles, WA	37
Bellingham, WA	28	Port Ludlow, WA	44
Blaine, WA	37	Port Townsend, WA	30
Bremerton, WA	76	Seattle, WA	67
Cape Flattery, WA	87	Tacoma, WA	86
Eagle Harbor, WA	67	Vancouver, BC	62
Everett, WA	62	Victoria, BC	30
Olympia, WA	112		

Several marinas on the islands provide moorage, fuel, and services for boaters. Numerous public boat launches are nearby on the mainland. There are launch ramps on San Juan, Orcas, and Lopez islands, although trailered boats are best put in on the mainland, rather than ferried to the islands for launching. Good anchorages are abundant, especially at the marine state parks.

As of 1995, the operation of jet skis (personal watercraft) is banned in San Juan County. This action was taken because of concern over noise and hazards to boaters and marine life. The jet ski industry has filed suit to halt the ban, so the issue will be decided in court. If you had planned to use such craft in the islands, be aware of the ban.

BOAT TOURS & CRUISES

Tours, cruises, charters, and rentals are ways to enjoy the islands by boat if you don't own a vessel of your own. Fees for boat rentals, charters, or tours range from around $25 for an afternoon to $10,000 for a week! Somewhere in that range there must be a boat to match your needs and budget.

Skippered tours and charters cost between $25 to $65 for a half day and $70 to $135 for a full day. The price range depends on the services offered and the size, type, and comfort of the boat. Group rates are available on large boats. Vessels range from a 16-foot outboard for two, up to 100-foot yachts that can accommodate up to 50 guests for the day or 17 overnight guests. Some charters provide drinks and light meals for half-day or sunset cruises, or full meals on all-day or overnight trips.

Bareboat charters run between $700 weekly for a basic, comfortably equipped boat into that $10,000 range for a large, posh yacht. All require a security deposit.

Off-season rates may be lower on all rentals, charters, and tours.

Negotiating around a boat can involve a bit of physical activity. Some boats can accommodate disabled persons or persons with some physical limitations. If you have any concerns, discuss them with the company at the time you rent or charter a boat.

Tours and cruises are all skippered, and normally leave at scheduled times and follow a specific itinerary or a defined goal—fishing, diving, or whale and wildlife watching are all popular in the San Juans. Boat size varies from small cruisers that accommodate a few people to large yachts complete with dining room and bar.

Of course, none of the fishing or wildlife cruises can guarantee that you'll catch salmon or see whales, but the folks that run these boats are well versed in the islands and will offer you a better chance than you may have on your own, as well as provide you with in-depth knowledge of the area itself.

Numerous tours to and through the islands originate in nearby cities. Those that are specifically focused on the San Juans are listed in this book, others may be located by checking with local travel agents. There is considerable overlap between businesses that list themselves as tours or cruises, and those that describe themselves as charters. If you're looking for a skippered boat trip around the islands, check out all descriptions.

Boat charters and rentals are available in all the nearby major cities, as well as at several San Juan harbors. With any type of rental or charter, be sure to inquire as to exactly the type of boat, its size, its power, sleeping accommodations, and what is included in the way of both marine and personal supplies.

Rentals are generally small boats for day use, and range from kayaks and rowboats up to small outboards for fishing or island exploring. **Charters** are larger boats that are contracted for a weekend or several weeks. They can be sailboats, cruising houseboats, or powerboats ranging up to posh yachts. These are classified as either "bareboat" or "skippered." On a **bareboat charter** you are the skipper; you plan your own itinerary and are fully responsible for the safety and well-being of yourself, your crew, and the boat. By law, chartered boats must be fully equipped with all US Coast Guard required safety devices such as fire extinguishers, life jackets, and flotation devices. They usually have fuel, radio, charts, and cooking utensils—everything necessary for a comfortable voyage. You provide your own food, bedding, and fishing gear, although these may be available through the company for an additional charge. Typically, rowing dinghys are provided, and outboard motors can be rented at an additional charge.

If this is your first time chartering with a company, you will normally be given a short "checkout" cruise to assure the company of your boat-handling abilities and to familiarize you with your craft. If you have questions or want suggestions about cruising in the islands, be sure to ask. Then you're on your own.

On a **skippered charter** you are essentially a guest. Unless your group is large, there may be other guests along. The boat owner is in charge of the boat, although some skippers will be happy to let you crew, or even take a turn at the helm. Meals and bedding are provided. Although the captain may have particular destinations in mind, the itinerary is usually flexible. If fishing is your goal, or if you're not an experienced boater, a skippered charter is a good way to go, because the boat owner knows all the best spots and will make sure you enjoy your cruise. Some charters specialize in other recreation where the skipper has particular experience or knowledge, such as scuba diving. Learn-to-sail skippered charters include lessons, giving you the skills to captain your own ship next time.

OFF-ISLAND BOAT & KAYAK TOURS, CRUISES & CHARTERS

ABC Yacht Charters
*1905 Skyline Way; Anacortes, WA 98221; phone – (800) 426-2313
or (360) 293-9533; fax – (360) 293-0313*

ABC has both power cruisers and sailing yachts, from 18 to 46 feet, available for bareboat charter. Larger custom yachts, ranging 50 to 120 feet, are chartered only with skipper and crew. Many items of equipment beyond USCG requirements are included with all boats. The company has staples and provisioning packages available on request, and will rent items such as bedding, barbecues, outboards, and fishing gear. One boat is specially equipped with wheelchair ramps and lifts to accommodate boaters with physical limitations.

Roche Harbor is a popular boating destination in the San Juans.

Adventure Pacific Charter Service
31607 44th Avenue South; Auburn, WA 98001; phone – (206) 939-8351;
cell phone – (206) 979-3230

The S.V. *Chinook*, a 45-foot long trimaran, is stationed in the San Juans during summer months. A telephone call to the boat's cellular phone is all that it takes to arrange for the boat to pick you up for half- or full-day excursions or three-day getaways. You name the adventure: sightseeing, watching marine life, scuba diving, kayaking, or whatever else fills your dreams. Kayaks can be lashed to the 28-foot-wide open deck of the boat for transport through strong tidal current channels to easier paddle routes. Bow nets between the pontoons of this fast, stable craft are great places for sunbathing as you relax to the sound of water rushing beneath you. Three-day getaway prices depend on party size; a maximum of six overnight guests can be accommodated.

Affordable Dreams Yacht Vacations
P.O. Box 581; Ferndale, WA 98248-0581; phone – (800) 354-8606

A variety of skippered cruises originate from the Bellingham/Anacortes area. Among the options offered are a sunset and guitar cruise for a romantic way to end the day, an overnight trip anchored in an island cove in the San Juans, a tent camping overnighter to one of the marine state park islands, a half-day sampler of the San Juans, a full-day cruise through the islands, a three-day adventure to selected places in the San Juans, or a full week on an itinerary of your choice that can include the San Juan Islands, Gulf Islands, or Victoria. Yachts are 28-foot or larger; the minimum party size is four. The company also acts as a booking agent for 75 bareboat charters in the area.

Anacortes Yacht Charters
P.O. Box 69; Anacortes Marina, Suite 2; Anacortes, WA 98221;
phone – (800) 233-3004 or (360) 293-4555

Over 80 power and sailboats, ranging between 26 and 55 feet, are available for bareboat charter from this mainland marina. Most boats are less than five years old; all are fully equipped with the required USCG safety equipment plus other essential gear. Clients can purchase supplies, groceries, and liquor within walking distance of the moorage, or on request the company will arrange for meals, staples, and bedding to be on board. The rate structure varies seasonally.

Bellhaven Marine, Inc.
9 Squalicum Mall; Bellingham, WA 98225; phone – (800) 542-8812; (360) 733-6636; fax – (360) 647-9664

Bellhaven Charters offers yacht brokerage, both power and sail, and bareboat sail charters from 28 to 43 feet. Provisions for your trip are readily available from nearby Bellingham supermarkets.

Bellingham Yacht Sales and Charters
174 Harbor Center; 1801 Roeder Avenue; Bellingham, WA 98225; phone – (800) 671-4244 or (360) 671-0990; fax – (360) 671-0992

This company charters a complete line of power boats between 32 and 45 feet. They will provide training in boat handling for bareboat charters, or can provide a skipper and crew for trips year-round to the San Juans, Gulf Islands, or farther north in Canadian waters. Off-season discounts are available.

Blue Water Yacht Charters
2130 Westlake Avenue North; Seattle, WA 98109; phone – (800) 732-7245; (206) 286-3618; fax – (206) 286-9154

As a charter broker, this company does not manage any boats, but instead maintains an agent relationship with more than 50 bareboat charter companies and thousands of crewed yachts-for-charter worldwide. The broker works with you to determine your requirements, then matches you to boats that Blue Water represents. To assure you a perfect vacation, the broker checks out the condition of all craft and the quality of the charter operation for any companies it represents.

Boom Town Enterprises
P.O. Box 4733 Blaine, WA 98230; phone – (360) 293-4248

The Resort at Semiahmoo is the departure point for the M.V. *Boom Town.* Jackie Goodsir, the U.S. Coast Guard licensed skipper of the spacious 38-foot cruiser, will take you on a day or sunset cruise. If your interest is wildlife watching, fishing, scuba diving, crabbing, or photography, she'll take you to the very best spots, and share her experiences with you. Fishing tackle and bait are provided. Day cruises feature a gourmet luncheon, and hors d'oeuveres are available on the sunset cruise.

Discovery Charters
P.O. Box 636; Anacortes, WA 98221; phone – (360) 293-4248

Sail from Cap Sante Marina in Anacortes aboard the *Discovery* for live-aboard two- to seven-day scuba diving tours in the San Juan and Gulf islands. Anchor in quiet harbors each night. Air fills to 3,000 PSI, low side exits, and an easy-boarding ladder add to the comfort and safety of dives. Three "home-cooked" meals a day, plus snacks, take care of creature comforts. Each dive explores different sites. The vessel accommodates up to 12 divers on trips of more than three days. Shorter whale watch and marine birdwatching charters are also available.

Grand Yachts Northwest
1015 Thomas Glenn Drive, Box #1; Bellingham, WA 98225;
phone – (800) 826-1430; (360) 676-1248; fax – (360)676-9059;
e-mail:gynw@pacificrim.net;
web: http:/www.marinenetwork.com/.www.html

Thirteen prestigious Grand Banks power yachts, ranging from 32 to 46 feet, and a 42-foot Krogen are available for either bareboat or skippered charter. Towels, linens, sleeping bags, and fishing gear may be rented from the company. Charter rates vary by yacht size and season.

Island Mariner Cruises
#5 Harbor Esplanade; Bellingham, WA 98225; phone – (360) 734-8866

On weekends from June 3 through September 10, and Tuesdays and Thursdays during July and August, come aboard the 110-foot *Island Caper* for a 90-mile whale search and nature watch cruise through the San Juan Islands. The vessel can carry up to 149 (a minimum group of 20 is required). Group charters for weddings, receptions, company picnics, and similar gatherings are also available. On board are a hot tub, complete galley seating 65 for dinner, a portable bar you can stock, a piano, sound system, TV, and VCR. Extended custom cruises can be accommodated using the seven two-person staterooms below decks.

Mosquito Fleet
1724F W Marine Drive, Everett, WA 98201; phone – (206)252-6800

The M.V. *Golden Spirit* can take up to 149 people for a 9½ hour adventure-filled day in the San Juan Islands. The vessel leaves the Everett Marina for a sail north up Saratoga Passage, through narrow cliff-rimmed Deception Pass, and on to Friday Harbor, in the heart of the San Juans. Here you have a choice of an afternoon of exploring nooks and quaint shops in Friday Harbor, or you can remain aboard for a three-hour nature cruise, with an opportunity to spot whales and other marine mammals. A naturalist on board makes your trip more interesting, and the vessel participates in a whale spotting service, which increases your chances of being in the right spot at the right time.

After picking up the shoreside visitors at Friday Harbor, the return trip follows the same route back to Everett. Sailings are daily from the end of May through the end of October. Weekend tours are offered during May. Sandwiches, soft drinks, beer, wine, and snacks may be purchased aboard. The Captain's Lounge, a private compartment with bar, restroom, video, and private outside deck, is available for groups up to ten.

Northwest Marine Charters
1500 Westlake Avenue North #110; Seattle, WA 98109;
phone – (800) 659-3048 or (206) 283-3040

This broker represents more than 50 boats, both power and sail, ranging from 23 to 72 feet, located in northwest waters from Seattle to Anacortes, Vancouver, and Comax, BC. Let them know your requirements, and they'll come up with the boat to meet your needs in a location near your desired vacation spot, thus saving you travel time.

Northwest Sea Ventures
P.O. Box 522; 2309 29th Street; Anacortes, WA 98221;
phone – (360)293-3692

See the San Juan Islands up close in a safe, quiet, and environmentally-gentle sea kayak. A variety of scheduled tour packages are available, ranging from short sunset trips to one- to five-day tours. In addition to these scheduled tours, groups of five or more can arrange trips tailored to their own special interests. Both scheduled and private classes in the basics of sea kayaking are offered. Classes include four hours of pool training and four hours of open water instruction. Beginners can rent both single and double kayaks for the day. Rentals include paddle, life vest, skirt, pump, and paddle float.

Orca Charters
Cap Sante Marina; Anacortes, WA 98221; phone – (360) 293-2129
or (360) 424-7410

Board the 63-foot *Entertainer* at Cap Sante Marina in Anacortes, where you and up to 47 other guests can enjoy a spacious yacht as it cruises through the scenic San Juans. A lounge offers a color TV, VCR, stereo system, and attentive service by the crew. A well-equipped galley ensures memorable meals, and two private staterooms with individual baths offer the ultimate in seclusion and comfort. A certified diving master is aboard to lead you to breathtaking underwater explorations.

Orca Cruises and Charters
9565 Semiahmoo Parkway; Blaine, WA; phone – (360) 371-3500

The M.V. *Odyssey* sails from the Semiahmoo Marina, on Drayton Harbor, for whale and nature searches, bottomfish charters, sunset and dinner cruises, working retreats, and other catered events. The vessel can carry up to 97 passengers on one-day cruises, but will cater to groups as small as 15. Two large interior salons, with stereo, TV, and VCR are comfortable group mingling areas; catered foods and snacks are available. For extended charters there are four double cabins sharing two full restrooms with tub or showers. Call for current schedules and prices.

P. S. Express
431 Water Street; Port Townsend, WA 98368; phone – (360) 385-5288

The 64-foot vessel *Glacier Spirit* departs daily from Port Townsend at 8:00 A.M. As it crosses the Strait of Juan de Fuca the tour passes close by Smith and Minor islands, then Castle Rock and the south side of Lopez Island. You are treated to a description of the natural history of the region as you view the abundant marine mammals and birds. After a cruise up San Juan Channel, on the east side of San Juan Island, the boat docks at Friday Harbor, where you can spend time onshore or remain on board for a two-hour whale watch excursion. After picking up its Friday Harbor explorers, the *Glacier Spirit* returns to Port Townsend via Mosquito Passage and Haro Strait, along the west side of San Juan Island. Up to 72 passengers can enjoy large viewing windows, fresh baked goods, snacks, and beverages throughout the trip. Overnight packages with San Juan B&Bs can be arranged.

Penmar Marine Company

2011 Skyline Way; Anacortes, WA 98221; phone – (800) 828-7337
or (360)293-4839; fax – (360) 293-2427

Year-round skippered or bareboat charters are available for one- or two-week trips to the San Juans or into Canadian waters. Powerboats run from 25 to 52 feet and sailboats between 30 and 46 feet. Either will provide never-to be-forgotten vacation trips to the San Juans, Gulf Islands, or Desolation Sound. Extensive yacht accommodations, over and above USCG requirements, are provided with each boat. On bareboat charters, linens, galley basics, provisions, fishing gear, and outboard motors can be supplied at extra cost.

Sail the San Juans, Inc.

1333 Lincoln Street, Suite 109; Bellingham, WA 98226;
phone – (360) 671-5852

Spend a week in the San Juans aboard the 42-foot sloop *Northwind*, sailing out of Bellingham. The skipper and crew will plan a trip to choice island locations, or will tailor the itinerary to your personal desires. Either relax and let the crew handle the boat, or actively join in the sailing experience. You will have an opportunity to spot and photograph whales, bald eagles, and other wildlife, to fish for salmon, or to drop a crab pot to catch the evening's dinner. The *Northwind* has two private staterooms for parties of two to four guests. Charter price includes all meals, fishing tackle, and whatever other gear is necessary to make your trip a memorable one.

San Juan Express, Inc.

Clipper Navigation, Inc.; Pier 69, 2701 Alaskan Way; Seattle WA 98121;
phone – (800) 888-2535 or (206) 448-5000

From mid-May to the end of September the passenger vessel *San Juan Explorer* makes a daily round-trip from Seattle to Friday Harbor, with an optional side trip to Rosario on Orcas Island. The schedule changes to Friday, Saturday, and Sunday only between April 1 and mid-May, and between the end of September and mid-October. For the remainder of the year, sailings are only on Saturday, Sunday and holidays. The outbound leg of the trip leaves Seattle at 7:30 A.M. for the cruise north up Saratoga Passage and through Deception Pass, then enters the San Juans via Thatcher Pass. After a three-hour layover in Friday Harbor (or the optional trip to Rosario), the vessel returns to Seattle via San Juan Channel, the Strait of Juan de Fuca, and Admiralty Inlet. The *Explorer* has an inside main deck with table seating for 135, picture windows, and an outdoor open deck. On-board food and beverage service and a friendly passenger attendant add to your comfort. En route the crew will describe landmarks and scenic attractions and point out marine mammals when spotted. Overnight packages with select inns and resorts are offered.

San Juan Island Shuttle Express
355 Harris Avenue, Suite 105; Bellingham, WA 98225;
phone – (360) 671-1137

During summer months, the Shuttle Express departs from the Bellingham Cruise Terminal daily at 9:15 A.M. and sails to Friday Harbor, with an intermediate stop at Obstruction Pass on Orcas Island. You can spend the afternoon touring Friday Harbor, or sign up for an optional three-hour-long trip through the islands to find and photograph orca and minke whales, porpoises, sea lions, seals, and a variety of sea birds. The whale watch tour leaves the Friday Harbor dock at 12:30 P.M. A return trip to Bellingham via Obstruction Pass departs Friday Harbor at 5:00 P.M.

Bicycles and kayaks are welcome on the boat, and group rates for transportation are available for parties of six or more. Overnight accommodations packages in Bellingham can also be arranged.

San Juan Sailing
#1 Squalicum Harbor Esplanade; Bellingham, WA 98225;
phone – (800) 677-7245; (360) 671-4300; fax – (360) 671-4301

Sailing out of Bellingham, you're only two hours away from the San Juans, where you can sharpen your sailing skills in its abundance of broad channels and enjoy a relaxing overnight anchorage at one of its marine state parks. Ten sailing yachts, ranging from 30 to 40 feet, are available for bareboat charter, and two larger sailing yachts, 48 and 51 feet, are for skippered charter only. All boats are generously equipped for safety and living comfort; add-on packages of linens, food staples, meal provisioning, and fishing gear can be arranged.

Victoria/San Juan Cruises
355 Harris Avenue, Suite 104; Bellingham, WA 98225;
phone – (800) 443-4552 or (360)738-8099

From mid-May to mid-October the 300-passenger *Victoria Star* makes daily round-trip cruises between Bellingham and Victoria, B.C. via the San Juan Islands. The ship leaves the Bellingham Cruise Terminal on Harris Avenue in the morning, arrives in Victoria's Inner Harbor around noon, then makes the return trip in the late afternoon. The route through the San Juans is different on the outward bound leg than it is on the return one, so scenery varies.

The impressive vessel has an open upper deck and an enclosed lower deck with a full bar, espresso and snack bar, table seating, and a duty free shop. If you spot whales or other interesting marine mammals or birds en route, the ship will stop for observation and photographing. Complimentary use of binoculars is provided. The *Victoria Star* is also available for private charter for dinners, dances, conventions, and parties.

Viking Cruises
P.O. Box 327; La Conner, WA 9825; phone (360) 466-2639

You'll skip the ferry lines by boarding the modern, 58-foot cruiser *Viking Star* in La Conner, 60 miles north of Seattle, and taking off for a scenic adventure in the San Juan Islands. The beautifully appointed vessel, which holds up to 49 passengers, has an enclosed, heated cabin with large viewing windows, and spacious outside decks. Up to a dozen people can join the captain in the upper deck wheelhouse. A variety of cruises are available, ranging from a 1½ hour "Shorty" in the La Conner vicinity, to a full day in the San Juans that includes a box lunch, tea, and coffee. A 3-day cruise package features two nights at Orcas Island's Rosario Resort.

You can soak up the sun and scenery, or wildlife watch. Field guides and binoculars are on hand, and a knowledgeable naturalist help you spot birds, whales, seals, and other wildlife. Group rates are available.

SCUBA DIVING SUPPLIES

You'll find scuba air refills at a few spots in the San Juan Islands, however equipment and repairs are hard to come by. Stop at either of these two mainland shops to be sure you're fully outfitted before heading for those prime dive spots around the islands.

Anacortes Diving and Supply, Inc.
2502 Commercial Avenue; Anacortes, WA 98221; phone – (360) 293-2070

Washington Divers, Inc.
903 North State; Bellingham, WA ; phone – (360) 676-8029

OFF-ISLAND MARINAS & LAUNCH RAMPS

Anacortes Marina

P.O. Box 486; Anacortes, WA 98221; phone (360) 293-4543

A privately owned, breakwater-protected marina on Fidalgo Bay has a fuel dock (gas, diesel, propane) and a pumpout station. The marina handles haulouts to 60 tons and offers a complete line of marine services, repairs, and supplies. Yacht charter and yacht sale companies are based at the marina. No transient moorage.

Blaine Harbor

275 Marine Drive; Blaine, WA 98230; phone (360) 332-8037

The city of Blaine sits on the US-Canada border, 15 nautical miles from the San Juans. The marina operated by the Port of Blaine has a 1,000-foot guest float, fuel dock (gas and diesel), pumpout station, and launch ramp. Boats up to 150 tons can be launched or hauled out, and there is adjacent dry storage. Land facilities include a marine chandlery and restrooms with showers. Fishing charters also operate out of the port facilities. From the harbor, the San Juan Islands are a leisurely day-cruise away.

Cap Sante Boat Haven

P.O. Box 297; Anacortes, WA 98221; phone – (360) 293-0694;
fax – (360) 299-0436; VHF channel 66; CB channel 5

The Port of Anacortes operates Cap Sante Boat Haven, on Fidalgo Bay. This moorage has 100 guest slips with power and water; restrooms, showers, and laundry facilities are at the head of the guest floats. The marina has a fuel dock (gas, diesel, premix, kerosene, propane) and a pumpout station. Haulouts to 30 tons can be handled; a full range of boat maintenance and repair services are available. The basin hoist launch takes boats up to 26 feet; dry storage is ashore. Groceries, ice, bait, hardware, and electronic gear are sold at the marina store. Downtown Anacortes, just a few blocks away, has restaurants and shops. Companies at the marina offer boat rentals and charters.

Semiahmoo Marina
9540 Semiahmoo Parkway; Blaine, WA 98230; phone – (360) 371-5700

Semiahmoo Marina, part of the extensive Semiahmoo Resort, lies on Drayton Harbor, near Blaine. Although it is primarily a permanent moorage marina, guest slips with power and water are available by reservation. The facility has security gates, a fuel dock (gas, diesel, propane), pumpout station, restrooms, showers, and laundry. The marina offers haulouts to 35 tons, dry storage, and a full range of marine maintenance, repair, and service. Shoreside shops carry groceries, bait and tackle, and marine hardware and supplies.

Skyline Marina
Flounder Bay; 2011 Skyline Way; Anacortes, WA 98221;
phone – (360) 293-5134; fax – (360)293-9458

For many boaters Skyline Marina is the jumping-off point for their trip to the San Juans. The full service marina is conveniently located on Fidalgo Island, at the north end of Burrows Bay. It provides fuel (gas, diesel, CNG, propane), pumpout station, small boat launch, guest moorage with power and water, restrooms, showers, and laundry. The marina can do haulouts to 35 tons and has dry storage and a complete range of marine repair and maintenance services.

Nearly everything a boater needs is right at hand: Shops in the marina complex sell marine hardware, groceries, ice, fishing tackle, bait, and licenses. A restaurant, yacht brokers, yacht charters, boat rentals, and fishing charters are within the marina complex, and a supermarket and liquor store are within walking distance.

Squalicum Harbor
P.O. Box 1737; Bellingham, WA 98227-1737; phone – (360)676-2500
or (360) 676-2542 weekends and after hours.

The second largest marina complex in Washington (next to Seattle's Shilshole Marina) is on the north end of Bellingham Bay. Two moorage basins have over 1,700 feet of guest moorage with power and water, restrooms, showers, and laundry. The older of the two basins, on the west, fronts on Squalicum Mall and Harbor Mall; both have a number of marine-oriented businesses offering parts and supplies, bait and tackle, haulouts, boat maintenance and repair, hoist launching, yacht sales, charters, two fuel docks, and two pumpout stations. The newer, east basin has guest moorage with power and water, restrooms, showers, and laundry.

Blaine Harbor, near the Canada-US border, is just a liesurely day-cruise from the San Juan Islands.

The main moorage dock leads ashore to Harbor Center, a covered esplanade with more marine-oriented shops including boutiques, tackle and bait shops, a small grocery, a marine chandlery, restaurants, and yacht sales and charters. On one corner of the basin is a four-lane boat launch ramp. During summer a passenger ferry service makes runs to the San Juans.

All the launch ramps described below are within 18 miles of the San Juans, making them ideal put-ins for day trips. They are listed from north to south.

Lighthouse Marine County Park Launch Ramp

This Whatcom County park is on the southwest tip of Point Roberts. To reach it, take Tyee Road south from the US-Canada border to Marina

Drive, turn west and follow Marina Drive, then Edwards Drive to the park. The ramp has two lanes and an adjacent boarding float. The ramp is 12 nautical miles north of Patos Island.

Port of Bellingham—Blaine Marina Launch Ramp

A two lane concrete ramp, with a loading ramp between lanes, drops to the jetty-protected basin on the east side of the Blaine Marina. From the north side of the town of Blaine, turn west from Peace Portal Drive onto Marine Drive. Follow it to the first intersection, then turn south on Milhollin Drive, which ends at the launch ramp parking area. From here, Patos Island is 16 nautical miles to the south.

Port of Bellingham—Squalicum Harbor Launch Ramp

A four-lane concrete launch ramp with two boarding floats is immediately east of the Harbor Center buildings at Squalicum Harbor. From downtown Bellingham head northwest on Holly Street to C Street. Turn left on C, and in one block, right on Roeder. Follow Roeder to the first entrance to Squalicum Harbor. There is ample parking above the ramp and to the south, beyond the Coast Guard station. The ramp is 13 nautical miles from the west tip of Orcas Island.

Larrabee State Park—Wildcat Cove Launch Ramp

Larrabee State Park has a single-lane launch ramp on its north shore. To reach it, from the south side of Bellingham follow signs to Highway 11 and Chuckanut Drive. Turn west on Cove Road ¾ mile north of Larrabee State Park; at a T-intersection the road south leads to the steep launch ramp on Wildcat Cove, a tiny inlet on Samish Bay. The west tip of Orcas Island is 11 nautical miles away.

Bay View Launch Ramp

Because the portion of Padilla Bay by the small community of Bay View becomes a mudflat at minus tides, this ramp is usable only by shallow-draft boats at high tide. To reach the ramp, take the Bay View-Edison Road north from Highway 20 to Bay View. A single-lane concrete ramp is just north of the intersection with Wilson Road. The ramp is 15 nautical miles from the entrance to Thatcher Pass.

Swinomish Channel Launch Ramp

An excellent two-lane concrete ramp with a boarding float is located under the bridge on the east side of the Swinomish Channel. Head west on Highway 20, and just before it starts over the Swinomish Channel bridge, turn right onto a road paralleling the north side of the highway. From here, Thatcher Pass in the San Juans is just 14 nautical miles away.

Washington Park Launch Ramp

This popular ramp at Sunset Bay in Washington Park is only 6 nautical miles from Thatcher Pass. At Anacortes, follow Highway 20 west toward the ferry terminal. Where the road heads downhill to the terminal, continue west on Sunset Avenue to Washington Park. The launch ramp is on the north shore, just inside the park.

Pioneer City Park Launch Ramp

This ramp drops into the east side of the Swinomish Channel at La Conner. At the south side of La Conner, turn south on Second, then west on Sherman to reach the concrete launch ramp. There is ample parking above the ramp. It is 17½ nautical miles to Thatcher Pass, via the Swinomish Channel.

Deception Pass State Park—Bowman Bay Launch Ramp

Deception Pass State Park has two launch ramps, one on the west side of the pass, and one on the east. To find the ramp on the west side, take Highway 20 south toward Deception Pass State Park. At the south end of Pass Lake, turn west on Rosario Road, then south on the road to the park's Bowman Bay area. A large parking lot and a single-lane concrete launch ramp are near the center of the bay. The ramp is 8 nautical miles from Lopez Pass.

Deception Pass State Park—Cornet Bay Launch Ramp

The eastern Deception Pass ramp is in the Cornet Bay marina area. From the south of the main entrance to the park, turn west from Highway 20 onto Cornet Bay Road, and follow it to the park. Just inside the park boundary is a launch ramp with boarding float. The ramp is nine nautical miles from Lopez Pass.

YACHT CLUBS & ANNUAL BOATING EVENTS

It's no secret that the San Juans are a boater's paradise. The three major islands have yacht clubs, and in addition there's the Friday Harbor Sailing Club and the Sailing Foundation. These organizations sponsor parades, races, regattas, and other rivalry and revelry throughout the year. Some races are white-knuckle serious, others are just for fun. Members of other yacht clubs may join in many events. They're a perfect way to get to know other boaters and enjoy the terrific boating in the islands.

Flying a spinnaker on a sunny San Juan day

For non-boaters, the races and parades are grand spectator events. Two of the major events are:

Opening Day of Boating Season

When: The first Saturday of May

Oil the teak and shine the brightwork! The yacht clubs of Orcas, Lopez, and San Juan islands kick off the boating season with local yacht parades. Boats are decorated for display and competition. Sailboat races and all-around parties are part of the festivities. You can register and compete for one of the prizes, or just get in line and join the fun.

The Lopez Island parade takes place in Fisherman Bay, The Orcas Island one in West Sound by the yacht club dock, and the San Juan Island parade is right in Friday Harbor.

Shaw Island Classic Sailboat Race

Where: The race begins and finishes at the Port of Friday Harbor docks
When: The second weekend in August

The Shaw Island Classic is one of the "for fun" races. Slack and flaky winds often result in few of the boats being able to finish the race in the prescribed time. The objective is to navigate the 16-or-so nautical miles around Shaw Island by whatever route the skipper chooses, depending on an assessment of tidal currents, winds, and the fickle finger of fate. Finish or not, most boats, skippers, and crews take it in a lighthearted spirit, and all participants join in a dinner sponsored by the San Juan Island Yacht Club to cap off the race and to award trophies. The event usually attracts over 100 entrants from all over the Northwest. It's a wonderful race to participate in as well as to watch. A portion of the course is along the ferry route, so the ferries provide good vantage points.

Lopez Island is sometimes refered to as the "Aspen of bicycling."

LOPEZ

The Friendly Isle

SKIP LOPEZ IF YOU'RE looking for a swinging scene; but if you want to laze away to a near-jellyfish state, you'll adore this place. Lopez, the first landing to be reached from Anacortes by the Washington State ferry, is less tourist-oriented than either Orcas or San Juan islands.

First-time visitors will find facilities at the ferry landing at Upright Head shockingly sparse. The small ferry office with outside waiting area may be staffed only when a boat is due. A tiny snack shack perched on the hillside beside the parking lanes provides burgers and colas during times of heavy ferry travel, but may be shut tight otherwise. A phone booth offers solace to stranded travelers.

Green forest flanks Ferry Road as it stretches south from the landing. Is there anything beyond? It depends on what you're looking for. This is the most slow-paced, most pastoral, and friendliest island of all. It boasts some outstanding lodging and restaurants, a few interesting shops, and, of course, the exquisite scenery that pervades all the archipelago. Bicyclists revel in the light traffic and gently rolling roads (don't be deterred by that short uphill grind from the ferry landing).

Midway down the west shore of the island one small hamlet, known as Lopez or Lopez Village, offers some limited services. Fisherman Bay, a well-protected anchorage, holds two excellent marinas that meet full

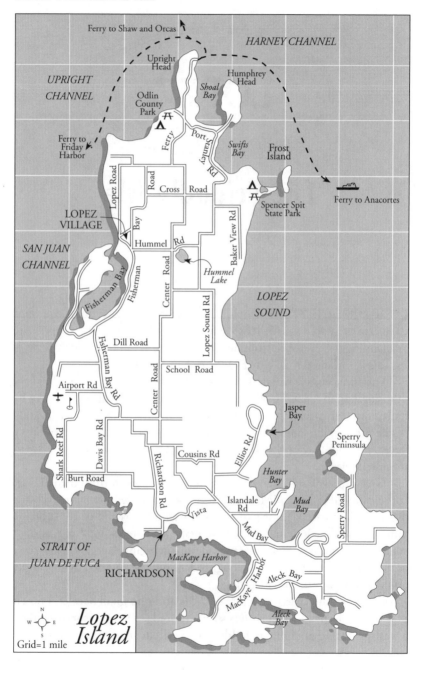

Ferry to Shaw and Orcas

HARNEY CHANNEL

Upright
Head

Humphrey
Head

UPRIGHT
CHANNEL

Shoal
Bay

Odlin
County
Park

Swifts
Bay

Frost
Island

Ferry to
Friday
Harbor

Ferry to Anacortes

Cross   Road

LOPEZ
VILLAGE

Hummel   Rd

SAN JUAN
CHANNEL

Spencer Spit
State Park

Baker View Rd

Lopez Road

Road

Ferry

Port Stanley Rd

Bay

Hummel
Lake

Fisherman Bay

Fisherman

Center Road

Lopez Sound Rd

LOPEZ
SOUND

Dill Road

School   Road

Fisherman Bay Rd

Airport Rd

Center   Road

Jasper
Bay

Sperry
Peninsula

Davis Bay Rd

Shark Reef Rd

Richardson Rd

Cousins Rd

Elliot Rd

Hunter
Bay

Burt Road

Vista

Islandale
Rd

Mud
Bay

Sperry Road

STRAIT OF
JUAN DE FUCA

MacKaye Harbor

RICHARDSON

Mud Bay

Aleck Bay

MacKaye Harbor

Aleck
Bay

N
W   E
S

Lopez
Island

Grid=1 mile

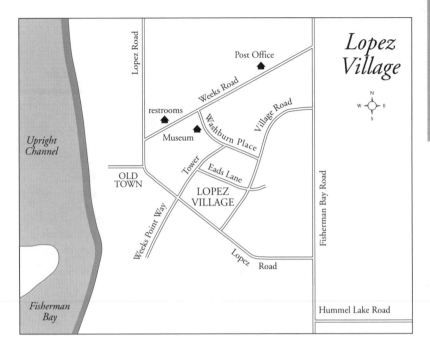

boating needs. Overnight lodgings are scattered throughout the island, while two parks beckon campers.

The handful of Lopez Island shops are largely concentrated in Lopez Village. Here you'll find Old Town (a few buildings on a spur road that dead ends at the water), Lopez Plaza (a long, low building on the southwest side of Lopez Road that holds a few shops), and a cluster of businesses and stores gathered on the northeast side of Lopez Road. A few additional businesses are scattered south, along Fisherman Bay Road.

And that's about all. For many visitors it's quite enough.

LODGING

●

*Prices quoted for accommodations are summer rates, double
occupancy, as of 1996, unless otherwise indicated, and are subject
to change. Lower rates are usually offered off-season.
A tax of 7.6% is added.*

Aleck Bay Inn

*Aleck Bay Road; Route 1, Box 1920; Lopez Island, WA 98261;
phone – (360) 468-3535; fax – (360) 468-3533; e-mail – abi@pacificrim.net*

Accommodations: 4 rooms and suites (all with private bathrooms and Jacuzzis,
    fireplaces, queen-size beds), TV. Children by arrangement, no pets, no smoking.
Extras: Full breakfast, sun deck, hot tub, beach, table tennis, billiards, games, cro-
    quet, badminton, volleyball, music, meeting room, bicycle and kayak rentals,
    facilities for small groups and weddings
Rates: $79 to $139. Credit cards accepted

Aleck Bay Inn provides gracious accommodations for your vacation,
weekend getaway, wedding, honeymoon, business meeting, or family gathering. The facilities are ideally suited for a small group gathering—the spacious, sunny game room also serves as a meeting room. Guests who want
more than reading on the sun deck or beachcombing will enjoy kayaking,
bicycling, brisk games of croquet, badminton, or volleyball, or more quiet
bouts of chess or checkers. Evenings may bring music fests around the piano. In addition to serving a generous breakfast, your hosts provide afternoon tea. Snacks are always available; dinner is served on request.

The inn, is on Aleck Bay, and has easy access to the beach. The exquisite, protected bay has good anchorages for boaters who want to come ashore
for a weekend of pampering, or who use the inn as a base for boat and island excursions.

How to get there: From the ferry landing follow Ferry Road south and
turn left (east) on Center Road. Center Road becomes Mud Bay Road as it
heads south. After approximately 8 miles, turn left on Lopez Sound Road,
which bends south and becomes Mud Bay Road. Continue on Mud Bay
Road and turn right on Aleck Bay Road. A blue sign marking the driveway
to the inn is on the right. Open year-round.

Blue Fjord Cabins

Route 1, Box 1450 (Elliott Road); Lopez Island, WA 98261;
phone – (360) 468-2749

Accommodations: *2 separate cabins (kitchenettes, queen-size beds, TV).*
Children OK, no pets, non-smokers preferred
Extras: *Shoreline deck and beach gazebo, beach, trails*
Rates: *$75 to $85, 3-night minimum July through mid-September, 2-night minimum at other times. No credit cards*

These Nordic chalet-style cabins are picture-postcard perfect. Nestled in an enchanting woodland setting, the property fronts on a remote cove on the east shore of Lopez Island. The scent of cedar, fir, and moist forest pervades. Both units enjoy forest views and total seclusion.

A short nature trail leads to Jasper Bay, a sheltered cove that holds a romantic waterside viewing deck with a gazebo, ideal for a private picnic. Spend a lazy afternoon looking for bald eagles; one or both of a resident nesting pair are often seen soaring overhead, sometimes scolding their young perched nearby. Watch otters playing along the shore, then linger to enjoy the evening sunset turn Mount Baker strawberry-ice-cream-pink.

Each cabin comfortably accommodates one or two persons; one child is welcome if parents provide sleeping arrangements. The units are well separated by forest for complete privacy. The beautiful, modern accommodations feature log walls with open beam ceilings, carpeting, kitchens, and decks. Because this is not a bed and breakfast, you must provide your own food; better yet, give yourself a real vacation and eat at one of the great local restaurants.

How to get there: From the ferry landing follow Ferry Road 2 miles and turn left on Center Road. Follow Center Road for 5¾ miles to a Y-junction, and turn left onto Mud Bay Road. After a short ½ mile turn left onto Cousins Road. In about 1 more mile turn left onto Hunter Bay Road. After ½ mile make a final left turn onto a private gravel road marked Elliott Road. One mile on Elliott Road brings you to the driveway of the inn, marked by a post lamp and a small wooden sign on the right. Total distance from the ferry landing is 10½ miles. Confirmed reservations are sent a map. Open year-round.

Edenwild Inn
Lopez Village; P.O. Box 271; Lopez Island, WA 98261;
phone – (360) 468-3238

Accommodations: *8 rooms and suites (private baths, most beds queen-size, some rooms with fireplace, all with either water or garden views), disabled access, courtesy van, no TV. Children OK, no pets, no smoking*

Extras: *Full breakfast, afternoon tea or coffee, facilities for small weddings, honeymoon suite, restaurant, walking distance to Fisherman Bay and shops of Lopez Village, bicycle rentals, kayak and boat rentals nearby*

Rates: *$100 to $140. Credit cards accepted*

Flowers spill from the surrounding gardens into the inn. Botanical prints decorate the walls and fresh or dried blossoms brighten tables. Soft, restful

Clematis and iris surround the door at Edenwild Inn.

flower tones of violet, rose, and blue sweep down the walls and over the elegantly furnished rooms.

The Lopez Village location is handy for shopping and dining. The inn's courtesy van will pick you up at the ferry, airport, or from a boat or seaplane in Fisherman Bay. Guests enjoy a full country breakfast. If you want romantic privacy, or are unable to pry yourself from the luxury of your bed, have breakfast served in your room. The restaurant at the inn serves lunches and dinners.

The garden makes a lovely setting for a wedding. Honeymooners can enjoy a romantic suite with a queen-size bed and fireplace. Complimentary flowers and champagne are included with the honeymoon package.

Enchanting is the only word for it. Purple and yellow iris crowd the brick path, and the covered verandah wears a delicate scarf of clematis. Leaded glass windows and lace curtains accent Victorian gingerbread. Although fashioned after a Victorian-era home, Edenwild Inn is recently built, providing charm without the creaky floors and recalcitrant plumbing of older structures. One room has disabled access.

How to get there: In Lopez Village, south of Lopez Plaza. Open year-round.

Hunter Bay House

P.O. Box 368; Lopez Island, WA 98261; phone – (360) 468-3636;
fax – (360) 468-3637; e-mail – SWIFTINN@aol.com

Accommodations: 1 bedroom home (king-size bed) fireplace, TV and VCR,
stereo system, full kitchen, laundry. No children, no pets, no smoking
Extras: Views everywhere, garden, hot tub, sun deck, robes
Rates: $195, 2-night minimum. No credit cards

The surrounding deep woods and fenced garden guarantee privacy, the stunning view of Lopez Sound guarantees memories. Once you sink into the living room's down-filled couch, you'll know you've found heaven.

Hunter Bay House, which is situated on a high bluff above the water, is owned by Robert Herrmann and Christopher Brandmeir, the same folks who have made the Inn at Swifts Bay a premier lodging. Their skilled touch shows here, too, with fine furnishings and thoughtful attention to the needs of their guests. The fully-equipped kitchen is the one you always wished you had, open to the view of Hunter Bay on one side, and the garden on the other. Basic food staples are supplied; you provide the main ingredients. For breakfast there's fresh, ready-to-bake muffins and juice waiting in the fridge.

The house is rented to two people only—it's the sort of place couples sneak away to for absolute solitude. Furnishings are a wonderfully eclectic assemblage of Northwest/lodge/antique/Ralph Lauren, with interesting collectibles ranging from Northwest Indian masks, to an old Pendleton blanket, antique furniture, and old sports equipment. The king-size bed is a handmade creation of unpeeled natural wood branches.

The passion for gardening of the previous owner shows in the beautifully landscaped grounds, which hold many rare and unusual plants. Even the bathroom looks out to a tiny garden.

How to get there: Hunter Bay House is located at the southeast end of Lopez Island. When you check in at the Inn at Swifts Bay (see following), you'll receive driving directions.

The Inn at Swifts Bay

Port Stanley Road; Route 2, Box 3402; Lopez Island, WA 98261;
phone – (360) 468-3636; fax – (360) 468-3637;
e-mail – SWIFTINN@aol.com

Accommodations: *5 rooms and suites (3 with private bath and gas-log fireplace, all with queen-size beds), spa, hot tub, 2 common areas with fireplaces, VCR. No children, no pets, no smoking*
Extras: *Full breakfast, robes, music and movie videotapes, private beach, exercise studio with sauna*
Rates: *$75 to $155. Credit cards accepted*

Max, an exuberant black Labrador, will greet you on your arrival at the Inn at Swifts Bay. Teddy bears lining a foyer settee offer a quieter, but no less friendly welcome. The Tudor-style brick home, embraced by three acres of lush forest and rhododendrons exudes Northwest hospitality and grace. The inn reposes on a hillside, across the road from Swifts Bay; a short walk provides beach access.

Each of the splendid rooms has an individual character; one holds wicker furniture and oriental rugs, an attic room has an antique sleigh bed and skylights for star viewing. Reserve the outdoor hot tub for private soaking—terry robes and slippers are available.

Evening brings romantic hand holding on the quiet patio, or casual gatherings around the fireplace in one of the two common rooms and a chat with other guests and your hosts. Feast on gourmet breakfasts, featuring fresh juices, homemade muffins, and dishes such as apple, ham, and brie omelets, crabcakes made from local Dungeness crab, or hazelnut waffles with fresh berries and crème fraîche. Ecstasy!

How to get there: From the ferry, drive south on Ferry Road for 1 mile and turn left (east) on Port Stanley Road. In about ¾ mile, as the road bends south, the mailbox #3402 and the sign for the driveway to the inn is on the right. Open year-round.

Island Farmhouse

Route 2, Box 3114; Lopez Island, WA 98261; phone – (360) 468-2864

Accommodations: *1 room (double bed, private bath, coffee maker, refrigerator), cabin (queen-size bed, refrigerator, coffeemaker, microwave, TV and VCR),. 1 child OK, no pets, no smoking*
Extras: *Walk to Lopez Village, bicycle rentals nearby*
Rates: *guest room $50, cabin $75. No credit cards*

These modern, country-cozy accommodations provide a nice option to the standard motel or inn. The room in the private home has a separate entrance and private bath to ensure privacy. The nearby cabin has basic cooking facilities where you can whip up a quick meal, and a deck for outside relaxation. Both accommodations are meant for two, although a foam floor mattress is available for a child.

As you down your breakfast coffee and fresh bakery muffins in your room, enjoy morning mists drifting over the pastoral view.

How to get there: On Hummel Lake Road, ¼ mile east of Lopez Village, on the south side of the road. Open year-round.

Islands Marine Center

P.O. Box 88, Fisherman Bay Road; Lopez Island, WA 98261; phone – (360) 468-3377; fax – (360) 468-2283

Accommodations: *3 units (some with queen-size beds, kitchenettes, fireplaces, TV), view deck. Children OK, pets OK*
Extras: *Bicycle and kayak rentals nearby. Moorage and boat launch available*
Rates: *1-bedroom $85 to $95, second connecting bedroom $35. Credit cards accepted*

These spacious, modern apartments are centrally located to all the marine activity on Fisherman Bay, making them an ideal base for visitors who want to take advantage of the San Juan's superb boating or fishing.

One suite that sleeps up to six has a hide-a-bed, trundle, and separate bedroom with a queen-size bed. Another unit has no separate entrance; it can be rented as an additional bedroom for guests in either of the two main suites. Each room looks west over Fisherman Bay, offering prime views of the islands' spectacular sunsets.

How to get there: On Fisherman Bay Road, immediately south of Lopez Village, on the second floor of the Islands Marine Center. Open year-round; 2-night minimum on 3-day weekends.

The Islander Lopez Marina Resort
Fisherman Bay Road; Lopez Island 98261; phone – (800) 736-3434;
(360) 468-2233

Accommodations: *32 rooms and suites (some with kitchenettes, TV). Children OK, no pets, no smoking*
Extras: *Marina, heated swimming pool, hot tub, laundromat, restaurant (breakfast, lunch, and dinner), meeting and banquet facilities, beach, bicycle or kayak rentals, charters (fishing, diving, or wildlife viewing)*
Rates: *$80 to $100, suites $170 to $275. Credit cards accepted*

The Islander Lopez offers the most complete range of facilities on Lopez Island, making it ideal for boaters' rendezvous and company retreats. A range of accommodations meet the varied needs of guests. New, deluxe rooms have water views and kitchenettes with wet bars and microwaves. Economy accommodations do not have views; all units have refrigerators and TV.

Lopez Village is just a stroll away, and various rental or chartering opportunities are right at hand. Boaters will welcome a chance to steady their sea legs in one of the comfortably furnished units, and soak in the resort hot tub. *See also* Restaurants *and* Marinas.

How to get there: The resort is immediately south of Lopez Village on Fisherman Bay Road. Open year-round.

Lopez Farm Cottages
P.O. Box 610, Fisherman Bay Road; Lopez Island, WA 98261;
phone – (360) 468-3555; fax – (360) 468-3558

Accommodations: *4 cottages (1-bedroom, queen-size beds, kitchenettes). A child OK, no pets, no smoking*
Extras: *Continental breakfast, farm atmosphere. Winery nearby. Bicycle and kayak rentals in Lopez Village*
Rates: *$110. No credit cards*

A stay in the country is guaranteed therapy for nerves frazzled from the big city rat race. This historic family farm provides just what you're looking for in a getaway. Sheep graze in the pastures, and you're almost sure to see deer foraging in the farm's 100-year old orchard.

The modern, newly-built guest cottages, nestled in an old cedar grove near the back of the 40-acre farm, are designed to fit right in with the rural ambiance, with country casual furnishings, charming front porches and back decks, and lots of privacy. Each of the spacious cottages holds a queen-size bed, gas fireplace, kitchenette, and a table and chairs. A futon is available if there's a child along. Breakfast is fresh muffins, jam, fruit, and other country goodies tucked in a basket that arrives in the special "breakfast box" at your front door. There's no need to even get out of your PJ's to chow down.

Lopez Village is 2½ miles away – perfect for a morning jog. Immediately across the road is Lopez Island Vineyards, where you can visit the tasting room, and then pick up a bottle of their award-wining wine to sip on the porch of your cottage as evening settles over the farm. Bliss!

How to get there: From the ferry landing follow Fisherman Bay Road south. The driveway leading to the inn is on the left in 2½ miles, across from the winery.

Lopez Lodge

Lopez Village; P.O. Box 117; Lopez Island, WA 98261;
phone – (360) 468-2500

Accommodations: 3 rooms (1- and 2-bed, some with shared bath, kitchenettes, queen-size beds, TV). Children OK, no pets, no smoking
Extras: Bicycle, kayak, and boat rentals nearby
Rates: $69 to $99. Credit cards accepted

These second-floor rooms above a small shopping plaza in Lopez Village are just the ticket for people looking for comfortable, reasonably priced accommodations. All rooms are spacious and clean, and have water views of the end of Fisherman Bay. The largest unit has two beds, kitchenette, a small living area, and private bath. The two smaller units (one with one bed, one with two) share a bathroom. Coffeemakers and coffee are provided in each unit. Daily, weekly, and winter rates are offered.

How to get there: In Lopez Village, next to Lopez Plaza. Open year-round.

MacKaye Harbor Inn

Route 1, Box 1940; Lopez Island, WA 98261; phone – (360) 468-2253

Accommodations: *2 suites and 3 rooms (2 rooms with private baths, 3 rooms share 2½ baths), no TV. Children over 8 OK, no pets, no smoking*
Extras: *Full breakfast, afternoon tea, guest refrigerator, barbecue, bicycle and kayak rentals (for guests only), kayak instruction and tours, binoculars*
Rates: *$89 to $139. Credit cards accepted*

Morning salt breezes drifting through lace curtains; languid, sunny afternoons; evening by the fireplace with a good novel—what could be nicer? MacKaye Harbor Inn offers even more. Although a country road separates the inn from the tranquil bay, the shore is part of the property. As a guest, you can enjoy evening strolls on the driftwood-strewn beach, or try to identify shorebirds with binoculars borrowed from the inn. If you want a few hours of exercise, your hosts have kayaks and bicycles available for a turn around the island, either by land or water. They'll even give you lessons in handling your kayak, and, if you wish, guide you on a tour of local waters.

The lovely Victorian farmhouse facing on MacKaye Harbor is one of the best-known and most highly praised of Lopez lodgings—and deservedly so. Your hosts will see to your every need, from the gourmet breakfast with different European entrées, to the fresh-baked afternoon snack, and the bedtime truffles. Because of its popularity, the inn is heavily booked in summer. But don't forget that off-season is a terrific time to visit the San Juan Islands, too.

How to get there: From the ferry landing follow Ferry Road south for 2 miles, and turn left (east) on Center Road. Center Road becomes Mud Bay Road as it heads south. In about 8 miles turn right on MacKaye Harbor Road. The water is reached in less than a mile. The inn is on the left, at the end of the beach. Open year-round.

Sarah's Garden

Port Stanley Road; Lopez Island, WA 98261; phone – (360) 468-3725

Accommodations: *1-bedroom suite (queen-size bed, private bath), no TV. Children OK, pets by permission, smoking OK*
Extras: *Walk to Odlin County Park, near ferry*
Rates: *$45. No credit cards*

Sarah's Garden is a bed and breakfast inn only a few minutes ride from the Lopez ferry landing. Its convenient location makes it ideal for cyclists arriving on the ferry to check in and drop off their gear. Then it's off to spend the day cycling the island's byways and exploring its nooks and crannies. Odlin Park, within walking or cycling distance, has one of the best beaches on the island for afternoon sunning or a romantic evening stroll.

Owner Jane Gamble's love of gardening spills over into her lodgings. Wake up in the spacious, cathedral-ceilinged bedroom, then enjoy your breakfast in a sun room amid dwarf fruit trees and hardy tropical plants. Fruit fresh from her garden will be on your breakfast tray.

How to get there: From the ferry, go south for 1 mile to the intersection of Port Stanley Road and turn left. Sarah's Garden is the first driveway on the right. Open year-round.

Village Guest House

Route 1, Box 2358; Lopez Island, WA 98261; phone – (360) 468-2191

Accommodations: 2 bedroom cottage with kitchenette, barbecue, TV, VCR. Children OK, no pets, no smoking

Extras: Deck, beachfront, walk to Lopez Village, bicycle, kayak, and boat rentals nearby

Rates: $90, $525 weekly (rate includes tax). 1-week minimum in summer. No credit cards

Your family can have a grand vacation in this nice little cottage at the mouth of Fisherman Bay. Steps lead down the moderate bank to the beach. The shops and restaurants of the Lopez Village are just a short stroll away, and kayak and bicycle rentals are right down the road.

The cottage sleeps four comfortably and has a spacious living room. Grill your burgers on the outside barbecue and relax in lawn chairs as you enjoy the sea breeze and spectacular sunsets. Boats negotiating the narrow channel into Fisherman Bay seem just an arm's length away from your front yard.

How to get there: Located on the water, two houses north of Old Town. Open year-round.

RESTAURANTS & CAFES
●

The Bay Cafe
Lopez Village; Lopez Island, WA 98261; phone – (360) 468-3700

Dinner. Beer, wine. Credit cards accepted; reservations recommended. $$

The setting is typically San Juan: cheery rooms in a former storefront decorated with an eclectic assortment of furniture and memorabilia. And the food is straight from heaven! You'll have difficulty selecting from the wide range of innovative dishes that draw on ethnic cuisines. Perhaps sesame-crusted pork tenderloin with Hoison glaze? Or chicken satay with curried noodles and Indonesian peanut sauce? Even traditional king salmon is graced with a sauce of Creole mustard cream. The dessert menu is equally varied, including refreshing sorbets and dazzling chocolate creations.

Bucky's Lopez Island Grill
Lopez Plaza; Lopez Island, WA 98261; phone – (360) 468-2595

Breakfasts, lunches and dinners. Beer, wine. $

Sit inside this cozy cafe, or grab one of the tables on the open deck overlooking Fisherman Bay. Stop by for lunch to find out what an Inside Out Rueben is, or to check out their claim that they make the best fish and chips in the San Juans. Dinner choices include ribs, fresh seafood, chicken, steak, burgers, and another chance to feast on fish and chips. Bucky's is the only place on Lopez you're sure to find open early for breakfast. All items are available for take out.

Gail's
Lopez Village; Lopez Island, WA 98261; phone – (360) 468-2150

Breakfast and lunch daily, dinner Thursday through Monday. Reservations recommended in summer. Beer, wine. Credit cards accepted. $$

If you're eating out on Lopez Island, don't miss Gail's. It's widely praised—and worthy of every word. The special care lavished on every dish is apparent. Homemade muffins and cinnamon rolls accompany your breakfast espresso and omelet. Organically-grown ingredients used in many dishes come from the restaurant's own garden. The varied menu features interesting dishes such a crab enchiladas, freshly made pasta with smoked salmon sauce, and cioppino overflowing with local seafood. London broil and chicken dishes round out the menu. The large, varied wine list features Northwest vintages.

Dine in the bright, airy dining room, with views of Fisherman Bay through etched-glass windows or on the vine-shaded verandah that looks out to the bay. Many of the excellent paintings and prints by local artists that hang on the walls are for sale.

The Galley Restaurant and Lounge
Fisherman Bay Road; Lopez Island, WA 98261; phone – (360) 468-2713

Breakfast, lunch, and dinner. Beer, wine, cocktails. Lounge with live entertainment on weekends. Credit cards accepted. $$

Here's where many local people hang out—what better recommendation can there be? Visiting boaters can tie up to the restaurant's dock on Fisherman Bay (moorage is free for patrons), saunter across the road, and chow down on a steak, burger, or the Galley's famous barbecued ribs. Down a cool one in the High Boat Room, swing your first mate around the dance floor to live music on Saturday night, or have a romantic meal under the stars in the rooftop dining area.

Irie Forrest Cafe
P. O. Box 1952; Lopez Island, WA 98261; phone – (360) 468-4743

Tuesday through Saturday 8:00 A.M. to 2:45 P.M. and 5:30 P.M. to 8:00 P.M. (deli open through the afternoon); Sunday 9:00 A.M. to 3:00 P.M. Closed Monday. Beer, wine. $$

Tourist heading down Lopez Island will be delighted to find there is now a restaurant on the south end. You'll enjoy your stop here as a soul-filling, as well as an appetite-satisfying experience. Ethnic music from Africa, Turkey, or other exotic countries plays quietly in the background, and tropical plants grace sunny corners. "Irie" in African-Jamaican means utmost contentment, or nirvana — the cafe is well named.

Guy and Janine will create a wholesome, energizing burrito, gourmet pizza, or sandwich for you. Their vegetarian selections, made from local, organically-grown produce, are especially popular; however, there are chicken and seafood choices, too. Eat in their pleasant cafe, or take your lunch away for a picnic at a scenic overlook. Lunches are casual, dinners are more elegant, with a selection of fine dishes. Sundays, an extended breakfast is offered until 3:00 P.M. You'll find the Irie Forrest Cafe at the intersection of Islandale and Mud Bay roads.

Islander Lopez Marina Resort

Fisherman Bay Road; Lopez Island, WA 98261; phone – (800) 736-3434
or (360) 468-2234

Breakfast, lunch, and dinner. Beer, wine, cocktails. Lounge, catering facilities.
Credit cards accepted. $$

Although the interior decor of the Islander Lopez hints at Polynesia, with Tiki torches and bamboo, the sweeping marine view from the spacious dining room or open patio is decidedly San Juan. An iced drink and hot appetizer start your meal. Then on to the main menu, which ranges from sandwiches to steaks, with a nice assortment of chicken and seafood dishes in between. Try seafood pasta (local seafood, of course) or a combination of barbecued ribs and shrimp. Children's menu available. This restaurant is part of the Islander Lopez Marina Resort complex, which has extensive lodging and moorage facilities.

A pair of whimsical cows on Lopez Island afirm the island's pastoral nature.

'Lil Upright

Lopez Ferry Landing; Lopez Island, WA 98261; phone – (360) 468-3822

Short-order snacks at the ferry landing. Enjoy your sandwich and cola at an open air table or in your car while waiting for the boat. For early risers catching the Red Eye ferry, there is fresh pastry and hot coffee. Hours very widely, depending on the season and ferry schedule.

Lopez Island Pharmacy

Lopez Village; Lopez Island ,WA 98261; phone – (360) 468-2644

Breakfast and lunch daily, except Sunday. Credit cards accepted. $

You may not drive up in your pink Chevy BelAir, but you'll still enjoy the nostalgia trip as well as the good food. The 50's style soda fountain has been a long-time standby at the Lopez Island Pharmacy—so much so that when they moved to new digs they packed up the fountain and its 15 stools and moved them too. Lunch fare includes homemade chili, corn dogs, chili dogs, and pastrami sandwiches to go with your soda, phosphate, or float. Enjoy coffee and pastry for breakfast.

Paradise to Go

Edenwild Inn; Lopez Island, WA 98261; phone – (360) 468-4080;
Inn: (360) 468-3238

Lunch daily, dinners 5:30 P.M. to 8:00 P.M Wednesday through Saturday.
Tuesday is burger night. Beer, wine. Credit cards accepted. $

Paradise it is! This deli and restaurant in the Edenwild Inn offers light lunches to carry out or to eat on the sunny adjoining patio. There's great gourmet food like Chinese chicken salad, tortellini salad, falafel, and healthy juice drinks or yogurt smoothies. Dinners are served Wednesday through Saturday.

Zephyr Espresso

1 Lopez Road, Lopez Village; phone – (360) 468-4114

7:30 A.M. to 4:30 P.M. daily, 9:00 A.M. to 4:00 P.M. Saturday, 9:00 A.M. to 2:00 P.M. Sunday. $

You won't have to do without first-rate espresso on Lopez Island. It's here at Zephyr Espresso. There's also bagels, cookies, other nibblies, and a selection of teas.

GROCERIES, DELIS, TAKE OUT & LIQUOR

Blossom Natural Foods
Lopez Village; Lopez Island, WA 98261; phone – (360) 468-2204

Before heading out for your day of bicycling or hiking on Lopez Island you'll want to stop at this shop in a gray clapboard house across from Edenwild Inn. They carry a great range of natural and organic foods such as dried fruits, nuts, bulk cheese, protein bars, and other healthy snacks. There's nice casual clothing, accessories, and gift items, too.

Holly B's Bakery
Lopez Plaza; Lopez Island, WA, 98261; phone – (360) 468-2133

Holly Bower has been purveying scrumptious fresh-baked goodies to tourists and islanders for over 15 years. Pick up some of her legendary cinnamon rolls or chocolate chip cookies to spirit back to your boat for breakfast, or enjoy them with coffee from a nearby espresso shop. Closed in winter.

Islandale/Southender
Mud Bay Road; Lopez Island, WA 98261; phone – (360) 468-2315

This small grocery serves people on the south end of the island. It's just the place to stop for picnic makings and cold beer after the bicycle trek down island. There's a public restroom (latrine) across the road, by the fire station, making it a doubly good place to stop.

Lopez Village Market
Lopez Village; Lopez Island, WA 98261; phone – (360) 468-2266;
fax – (360) 468-2445

This is the largest, most complete grocery on Lopez Island. You'll find all you need here to restock your boat galley, including ice. The store also carries a selection of basic drug, toiletry, hardware, and kitchen items; you should be able to find here whatever it was you forgot to bring from home.

Washington State Liquor Store
Lopez Village; Lopez Island, WA 98261; phone – (360) 468-2407

Located in the new section of Lopez Village on Washburn Place, immediately across the street from the historical museum.

SHOPPING

Archipelago

Lopez Plaza; Lopez Island, WA 98261; phone – (360) 468-3222

This interesting little shop offers ethnic clothing imported from India and other foreign countries. You'll find a nice selection of imported jewelry and handmade cards.

Chimera Gallery (Lopez Artist Cooperative)

Lopez Plaza; Lopez Island, WA 98261; phone – (360) 468-3265

A number of local artists and craftspeople display their creations at this gallery. You'll see a wide range of artworks of uniformly high quality, including blown glass, pottery, Northwest Indian carvings, paintings, glass necklaces, woodblock prints, photo prints, weaving, and more. There are items unlike anything you'll find elsewhere. Look for Tamara Schoen's whimsical walking sticks handcarved from ocean spray wood and decorated. There are also exquisite drawings of butterflies by local nature illustrator Vrobik.

Enchanted Needle

Old Town Lopez; Lopez Island, WA 98261; phone – (360) 468-2777

Needleworkers looking for a knitting or embroidery project to while away quiet evenings will find everything needed here. Fabrics, yarns, thread, pattern books, and stitchery and craft supplies are all stuffed into one happy store. It's a fun and unique place to shop.

Grayling Gallery

Hummel Lake Road; Lopez Island, WA 98261; phone – (360) 468-2779

This exclusive gallery carries excellent paintings, prints, pottery, jewelry, and other works by Northwest artists. It's open from 10:00 A.M. to 5:00 P.M. every day except Wednesday. The owner is an artist herself, who creates realistic paintings in both oils and watercolor.

Island Shirts and Caps

Lopez Village; Lopez Island, WA 98261; phone – (360) 468-2828

You'll notice a couple of odd-shaped, two-story wooden towers in Lopez Village. These are former water towers that are now abandoned, or converted to other uses. These towers were constructed in the early 1900s. A gasoline engine pumped water from wells into the towers, and gravity carried the stored water to where it was needed.

Island Shirts and Caps is in one of these old buildings. Stop in, if for no other reason than to see what the inside of a water tower looks like. The shop carries preprinted T-shirts, sweatshirts, hats, etc. Or you can chose a motif and shirt and they'll do custom printing and lettering for you.

Lopez Island Pharmacy
Lopez Village; Lopez Island, WA 98261; phone – (360) 468-2644

Lopez Pharmacy recently relocated from its long-time site near the south end of Fisherman Bay to a new building in Lopez Village—and brought its well-known 50's-style soda fountain along in the move! The store stocks the standard drugs and sundries as well as a nice line of gift items, including some very nice things by local craftspeople. The fountain offers sandwiches and sodas that will transport you back to the days of bobby socks and poodle skirts. *See also* Restaurants and Cafes.

Lopez Island Vineyards
Fisherman Bay Road; Lopez Island, WA 98261; phone – (360) 468-3644

Hours: *Noon to 5:00 P.M.; Wednesday through Sunday, Memorial Day through Labor Day; Friday and Saturday, Labor Day to Christmas and mid-March to Memorial Day; or by appointment.*

In early days the San Juan Islands were widely known for the orchards that flourished here. Lopez Island Vineyards, a small family run vineyard, continues this heritage by producing premium wine from grapes grown on their own estate here on Lopez Island, and in eastern Washington. You can stop by to pick up a bottle or two, or can dally in the wine-tasting room and tour the vineyards.

Madrona Farms
Corner of Richardson and Davis Bay roads; Route 1, Box 1800; Lopez Island, WA 98261; phone – home: (360) 468-3301; field: (360) 468-3441

Every spring and summer when the flower fields of Madrona Farms burst into bloom, Lopez Island becomes doubly beautiful. It's a mini-Skagit Valley! The folks at Madrona Farms grow their flowers and berries at two locations. Fields of daffodils and tulips, which bloom from mid-March to mid-May, are at the corner of Alex Bay and Watmough roads. The main farm, on Davis Bay Road just west of its intersection with Richardson Road, raises summer-bloomers such as delphiniums, sweet Williams, Asiatic lilies, gladiolus, and snapdragons, as well as the scrumptious organically grown berries that go into their jams and jellies.

You're welcome to stop and walk through the fields and chat with the owners if they're around. Many of the blossoms are destined for Seattle's Pike Place Market, but you'll also find them for sale at local stores. Group tours are available if you call and make arrangements; they'll have flowers and berry preserves available for sale. If their roadside stand isn't open for business, look for their many flavors of Madrona Farm jams, jellies, and syrups in stores at Lopez Village, Eastsound, and Friday Harbor.

Panda Books and More
Village Center Building; Lopez Island, WA 98261; phone – (360) 468-2132

Kids can cuddle up on a pillow in this store's cozy bay window to read or play a quiet game while parents browse. The excellent selection includes new books as well as some used paperbacks. You'll also find a good selection of books of regional interest. The "and More" indicated by the shop's name covers cards, prints, posters, calligraphy, cassette tapes, CD's, and maps.

Side Street Gallery
Friendly Isle Building; Lopez Island, WA 98261; phone – (360) 468-2911

You'll find sculpture and paintings by some of the exceptional local artists at this gallery on the south side of the Friendly Isle Building. Fine quality handmade jewelry is designed and made right on the premises.

Village Apparel
Friendly Isle Building; Lopez Island, WA 98261; phone – (360) 468-2022

Spiff up your vacation wardrobe at this women's clothing shop, or find a personal gift for a friend back home. Maybe a new beach bag, scarf, or some bright jewelry is just the finishing touch you're looking for. Village Apparel also carries an excellent line of imported sheepskin items and a selection of adorable handmade dolls.

Village House Antiques & Collectibles
Lopez Village; Lopez Island, WA 98261; phone – (360) 468-2338

This antique shop is crammed with all manner of treasures from Grandma's attic—dishes, salt and pepper shakers, Fiestaware, sandwich glass, old clothing, books, furniture. Who knows what other special finds? The shop shares the space with a barber, so if you need a quick trim too, here's the spot. It's in Lopez Village in a new building north of the public restrooms.

Willow Farm
#10 Bay Building, Lopez Village, WA 98261; phone – (360) 468-4050

Willow Farm, in the corner of the Bay Building, offers things to beautify the home, garden, and body. There are fine European soaps, aromatherapy products, candles, incense, lamps, greeting cards, gift wrapping and ribbon, baskets, mirrors, prints, crystal, and glassware. They'll make a custom silk and dry flower arrangement just for you. You're sure to find something you can't resist for yourself or a friend.

EVENTS & ATTRACTIONS

Fourth of July Parade

If you're jaded by mega-events like the Rose Bowl Parade or Macy's Thanksgiving Parade, stop by the San Juans to discover what a hometown Fourth of July parade is really meant to be. The whole island turns out to either participate or watch, as the marchers join ranks and wend along the two-mile parade route. Fireworks! Flags! Clowns! Hometown bands! Kids in costumes! Funny old cars! Hot dogs! Ice cream! Where else could you have so much fun? Or eat so much?

Lopez Island Historical Museum
P.O. Box 163; Lopez Island, WA 98261; phone – (360) 468-2049
or (360) 468-3447
Hours: *Noon to 4 P.M.; Friday through Sunday, May, June, and September; Wednesday through Sunday, July and August*

This museum gives you insight into early life on Lopez Island. Old farm machinery, boating and fishing paraphernalia, household goods and gadgets, and photographs are beautifully displayed to portray long-ago residents and their daily activities.

You'll find a couple of picnic tables outside, a reef net boat on the lawn, and an old tractor on the other side.

How to get there: The building is on Weeks Road, in Lopez Village.

ON-ISLAND TRANSPORTATION

Angie's Cab Courier

P.O. Box 254; Lopez Island, WA 98261; phone – (360) 468-2227

Angie's cab will provide transportation to and from anywhere on the Lopez Island. For visitors on an extended stay who find they have forgotten some key essential that is not available at local stores, the courier part of Angie's business makes a once-a-week trip to the mainland to fill customers' shopping lists. The company also has a car available for on-island rental.

Bike Shop on Lopez

School Road: Lopez Island, WA 98261; phone – (360) 468-3497

A varied stock of bikes – 5-speeds, 10-speeds, cross bikes, and mountain bikes – are but a phone call away on Lopez Island. The Bike Shop will take your telephone order and then deliver the bikes wherever you want them on Lopez. Call in advance from the mainland, and they can be waiting for you at the ferry landing. A charge for delivery and pick-up is added to the normal daily rental fee. Helmets and water bottles come with each bicycle.

Cycle San Juans

Route 1, Box 1744; Lopez Island, WA 98261; phone – (360) 468-3251

Crossroads bicycles with sturdy tires, water bottles, helmets, and a bar bag with a munchie inside are all yours for a phone call at Cycle San Juans. Rentals are by the half day, full day, or more. They deliver your rental to you free of charge.

Lopez Bicycle Works

*Route 2, P.O. Box 2700; Fisherman Bay Road; Lopez Island, WA 98261;
phone – (360) 468-2847*

Lopez Island has been referred to as the "Aspen of bicycling," and this shop provides for cyclists' every need. For those that want to sample the sport, there are over 100 bicycles for rent. A fully equipped repair shop can assist you with problems. The shop sells custom-built bikes, and they carry a full line of bicycle products and accessories. The Bicycle Works is located just south of Lopez Village, on Fisherman Bay Road, across the street from the Islander Lopez.

BOAT & KAYAK TOURS, CRUISES & CHARTERS

Harmony Charters
Box 211; Lopez Island, WA 98261; phone – (360) 468-3310

Join the captain and crew aboard the 68-foot ketch *Harmony* for a sailing tour to your choice of vacation spots in the San Juan Islands. Pick a secluded anchorage to try your hand at crabbing, clamming, or fishing. Guest amenities include three double berths, a shower, and prepared meals designed to your tastes, featuring fresh vegetables from the cook's garden. Added attractions include a piano for evening song fests and a ski boat for day-time fun. For those interested in briefer excursions, a 32-foot Bayliner is available for fishing charters, water taxi service, or day trips through the islands.

Kismet Sailing Charters
P.O. Box 111; Lopez Island, WA 98261; phone – (360) 468-2435

You have a choice of skippered day-sails aboard the 23-foot sloop *Moshulu* or overnight trips aboard the 36-foot ketch *Kismet*. The yacht accommodates four to six guests for overnight or extended cruises in the San Juans or Gulf Islands. The spacious lounge has a wrap-around couch and a piano. All meals are included.

Lopez Diving Service
Shark Reef Road; Lopez Island, WA 98261; phone – (360) 468-2054

This company specializes in commercial diving; however, they will provide scuba air refills. The owner does not have a high-compression air source for rapid tank fills, but if you leave your tanks they'll be filled within a few hours, ready for tomorrow's early morning dive. Call ahead.

Lopez Kayaks
Fisherman Bay Road; Lopez Island, WA 98261; phone – (360) 468-2847

The south end of Lopez Island, with its many caves and islands, is one of the most breathtaking areas in the San Juans to explore by kayak. Lopez Kayaks, located at the Lopez Bicycle Works on Fisherman Bay Road, is the only company in the San Juans that rents boats for individual use. Both single and double sea kayaks are available, and all come fully equipped with dry bags, hatch tarps, and safety equipment. In addition to rentals, the company offers guided half-day and sunset tours.

Mystic Sea Charters

*Route 2, Box 3026; Lopez Island, WA 98261; phone – (800) 553-2075,
or (360) 468-2032; fax: 468 2030*

The M.V. *Mystic Sea* is a 100-foot vessel operating out of Fisherman Bay on Lopez Island. Charter it for a host of activities such as large group meetings and parties, long distance sightseeing trips, wildlife tours, scuba diving expeditions, fishing trips, or inter-island transportation. The vessel sleeps up to 14 persons for overnight trips and accommodates up to 42 guests for shorter cruises. A TV, VCR, stereo system, wet bar, espresso bar, and fully-catered meals are among the creature comforts.

MARINAS & LAUNCH RAMPS
●

Islander Lopez Marina Resort

P.O. Box 197; Lopez Island, WA 98261; phone – (360) 468-2233

The Islander Lopez Marina Resort is part of a resort complex on Fisherman Bay, on the west side of Lopez Island. The recently rebuilt moorage has 50 guest slips with water and power, a fuel dock (gas), and restrooms, showers, and laundry. The resort's excellent restaurant and lounge sit above the moorage. Overnight accommodations are available at the resort; moorage guests may use the heated swimming pool and hot tub. Groceries and bicycle rentals are nearby. *See also* Lodging.

Islands Marine Center

*P.O. Box 88; Lopez Island, WA 98261; phone – (360) 468-3377 or
(360) 468-2279; fax – (360) 468-2283;
VHF Channels 16 and 69; CB Channel 9*

This full-service marina on Fisherman Bay, on the west side of Lopez Island, has 50 guest slips with power and water, restrooms, showers, laundry, a launch ramp, and pumpout station. Boat repair and maintenance, haulouts to 15 tons, and dry storage are available. The marina sells and services small boats and outboard motors, carries marine hardware and supplies, bait and tackle, and ice, and offers a tow boat service. Yacht charters are available out of the marina. On request, courtesy van service is provided to Lopez Village, the airport, the golf course, and the ferry landing. *See also* Lodging.

Odlin County Park Launch Ramp

San Juan County Parks and Recreation; Friday Harbor, WA 98250;
phone – (360) 378-4953

This single lane launch ramp faces on Upright Channel, on the northwest side of Lopez. To reach it from the ferry landing, follow Ferry Road south to the intersection with Port Stanley Road. Turn west and follow the road downhill to Odlin County Park. The ramp is on the north side of the park, just as the road meets the water.

Hunter Bay Launch Ramp

The Hunter Bay launch ramp is adjacent to a county dock on the southeast side of the island. To find it, take Center Road south down the middle of Lopez Island to Mud Bay Road. Head east on this road, and in two miles turn east on Islandale Road. Follow this downhill to its end at the dock and single-lane launch ramp.

MacKaye Harbor Launch Ramp

Kayakers especially like this launch ramp, as it allows them access to several bays and islands on the south end of Lopez. Reach the ramp by following Mud Bay Road east to Islandale, then turning south on MacKaye Harbor Road. After a few hundred feet, head west on a gravel road that leads down to a single-lane concrete launch ramp on the northeast side of MacKaye Harbor.

Opposite: Docks at a marina on Fisherman Bay provide overnight moorage to Lopez Island visitors.

PARKS, CAMPGROUNDS & CAMPS

Camp Nor'wester

Route 1, Box 1700; Lopez Island, WA 98261; phone – (360) 468-2225

Age: *Boys and girls age 9 to 16*
Fees: *4-weeks, $2050, 8-weeks, $3950, $150 sibling discount*
Facilities: *Lodging in 16-person units (including tents or teepees) with counselor and assistant, restrooms and showers, main lodge, dining hall, saltwater swimming pool, barn, stables with 28 horses, riding ring, rifle and archery ranges, craft center, adobe oven, health center, trading post, play fields, trails, rock climbing areas, dock, beach, 35-foot Indian canoe*
Activities: *Camping, swimming, nature study, boating (sailing, rowing, canoeing), soccer, baseball, basketball, volleyball, music, drama, crafts (woodworking, ceramics, weaving, spinning, painting, tie dye, batik, basket making, more), photography, baking, riding (English and Western), bicycling, archery, riflery, hiking, rock climbing, mountain climbing, ropes and challenge course, out-of-camp trips*

Here's a site made in campers' heaven—Indiana Jones would have gone here when he was a kid! Once the narrow isthmus that links the 387-acre peninsula to the southeast tip of Lopez Island is crossed, the everyday world vanishes, and only the realm of outdoor adventure remains. The camp's distinct Northwest bent reflects the culture of Native Americans who lived here long before the peninsula became a summer playground for youngsters. Totem poles grace the entry, and the camp's 35-foot canoe is carved in the authentic Haida Indian manner.

Extended trips, available to older campers, include bicycle treks to Canada's Gulf Islands, alpine hiking in Mount Baker-Snoqualmie National Forest, or a real mountain climb to the glaciated summit of Mount Baker. The season is divided into two four-week sessions, beginning mid-June and ending mid-August; campers may sign up for one or both.

As of early 1996 the Camp Nor'wester property is for sale. Whether the new owners will continue the camp is not known.

Spencer Spit State Park
Lopez Island, WA 98261; phone – (360) 468-2251

Facilities: 45 campsites, picnic shelters, picnic tables, fireplaces, restrooms and pit toilets, trailer dump, 16 mooring buoys, hiking trail

The fascinating sandy spit that wraps around a saltwater lagoon is the premier attraction of this fine park on Lopez Island's northeast side. You'll find campsites on the hill above the beach, and picnic tables along the shore. For boaters, there're numerous mooring buoys for tying up, and when those are filled there's ample room for anchoring.

How to get there: From the ferry landing drive 1¼ miles south and turn east on Port Stanley Road, which curves south. At 3¾ miles head west on Baker View Road and follow it to the park. Total distance is 5 miles.

Odlin County Park
Route 2, Box 3216; Lopez Island, WA 98261; phone – (360) 468-2496

Facilities: 30 campsites, picnic shelters, picnic tables, fireplaces, pit toilets, boat launch ramp, dock, sports field, children's play equipment, hiking trails

This pretty little county park holds 30 campsites on an 80-acre wooded site on the northwest shore of Lopez Island. The protected sandy beach offers excellent wading and swimming. A baseball diamond, oodles of picnic tables, picnic shelters, and fireplaces attract day-time users, too. A boat launch ramp and dock sit at the north edge of the property.

How to get there: The park is 1¼ miles from the ferry landing. To find it, turn west off Ferry Road onto Odlin Park Road (well signed) and follow it 300 yards downhill.

The rustic general store at Shaw Island carries all manner of island necessities.

Simply
SHAW

ALTHOUGH THE FERRIES touch down at Shaw, the island doesn't offer much for tourists. Residents stoutly resist any commercialization of their corner of the archipelago. However, it's an interesting spot, and if you have time, you'll probably enjoy a brief turn around its roads before going on to the larger islands.

As the ferry nuzzles up to the landing, first-time visitors are often startled to see a Catholic nun deftly lowering the car ramp. Members of the Franciscan order live on the island and operate the ferry terminal and Shaw's sole commercial enterprise, The Little Portion Store at the ferry landing.

Most roads are inland, rarely offering scenic glimpses of the water. You'll discover an interesting museum and an historic schoolhouse at a crossroads near the middle of the island. There are no commercial lodgings on Shaw; the only overnight "facility" for visitors is a small campground facing on Upright Channel. Canoe Island, off the southeast shore of Shaw Island, is the site of a youth camp.

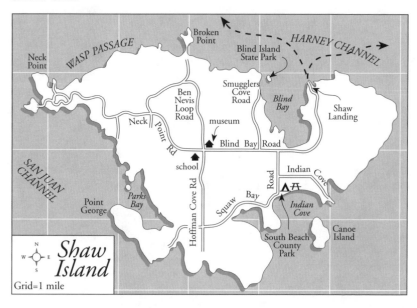

SHOPPING & FOOD

The Little Portion Store
Shaw Island, WA 98286; phone – (360) 468-2288

The many hats worn by this combination ferry terminal/general store/ gas station/marina/post office contribute to its rustic country store atmosphere. You'll find aisles and walls lined with tourist trinkets along with living necessities ranging from garden tools to pantyhose. Snacks and sandwich fixings are available.

ATTRACTIONS

Little Red Schoolhouse

Your great-grandparents may have learned their three R's in a one-room schoolhouse similar to the one that sits mid-island at the intersection of Blind

Bay Road and Hoffman Cove Road. This Shaw Island building, which is on the National Register of Historic Places, is a still-operating example of these classic schools.

Across the road's intersection is the island library; a tiny log cabin that adjoins it houses historical displays of earlier island times.

MARINAS & LAUNCH RAMPS

Shaw Island Franciscan Services
Shaw Island Ferry Landing; phone – (360) 468-2288

This little marina on Harney Channel, adjacent to the Shaw Island ferry landing offers a limited number of guest moorage slips by advance arrangement. Find groceries, hardware, bait, and tackle at the small store at the head of the dock.

A log cabin houses displays of the Shaw Island Historical Museum.

South Beach County Park Launch Ramp

The only public launch ramp on Shaw Island is at South Beach County Park. To reach it from the ferry landing, continue on Blind Bay Road to its intersection with Squaw Bay Road. Turn onto the latter and follow it south to Indian Cove Road. Here turn west, and shortly reach the county park and a single lane launch ramp into Indian Cove. Because of the long shallow beach, the ramp is only usable at high tides.

PARKS, CAMPGROUNDS & CAMPS

Canoe Island French Camp
P.O. Box 170; Orcas, WA 98280;
summer phone Canoe Island: (360) 468-2329,
winter phone Seattle (206) 860-8405

Age: Boys and girls age 9 to 15
Fees: 2 weeks, $1,200; 3 weeks, $1,800
Facilities: Lodging in 3-4 person teepees with counselor, restrooms and showers with electricity, heated swimming pool, dining room, library, health center, craft room, photography dark room, tennis court, volleyball court, dock, beach
Activities: French-based singing, dancing and cultural activities, camping, crafts (including pottery and photography), boating (sailing, canoeing, kayaking), swimming, archery, fencing, drama, music, tennis, volleyball, campfires, nature study, out-of-camp trips

Has there ever before been such a great way for a kid to learn a language? French Camp, founded in 1969, is located on Canoe Island, its own private 50-acre island immediately south of Shaw Island. This camp uses the French language and culture as a unique springboard for summer activities.

Campers may enroll for two- or three-week sessions that run from late-June to late-August; two or more sessions may be added together for longer stays. Even youngsters who don't know French will feel at home as they become acquainted with the language through activities that revolve around French themes.

South Beach County Park

San Juan County Parks and Recreation; Friday Harbor, WA 98250;
phone – (360) 378-4953

Facilities: *12 campsites, water, pit toilets, picnic shelter, fireplaces, picnic tables,*
boat launch ramp

This small park tucked in a remote corner of Shaw is often by-passed in favor of larger, better-known campgrounds. As a result, you may find space here when other areas are filled. Even if you don't plan to camp, it's a great place to stop; the beach is one of the best in the San Juans, and in summer the shallow water is often warm enough for wading or swimming.

How to get there: Head south from the ferry landing on Blind Bay Road, and in 1¼ miles turn left onto Squaw Bay Road. In ¼ mile a side road to the left, which is usually signed, leads to the park.

SHAW ISLAND
Parks, Campgrounds & Camps

The Orcas Hotel at Orcas Landing, which is on the National Register of Historic Places, still operates as a gracious hotel.

ORCAS

Tourist Nirvana

IF ASKED TO CHOOSE the best of the San Juan Islands, many visitors would undoubtedly say it is Orcas. While that assessment could be argued long and passionately, there is no question that Orcas offers much to tourists: superlative scenery, terrific recreation, and a diversity of accommodations, restaurants, and shopping.

For at least several centuries Orcas has been a "tourist destination." Although the long-ago Native Americans who originally summered here were, undoubtedly, most interested in tucking the local flora and fauna into their winter larders, they certainly must have appreciated the island's uncommon beauty. In the late 1800s the island became a getaway for mainland vacationers who came here to relax by tents and campfires on the beach or in the cedar-scented forest, or to stay in one of the inns that had sprung up on the shores. Some of those inns still welcome visitors today.

Three small "centers of commerce" are at Orcas Landing, Eastsound, and Deer Harbor. A few restaurants and other businesses are scattered about at other spots on the island, mostly at the intersections of main roads. The several shops and eateries at Orcas Landing attract tourists who (wisely) arrive early, in anticipation of the ferry. Overnight accommodations are also nearby. Deer Harbor, on the west side of the island, has facilities for people who live on that end of the island or who stop at the resort and marina.

The largest village—and major business center—is Eastsound, at the head of the long, fjord-like waterway named East Sound. The extreme head of the bay is quite shallow; however boaters wanting to stop at Eastsound

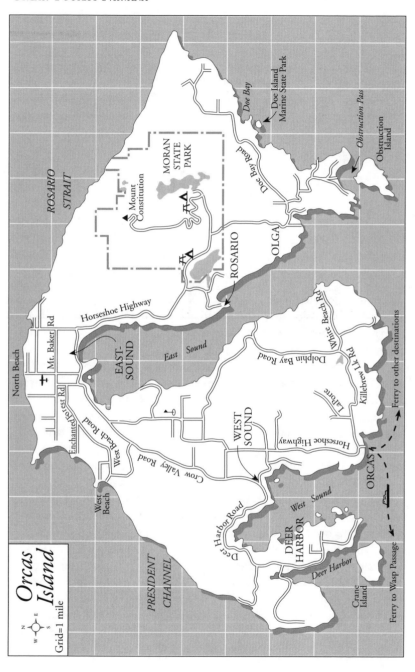

Orcas
Island

Grid=1 mile

N
W E
S

ROSARIO STRAIT

PRESIDENT CHANNEL

Doe Bay

Doe Island Marine State Park

Obstruction Pass

Obstruction Island

MORAN STATE PARK

Mount Constitution

ROSARIO

OLGA

Horseshoe Highway

North Beach

Mt. Baker Rd

Enchanted Forest Rd

EAST-SOUND

East Sound

West Beach Road

Crow Valley Road

West Beach

WEST SOUND

Deer Harbor Road

DEER HARBOR

Deer Harbor

West Sound

Crane Island

Dolphin Bay Road

White Beach Rd

Killebrew Lk Rd

LaBore

Horseshoe Highway

ORCAS

Ferry to other destinations

Ferry to Wasp Passage

can anchor near the head of the bay and take a dinghy to the public dock on the west side of Madrona Point. From there it's just a nice leg-stretch (about two blocks) to the shops, groceries, and restaurants of Eastsound.

A good deal of the eastern lobe of the island is devoted to Moran State Park, a 4,600-acre mountainous treasure that provides recreation and scenic splendor to both residents and visitors.

Orcas Island roads have a good deal more twists and turns and ups and downs than those on the other islands. That's part of its charm. Around any bend may lie a jewel of a bay, or at the top of a rise a breathtaking marine vista may appear. The perversity of the roads is not enough to deter bicyclists, who flock here by the thousands—some even make it to the 2,407-foot-high top of Mount Constitution.

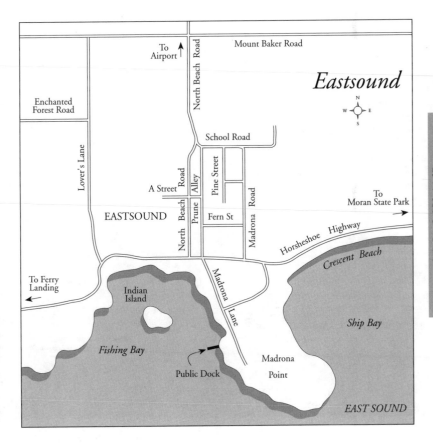

The island's somewhat unusual "saddlebag" shape makes getting around a bit complicated. The landmass is divided nearly in two by East Sound, and to a lesser extent sliced again by West Sound and Deer Harbor. All roads must loop around these waterways; few roads go true east/west or north/south, thus getting from the far east side of Orcas to its far west side requires a somewhat circuitous route. The main road, Horseshoe Highway, runs north from Orcas Landing around East Sound to the village of Eastsound, then continues on to the community of Olga. Deer Harbor Road curves around the end of West Sound, heading for Deer Harbor, and Crow Valley Road provides an alternative north/south route on the west side of the island.

Sunrise on East Sound, as seen from Double Mountain Bed and Breakfast.

LODGING

●

Prices quoted for accommodations are summer rates, double occupancy, as of 1996, unless otherwise indicated, and are subject to change. Lower rates are usually offered off-season. A tax of 7.6% is added.

Bartwood Lodge

Route 1, Box 1040; Eastsound, WA 98245; phone – (360) 376-2242

Accommodations: *16 rooms and fireplace suites (some with water views, some with private patios; all have cable TV). Children OK, no pets, smoking and nonsmoking.*
Extras: *Bartholomew's Bar and Grill (dinner year-round, breakfast and lunch in summer), championship tennis court, beach, boat dock and fuel, launch ramp, mooring buoys*
Rates: *$80 to $125. Credit cards accepted*

Arrive by either car or boat at this small resort on Orcas Island's north shore. Comfortable, modern rooms and suites await you in a three-story unit facing directly on the water. Patio Rooms, away from the water side of the lodge, have private patios where you can watch the evening stars. Waterfront Rooms and Fireplace Rooms all enjoy expansive views north to Sucia and Matia islands, the Gulf Islands, and peaks of Canada's Coast Range.

The rocky beach of the resort offers interesting tide pool exploration. Whales frequent these outer San Juan waters, and with luck you may sight orcas or dolphins offshore. Charter a boat to take advantage of some of the best fishing in the San Juans just offshore; evenings can include drinks, dinner, and bragging about the day's catch with friends at Bartholomew's.

How to get there: From Eastsound drive north on North Beach Road to Andersen Street and head east for ½ mile. Open year-round.

Beach Haven Resort

Enchanted Forest Road; Route 1, Box 12; Eastsound, WA 98245; phone – (360) 376-2288

Accommodations: *18 units (1- to 4-bedroom units), including log cabins, 2 modern apartments, "honeymoon cottage" with Jacuzzi tub, large A-frame home sleeps up to 10. All have private baths, kitchens, wood stoves (wood furnished), no TV, no phones. Children welcome, no dogs, smoking and nonsmoking. A-frame and lodge are disabled accessible*

Extras: Beach, forest, deer, otters, eagles, playground, rowboat and canoe rentals,
   free mooring buoys, romantic atmosphere, adult section
Rates: $85 to $145 (some units sleep up to 8); $200 for A-frame home that sleeps
   10. One-week minimum July and August. Credit cards accepted

Twilight may find a deer on your doorstep or an otter sleeping under
your deck at this perfect rustic family hide-a-way tucked into an old-growth
forest setting. Thirteen well-maintained log cabins, an A-frame cedar home,
two modern apartments, and a romantic "honeymoon cabin" are just steps
from a long, sloping pebble beach on Orcas Island's west shore.

Here's the ideal site for either a secluded retreat or a family vacation.
Cabins are well-separated. Four one-bedroom cabins in the adult section
offer privacy. Honeymooners will love one especially romantic cabin that
features skylights, a Jacuzzi, heated tile floors, and a private beach area hidden by wild roses.

Wade or swim on summer days, or explore President Channel in a rowboat. Enjoy breathtaking sunsets or stroll the private beach. All cabins are
completely furnished and have electric heat; air-tight wood-burning stoves
(wood supplied) add a cheery note to chill evenings.

Behind the family section lies a large playground, where children run,
play, and easily become pals. The two-story fort set, Burma bridge, swings,
slides, table tennis area, and horshoe pits keep them busy all vacation long.
An ongoing summer project is a beach driftwood fort that youngsters begin
in May. New arrivals expand it, until by summer's end it's a work of art.
Winter storms dismantle the structure, so a new one begins the following
summer.

How to get there: (Mileages given are distance from ferry landing.) From
the Orcas ferry landing drive north on Horseshoe Highway. In 2½ miles
turn left on Deer Harbor Road, at 3¼ miles, at a T-intersection where there
is a deli, go right (north) on Crow Valley Road. After 6¾ miles, turn left at
a stop sign onto West Beach Road. In 8 miles, at a T-intersection, turn right,
and at 8¼ miles turn left onto Beach Haven Road, which ends at the resort.
Total distance from the ferry is 8½ miles. Open year-round; 7-night minimum in summer, special off-season rates.

Buck Bay Farm Bed and Breakfast
Star Route 45; Olga, WA 98279; phone – (360) 376-2908

Accommodations: 5 bedrooms (3 with private bath, 2 with shared baths, queen-
   size beds, TV in sitting room). Rooms on lower level are disabled accessible.
   Children OK, no pets, no smoking.

Extras: *Full breakfast, sun room, firepit in backyard and gas barbeque on deck for guest use, farm ambiance, near Moran State Park*
Rates: *$75 to $95. Credit cards accepted*

This is the farm you wish you had lived on as a kid (or perhaps retire to now), with sheep peacefully grazing in a meadow, evening barbeques in the back yard, comfy beds to snuggle in, and a tummy-warming hearty breakfast awaiting you in the morning. The amazing thing is that this was formerly the farm's barn. Owners Rick and Janet Bronkey have magically transformed it into an airy, elegant inn, with wide decks overlooking meadows and an orchard where guests can bask in the summer sun or marvel at the evening starlight extravaganza. Common areas include a sun room and a sitting room with piano and TV, so there's plenty of room to socialize with other guests or to find your own private niche for reading or zoning out.

Knotty pine ceilings provide a fresh counterpoint to walls of deep rose, burgundy, and white. Alder and Rose rooms are exceptionally spacious; each has a sitting area and a daybed that can accommodate an extra guest. Garden Suite is two bedrooms sharing a bath, which can be rented as a suite for a group of four. Maple Room has a private bath and queen-size bed.

The home-style breakfast, prepared on a huge, commercial gas range, may feature a quiche or pancakes, French toast, and eggs to order, along with fresh fruit, sausage, hash browns, hot muffins, and jam. Janet Bronkey, who raised five children, promises you'll rarely be served anything you can't pronounce.

How to get there: Follow Horseshoe Highway east and then south from Eastsound, through Moran State Park. At the Olga junction head west on Point Lawrence Road. The inn is on the right, ¾ mile from the junction. Total distance from Eastsound is 8 miles.

Cascade Harbor Inn
Rosario Way; Eastsound, WA 98245; phone – (360) 376-6350; fax – (360) 376-6354

Accommodations: *48 units (studio units with full kitchens, 1-bedroom, suites with full kitchens, TV). Children OK, no pets, no smoking.*
Extras: *All units have private balconies with views of Cascade Harbor; suites have fireplaces. Walking distance to Rosario Resort; trail leads to Moran State Park*
Rates: *$90 to $270. Credit cards accepted*

Sip a chilled martini on your private balcony as you watch eagles soar above the treetops, or curl up by the fireplace with a book and a bowl of popcorn. These well-appointed, modern waterfront units overlooking Cascade Harbor will beautifully fill your needs for an overnight, weekend, or extended stay. Various combinations of adjoining rooms allow for creating larger suites for families or groups. Bedrooms have either one or two queen-size beds, studio units have comfortable, pull-down, double-size Murphy beds.

You can whip up a meal in your fully-equipped kitchen or stroll down to Rosario Resort, just below; to can dine in their fine restaurant. (The other facilities of the resort are available for a fee.) More restaurants, as well as shopping, are in Eastsound. Moran State Park, with its hiking, swimming, biking, fishing, sightseeing, birdwatching, and wealth of other recreation, is just up the road.

How to get there: From Eastsound continue east for 4 miles and go right (south) on Rosario Road. Follow it downhill for 1¼ miles to Rosario Resort and turn left at a chain link fence covered with ivy. At a Y in the road, stay right. The office is in the Port Building. Open year-round

Chestnut Hill Inn
P.O. Box 213; Orcas, WA 98280-0213; phone – (360) 376-5157

Accommodations: 4 rooms (queen-size beds, private baths, fireplaces), no TV, VCR movies in sitting room. No children, no pets, no smoking.
Extras: Full breakfast, picnic baskets, afternoon tea, lunch and dinner to guests (by arrangement), evening apéritifs, guest refrigerator, in-house massage, robes, and slippers, pond, use of rowboat or bicycles; chapel nearby
Rates: $135 to $145. Credit cards accepted

If we were awarding five stars for being romantic, Chestnut Hill would get at least ten. Innkeepers Marilyn and Dan Loewke have a sense for details, both in home furnishings and personal attention, that adds up to an exceptionally rich experience for their guests.

The inn looks out to a rolling meadow and a pond with a little island and dock. Horses boarded in the stable adjacent to the pond add a note of country elegance. Each of the four bedrooms has a four-poster, canopy bed, Egyptian cotton sheets, and gas fireplace. The name and decor of each room is dictated by its view: Pond Room (fresh green wall, ivy, and frogs), Stable Room (cranberry red walls, plaids, and equestrian painting), and Garden Room, on the main floor (floral prints and accents of green and daffodil yellow). Chapel Room, which is the most romantic of all, is gold and white with a lace canopy on the bed, and subtle touches of cherubs.

This may be the greatest place in the islands for a wedding. The tiny white chapel on the adjacent property, which seats up to 50, can be rented for intimate weddings, or the inn's gazebo can be the stage for lovely outdoor nuptials.

A gourmet, multi-course breakfast will start your day. If you plan to go bicycling or sightseeing, picnic basket lunches are available. Dinners are available, by arrangement (candlelight too, for the romantically inclined). On winter afternoons, tea, sweets, and savories are served guests. Several common rooms ensure that you'll find just the right personal space for socializing or solitude.

How to get there: Chestnut Hill is 1¾ miles from the ferry landing. Exit the ferry, turn *right* (the attendants direct traffic left, but if you signal they will permit you to go right). Drive 1 mile to the first left and turn on LaPorte Road. Continue on La Porte for ½ mile to a Y. Stay left at the Y, putting you on John Jones Road. At a break in the trees in ¼ mile, the signed driveway leading to the big yellow inn on the hill is on the right.

Deep Meadow Farm Bed and Breakfast
P.O. Box 321; Deer Harbor, WA 98234; phone and fax – (360) 376-5866

Accommodations: 2 rooms (private baths). Children over 12 OK, no pets, no smoking.
Extras: Full breakfast, pastoral setting, hot tub, hiking trails, walk to Deer Harbor
Rates: $100 to $110. No credit cards

The name "Deep Meadow" beautifully describes the pastoral setting of this bed and breakfast inn. Yet it's close enough to Deer Harbor for you to join in the nautical atmosphere too. Deep Meadow is a 40-acre former dairy farm that was homesteaded in 1900. The current home has been extensively remodeled and updated. Inkeepers Gary and Anna Boyle maintain the charming ambiance of a country farmhouse with antiques acquired in the Midwest and family heirlooms. Two spacious guest bedrooms on the second floor have lovely views of the farm.

Settle on the verandah in the evening and watch twilight creep over the island as crickets tune up their fiddles and deer saunter through the pasture. In daytime watch for eagles and hawks soaring overhead or perched in treetops. A hearty farm breakfast served the next morning will prepare you for a day bicycling around the island, paddling a kayak in Deer Harbor, hiking trails in Moran State Park, or simply lazing on the verandah.

How to get there: Follow Deer Harbor Road west. Three miles from the Crow Valley Road junction turn right onto Cormorant Bay Road. The inn is reached in ¼ mile. Open year-round.

Deer Harbor Lodge and Inn
P.O. Box 142; Deer Harbor, WA 98243; phone – (360) 376-4110

Accommodations: *8 rooms in a 2-story log lodge (private baths), shared sitting rooms, no TV. No children, no pets, no smoking*
Extras: *Water view, continental breakfast, Deer Harbor Inn serves dinner*
Rates: *$95. Credit cards accepted*

When tourists arrived at Deer Harbor Lodge in your grandfather's day, they stayed at the gracious lodge on the hillside above the harbor. Alas, the old inn is past its prime for lodging, and only the restaurant portion still serves the public. A handsome two-story log cabin in an old orchard near the inn now provides accommodations to tourists.

Constructed of huge peeled logs, with high ceilings and spacious rooms, the lodge provides elegance with a country flair. Fresh white muslin, puffy comforters, and rugged, natural wood create an inviting mood. Both floors of the lodge share common sitting rooms. Wide decks look out to Deer Harbor and the surrounding forested mountains.

Breakfast arrives at your door in a charming picnic basket, so you can enjoy your coffee and muffins in bed. For dinner, stroll through the old orchard to the inn to enjoy one of their fine meals.

How to get there: From the Orcas ferry landing head north on the Horseshoe Highway, and in 2 miles turn west on Deer Harbor Road. Follow this road as it curves around West Sound. The entrance to the inn is on the left, about ½ mile before reaching Deer Harbor. Open year-round.

Deer Harbor Resort and Marina
P.O. Box 200; Deer Harbor, WA 98243; phone – (360) 376-4420

Accommodations: *25 units (bungalows, cottages with private spas on decks, or villas, many with fireplaces, TV). Children OK in villas, no pets, smoking and nonsmoking*
Extras: *Hemingway's by the Sea (breakfast, dinner, and Sunday brunch, March through October), grocery and deli, pasta and pizza bar, heated pool, massage, gift shop, beach, boat dock and fuel, marina, small boat rentals, boat charters, kayak trips, sightseeing charters*
Rates: *$99 to $229. Credit cards accepted*

One of the longest-established resorts in the San Juans, the facilities at Deer Harbor have been regularly updated to provide modern accommodations and all the creature-comforts one might want in a complete vacation destination. The 25 modern units offer a range of amenities from fireplaces and private spas to snuggly feather beds. All boast great views of the off-shore islands and of boats bobbing in the protected harbor.

There's no lack of things to do—boat charters ranging from kayaks to yachts originate here, and the beach is open to guests for clamming, exploring, or just walking. Evening brings glorious sunsets as shadows fall across the pink-glowing water of Deer Harbor. The resort's restaurant, Hemingway's by the Sea, offers evening meals on an outside deck.

How to get there: From the Orcas ferry landing head north on the Horseshoe Highway, and in 2 miles turn west on Deer Harbor Road. Follow this road as it curves around West Sound and in 9 miles arrives at Deer Harbor. Closed mid-December to mid-January; some units closed in winter

Doe Bay Village Resort and Retreat
Star Route 86; Olga, WA 98279; phone – (360) 376-2291 or (360) 376-4755

Accommodations: 19 units (1- to 3-bedroom cottages, tent-cabins, some units with kitchenettes, bathrooms, and wood stoves); 1 dormitory-style hostel (central shower); group accommodations; guest kitchen with stove, refrigerator, and cookware; no TV or phone. Tent and RV camping. Children OK, pets on leash, no smoking

Extras: Hot mineral baths, sauna, massage, convenience store, cafe (breakfast and dinner), volleyball courts, 2 beaches, picnicking, trails, scuba diving, guided kayak trips

Rates: Wide range of prices running from $14.50 per person for dormitory lodging to $91.50 for a 3-bedroom guest house that sleeps 6. Credit cards accepted

Doe Bay offers alternative accommodations for those seeking inexpensive lodgings and informal surroundings. This does not mean the setting is any less enticing—in fact it is one of the most splendid, with cabins clustered in a wooded setting on the rim of a small, rocky cove. Some units have water views; all are permeated by the bracing scent of cedar, fir, and salt air. Although a few of the cabins have better appointments, accommodations range toward the rustic and spartan.

There is a great sense of camaraderie—shared interests make for quick friendships. Due to its livelier atmosphere and lower cost, the resort attracts a younger crowd than more up-scale resorts elsewhere in the islands. Tubs and sauna are clothing optional. Non-guests may use the hot tubs for a fee. Seats and picnic benches above the beach invite a private afternoon with a favorite book or a snack with a gull or two.

A kayak rests on the lawn at Doe Bay Village Resort and Retreat.

How to get there: From Eastsound drive east, following the Horseshoe Highway for 18 miles through Moran State Park to Doe Bay. Open year-round

Double Mountain Bed and Breakfast
P.O. Box 614; Eastsound, WA 98243; phone – (360) 376-4570

Accommodations: 3 rooms and suites (1-bedroom with king-size bed and private bath, 1-bedroom with queen-size bed and bath in adjacent hall, 2-room suite with private bath, kitchen, sleeps 4). Children OK, no pets, no smoking
Extras: *Full breakfast, views, birdwatching, hiking nearby*
Rates: *$85 to $125. No credit cards*

Double Mountain Inn has, in our estimation, the most breathtaking view of any lodgings in the San Juan islands. The 180-degree panorama stretches from the Canadian mountains down the length of East Sound to islands beyond. Across the valley, the tree-clad slopes of Buck Mountain and Mount Constitution rise. At night tiny lights of remote homes twinkle on Buck Mountain, and the village of East Sound glows below. Airplanes landing at the small airport look like children's toys.

This modern private home situated on the side of Double Mountain offers excellent accommodations in one of two spacious bedrooms on the main floor or a lower-level suite. Windows and a deck stretching along one side of the house take full advantage of the view. You'll feel at home instantly in the country modern furnishings. For breakfast, innkeeper Gail Koher may whip up some of her specialty "Dutch babies" with powdered sugar and homemade jam, as she did for us.

How to get there: From Orcas Landing follow Horseshoe Highway for 8 miles. ½ mile before reaching Eastsound a gravel road angles up the hillside. You'll notice some large spaceship-type sculptures hanging in the trees. Follow the road uphill for ¾ mile to the inn, on the right. Drivers unaccustomed to Orcas Island backroads may at first be intimidated by the steep drive up the gravel road. However, it's only a short distance, and the fine inn awaits.

Frog and Sparrow (to say nothing of Columbine)
Vacation Houses at Obstruction Pass

P.O. Box 247; Olga, WA 98279; phone – (360) 376-4671

*Accommodations: 2 small homes and a rustic 1-room cabin. (The houses have
    full kitchens, the cabin has light cooking facilities; all have double beds,
    baths, and wood stoves.) Children possible, no pets, no smoking*
*Extras: Beach, water views, woods nearby. Groceries, boat moorage, and kayak rental
    within walking distance at Lieberhaven Marina; sailing charter package available.*
Rates: $85 to $110, discount for full week. No credit cards

The whimsical names give you a hint about these charming accommodations situated on the most scenic corner of Orcas Island. Each of the little house has something unique. *Sparrow*, on a wooded hill with a lawn and pretty garden, has a sleeping loft for an extra person or two. It has two decks and charming sheds built of split cedar and driftwood by local artists. Take a sleeping bag to the sleep shed, and awaken to the mewing of gulls.

Frog, which sits right on the beach, is a shingled cottage dating from the 40s. You can watch the sun rise over Obstruction Pass from your bed in this quaint cottage. A guest or child can be accommodated in a tiny bedroom. Directly behind *Frog* is *Columbine*, a one-room rustic cabin with a bath and a cedar and driftwood deck. The deck, fence, and cedar-slab counters were all built by local artists.

All three cottages have double beds, made up with flannel sheets and lots of pillows and are furnished with antiques. Flowers and/or handrolled beeswax candles are provided, according to the owner's whim.

A special boat charter package with Brisa Charters, based at Obstruction Pass, includes a three-hour tour of the islands on a classic 45-foot sloop. (*See* Orcas Island Boat & Kayak Tours, Cruises & Charters.)

How to get there: From Eastsound, drive through Moran State Park, on the Horseshoe Highway, for 8½ miles to the intersection with Obstruction Pass Road. Turn south (right) and follow this road to the Obstruction Pass public dock in 2 miles. One cottage is east of the public dock, the other is west, past Lieber Haven Resort. Open year-round.

Glenwood Inn

Route 1, Box 110; Eastsound, WA 98245; phone – (360) 376-2671

Accommodations: 5 waterfront cabins (largest sleeps 8, kitchenettes, fireplaces, no TV). Children OK, no pets, no smoking. No credit cards, $$.
Extras: Beach, forest
Rates: $420 to $620 per week. No credit cards

What greater testimonial is there for a resort than to have guests return year after year? That's the case for this quiet spot on a 65-acre forested enclave on Orcas Island's north shore. The five cabins, located above the beach and on a slight bluff, all boast water views. The largest A-frame unit, which sleeps 8, has a loft and both queen-size and single beds. Llamas, which are kept on the property, add a bucolic note.

The resort's ½-mile-long sandy beach faces north to Sucia Island and Canada's Gulf Islands. Walk the beach west to reach Point Doughty, a long rocky spit that attracts scuba divers. Eagles, which nest nearby, often are seen soaring overhead or perched in tall snags.

How to get there: From Eastsound, drive north on either Lovers Lane or North Beach Road and turn west on Mount Baker Road. Follow this road and head north (right) on Glenwood Inn Road, which is the last road before YMCA Camp Orkila. Open end of May to October; 2-day minimum stay spring and fall, 1-week minimum in summer

Hazelwood Bed and Breakfast

P.O. Box 835; Orcas, WA 98280; phone and fax – (360) 376-6300

Accommodations: *2 rooms (queen-size beds, 1 with private bath, 1 with designated bath in hall), no pets, no smoking*
Extras: *Full breakfast, Jacuzzi, view, seclusion, beautiful forest*
Rates: *$ 85 to $95. 2-night minimum in summer. Credit cards accepted*

A unique geodesic dome tucked into 12 acres of secluded madrona and fir offers lodgings for escapees from work-a-day tensions, or couples who want a romantic retreat, or to sample the beauty of Orcas Island life. The opportunity to enjoy the unique space of the large dome is worth the stay in itself, not to mention the "southern hospitality" innkeepers Dan and Susan Smith offer. A wide cedar deck that wraps around the dome, at tree top level has a 160-degree view that includes the Olympic Mountains, Straits of Juan de Fuca, and extends clear to Mount Rainier!

The Smiths are Airforce retirees who have traveled world wide. Many of the fascinating furnishing are things they've gathered from distant places. Bedrooms are beautifully furnished with antiques in a lodge style that blends perfectly with the forest surroundings. There are special touches everywhere, such as the pair of antique ski poles that serve as a curtain rod in one bedroom.

Breakfasts are wholesome fare including fruits, juices, and homemade breads, muffins, and scones that will charge you up for the day. Evening brings a chance to relax and watch deer in the meadow below, and settle into the 6-person Jacuzzi.

How to get there: From the ferry landing turn right (regular traffic is directed left), and drive 1 mile to LaPorte Road. Turn left and in ½ mile at a Y in the road go left on John Jones Road for 200 yards to the wooden posts of Victorian Valley Drive. Turn left onto Victorian Valley Drive and go 300 yards to the first driveway on the right, which is the entrance to Hazelwood.

Joy's Inn

Route 1, Box 76; Eastsound, WA 98245; phone – (360) 376-4292

Accommodations: *2 bedrooms with queen-size beds (one is a modern waterbed, shared living room and kitchenette, shared bath), no TV. Children OK, no pets, no smoking*
Extras: *Continental breakfast, piano, country atmosphere, pond, swing*
Rates: *$65 to $75. No credit cards*

You'll be ready to move to the country permanently after a stay at this lovely home sited on eight acres near the middle of Orcas Island. The guest quarters, on the lower level of the home, open out onto a deck facing a pasture, pond, and orchard. You'll love watching birds on the pond, and deer grazing in the pasture or mooching apples off trees. Evenings bring the bright starry skies.

The two rooms share the bath, common living area, and kitchenette. The common area has a hide-a-bed, so the lodgings are ideal for a family with several children, or two families with children. For evening fun, there's a woodstove to add a real country touch, or a piano for evening sing-a-longs. Or stroll down to the pond, lie on the grass and listen to the crickets sing.

How to get there: From the Orcas ferry landing, follow the Horseshoe Highway north for 6½ miles. The inn is on the west (left) side of the road, just past the golf course. Open year-round.

Kangaroo House
P.O. Box 334; Eastsound, WA 98245; phone – (360) 376-2175

*Accommodations: 5 rooms (1- and 2-beds, private and shared baths), no TV.
    Children OK, no pets, no smoking*
*Extras: Full breakfast, hot tub, game room, sunny deck, guest refrigerator, robes,
    near Eastsound*
Rates: $70 to $110. Credit cards accepted

The kangaroo hasn't lived here for quite some time (some 40 years ago "Josie" was the pet of a former owner), but the memory of her remains in the name of the inn and the few quaint kangaroo knickknacks around. Even without a real live kangaroo your stay here will be memorable.

The inn is a turn-of-the-century Craftsman-style home with a lovely old field stone fireplace and beamed ceilings. The five bedrooms are delightfully furnished with antiques, lace curtains, and flowered coverlets. Owners Jan and Mike Russillo make sure your every need is attended to. Spend evenings around the fireplace, in the adjacent sitting area of the spacious living room, or in the game room thoughtfully stocked with books and board games. A hot tub in the garden is for the exclusive use of guests. You can sign up for a private time; robes and towels are provided.

Breakfast in the sunny dining room is a multi-course affair. We protested we would only eat a light breakfast because we were catching an early ferry, but we couldn't resist demolishing the entire breakfast, including scrumptious French toast filled with cream cheese and served with homemade apricot sauce.

Two resident squirrels may scamper down the overhanging evergreens outside, or deer may saunter across the backyard as you dine. The inn property backs up to the Orcas airport, so there may be an occasional drone of a small plane. It's fun to watch the planes, and the nearness of the airport is an advantage for guests arriving or departing via this route.

How to get there: From Eastsound drive north on North Beach Road. The Inn is on the left, in a little less than a mile. Open year-round.

L'Aerie Bed and Breakfast

Rosario Road; Eastsound, WA 98245; phone – (360) 376-4647

Accommodations: 2 rooms (private baths; Garden Room has pot-bellied stove, queen-size bed and daybed; Tower Room has king-size bed), cable TV. Children and pets by permission, no smoking
Extras: View, garden, ½ mile from Moran State Park
Rates: $75 to 100. No credit cards

As soon as you step inside this bed and breakfast perched on the hillside above Cascade Harbor you'll understand how it came by its name. The soaring view of mountains and water is, indeed, like that from an eagle's aerie. Flower-filled gardens edge the house, and a short rustic path reaches a charming greenhouse that graces one corner of the house. Follow the path farther and you'll discover a small waterfall.

The casual comfort of this ranch-style home's decor will immediately make you feel at home. Both of the inn's rooms are exceptionally spacious. The Garden Room has a sitting area with wicker chairs and a table where you'll enjoy the view. It also has a refrigerator, toaster oven, and coffee maker tucked in a closet so you can make an afternoon snack. The private entrance opens into the garden. The exceptional comfort and privacy of this suite makes it ideal for honeymooners. The Tower Room on the upper level is also spacious, and boasts a higher view and a king-size bed.

A full breakfast is served in the living room, where owner Louise Smith displays her beautiful collection of antique cut glass, china, and silver.

How to get there: From Eastsound, drive west on the Horseshoe Highway. In 4 miles, just before entering Moran State Park, turn south (right) on Rosario Road and follow it downhill for ¾ of a mile. The mailbox with the inn's name is on the right, the pretty yellow and white home itself is on the left.

ORCAS ISLAND
Lodging

Landmark Inn
Route 1, Box A-108; Eastsound, WA 98245; phone – (800) 622-4758;
(360) 376-2423

Accommodations: 15 suites (1- and 2-bedroom condominium-style suites, full
  kitchens, queen-size beds and hide-a-beds, fireplaces, balconies with water
  views, cable TV), cribs available, bicycle storage. Children OK, no pets,
  smoking and nonsmoking
Extras: Beach access, in Eastsound
Rates: $120 to $150, discount for full week. Credit cards accepted

This modern, three-story inn offers large, fully-equipped condominium
units within easy walking distance of the restaurants and shopping of Eastsound. The largest unit, which has two bedrooms and two baths, sleeps eight
vacationers. Bicycle storage is available for those who choose this mode of
touring the islands. Immediately across the road from the inn is a small park
with a beach and waterfront trail.

Views from the third story are the grandest. Most units look out to for-
est-embraced hills reflected in East Sound. Ground level units will appeal
to those who have difficulty negotiating stairs.

How to get there: From the Orcas ferry landing, follow the Horseshoe
Highway north to Eastsound. The inn is on the left as you enter town. Open
year-round

Liberty Call Bed and Breakfast
P.O. Box 232; Orcas, WA 98280; phone – (360) 376-5246

Accommodations: 2 suites with water view (private baths), TV. Children OK,
  no pets, no smoking.
Extras: Full breakfast, animals, walking distance to Orcas Landing
Rates: $85. No credit cards

While many bed and breakfast inns aren't equipped to handle children,
Liberty Call welcomes them. Some families return year after year, their youngsters eagerly looking forward to the friendly, familiar surroundings.

Three pygmy goats living at the inn provide great entertainment. Deer,
wild rabbits, and squirrels also frequently drop by. When everyone needs
some exercise, there's a bicycle rental shop a few steps down the road, and
the shops and restaurants of Orcas Landing are just beyond. If you want a
quiet evening, play one of the games on hand.

The inn sits on a hillside overlooking Harney Channel, embraced by evergreens. A wide, sunny deck overlooking the water offers great views of ferry and boat traffic below. The home's decor is nicely understated nautical. Adults will enjoy the gracious, comfortable furnishings, but parents won't have to worry about children spilling Coke on a precious antique.

How to get there: Head east from Orcas on White Beach Road. In ½ mile the driveway to Liberty Call is on the left. Open spring through fall.

Lieber Haven Marina Resort
P.O. Box 127; Olga, WA 98279; phone – (360) 376-2472

Accommodations: 12 units (1- and 2-bedroom cabins and apartments, all with kitchenettes and patios or decks with picnic tables and barbecues); no TV. Children OK, no pets, nonsmoking

The morning sun warms a relaxed visitor at Lieber Haven Marina Resort.

Extras: Convenience store, boat rental, marina, beach, fishing, scuba diving, kayak tours; sailing, fishing, and whale watching charters; boat launch nearby
Rates: $80 and up. Credit cards accepted

Intimate is the word for this corner of Orcas Island. Obstruction Pass is a ¼-mile-wide dog-leg channel that sees less boat traffic than Thatcher Pass, to the south (although ferries have been known to make a breathtaking detour through here at high tide). Lieber Haven, the small resort facing on the pass offers a casual, nautical setting ideal for a family holiday or a couple's private retreat. The accommodations are spacious and generously furnished. Most units are strung along the waterfront, others are just a step away. The exceptionally congenial owners also run the small marina and convenience store. A collection of driftwood, statues, and flowers scattered along the shore and dock enhances the nautical aura.

The natural setting offers a wealth of kid adventures—search the beach for wave-tossed treasures, build fantasylands from driftwood, lure fish to baited hooks dropped from the dock, or check out pilings for bizarre marine life. Moran State Park, with its lakes and hiking trails is nearby. And for grownups, benches on the dock and shore invite relaxation and watching the long fingers of evening caress the islands.

How to get there: From Eastsound, drive west on the Horseshoe Highway for 8 miles to the intersection with Obstruction Pass Road. Turn south (right) and follow this road to its end at the Obstruction Pass public dock and launch ramp in 2 miles. The resort is west of the launch ramp. Open year-round.

North Beach Inn
P.O. Box 80; Eastsound, WA 98245; phone – (360) 376-2660

Accommodations: 11 units (1- to 3-bedroom cottages, kitchenettes), no TV. Children OK, pets OK, smoking and nonsmoking
Extras: Beach, seclusion
Rates: $90 (2-person studio) to $165 (4-person cottage). No credit cards

North Beach Inn is a grand old standby on Orcas Island's north shore. The main lodge that is the focal point of the resort once served as a dining hall for a summer camp. Now it is the owner's private home, and visitors may either cook their own meals in their cottage's kitchenettes or repair to a local restaurant.

A long private lane leads to rustic cottages strung along the beach. You'll find it just the spot for a complete escape from the world. Stroll the long gravel beach in the cool of the evening, or settle down among the driftwood for an afternoon of solitude with a thick novel.

Facilities vary from older, quite rustic cottages to larger, better appointed lodges big enough to accommodate a family of six or seven. All units have fireplaces and electric heat and come equipped with bedding and cooking utensils.

How to get there: From the Horseshoe Highway, on the west side of Eastsound, turn north on Lovers Lane. Drive to a T-intersection and head west on Mount Baker Road. The entrance is signed. Open year-round, except closed December 1 to Valentine's Day weekend (open for Valentine's Day); renting Saturday to Saturday in summer season (unless there are cancellations), 2-day minimum otherwise.

Northshore Cottages

Sunset Avenue; P.O. Box 1273; Eastsound, WA 98245;
phone – (360) 376-5131; fax – (360) 376-6535

Accommodations: 2 cabins (kitchenettes, fireplaces, hot tubs) big-screen TV, VCR, telephone. Children OK, pets OK
Extras: Beach, hot tub, walk to Eastsound
Rates: $110 to $120; 2-night minimum. No credit cards

Two pretty little cabins above the water offer private lodgings for couples. Both units have their own deck and hot tub. The owners are antique collectors, and have filled the cottages with a selection of lovely antique furniture. The smaller unit has a clean, cozy gas-burning fireplace. The larger of the two cottages, which can accommodate two couples, or a couple with children, boasts a gorgeous fire-view "Soapstone" wood-burning stove.

Fix dinner in your kitchenette and enjoy it on your deck as you watch evening settle over the islands. To the north is Sucia Island and the Canadian Gulf Islands. You may even see whales offshore. Finish the day with a relaxing soak in the outdoor hot tub, or follow the path down to the beach, stretch out, and stargaze. You'll never see skies more brilliant! Then it's off to dreamland in the cozy warmth of your bed.

How to get there: Drive north from Eastsound on North Beach Road. Just opposite the sign to Smuggler's Villa turn right onto Sunset Avenue. The cabins are on the left in about ¼ mile. Open year-round.

ORCAS ISLAND
Lodging

The Old Trout Inn

Route 1, Box 45A, Eastsound, WA 98245; phone – (360) 376-3626

Accommodations: *4 rooms and guesthouse (2 bedrooms with queen-size bed and private bath, 1 bedroom with queen-size bed, and shared bath, 1 bedroom with twin beds and shared bath; guesthouse has 1 queen-size bed, mini-kitchen, hot tub, gas fireplace), TV in sitting room. No small children, no pets, no smoking*
Extras: *Full breakfast, afternoon snacks, Jacuzzi, 3-acre pond, birdwatching*
Rates: *$85 to $135. Credit cards accepted*

Exquisite settings in the San Juans aren't required to have a beachfront location, as is proved by the Old Trout Inn. A beautiful three-acre pond, complete with cattails and a small waterfall, is the focal point for this fine lodge. The main house edges right on the pond, and the living room and wide deck provide perfect spots for watching wild birds that stop by (binoculars are on hand). This would be a beautiful spot to have a wedding. All rooms are beautifully decorated with a few period pieces and lots of comfortable, country touches. Innkeepers Dick and Sandra Bronson love to travel; you'll enjoy looking at the interesting mementos of their trips.

One of the main floor bedrooms, which opens onto a sunny garden room, has a private bath. The other two bedrooms on the main floor share a bath; one has a queen-size bed, the other has twin beds, so they would make ideal accommodations for a family. A downstairs suite has a luxurious queen-size canopy bed, a private bath and sauna. The private living room in this unit boast a stone fireplace, wet bar, and VCR. This suite opens up to the lower deck, with a hot tub overlooking the pond. The nearby guesthouse, which sleeps two, has a hot tub on the outside deck, gas fireplace, kitchen, and glassed-in sitting room.

Breakfast is served in the handsome dining room, with the pond in full view. You'll want to take a break from your relaxation or island exploration for afternoon snacks on the deck.

How to get there: From Orcas ferry landing follow Horseshoe Highway north for 2½ miles. The inn is on the left.

Olympic Lodge

P.O. Box 339; Deer Harbor, WA 98243; phone – (360) 376-3199

Accommodations: *5 rooms (2-bedroom bungalow with kitchen; 3 rooms in lodge, 2 with shared bath). TV in cottage and sitting room. Children OK in bungalow, no pets, no smoking. Bungalow is disabled accessible.*
Extras: *Continental breakfast for guests in lodge, tennis court, beach, mooring buoy for guest boats; restaurants and marina nearby*
Rates: *Bungalow $125 ($150 for 4 persons), rooms $65 to $85. 10% discount for week-long stay. No credit cards*

You'll be transported back to bygone times as you enjoy the sun setting over the Olympic Mountains from the old-fashioned porch that wraps around the front of Olympic Lodge. This historic Craftsman-style home on the Deer Harbor waterfront was built in 1914 by early homesteader Henry Cayou. When they remodeled and updated the inn in 1995, owners Phillip and Ronda Greenawalt made every effort to retain the historic character of the home, yet provide guests with all modern creature comforts. Rooms are beautifully furnished with antiques and fine reproductions.

A family will have a glorious vacation in the beachfront bungalow, which has two bedrooms, one with a queen bed, one with twin beds. The cottage also holds a full kitchen, a sitting room with fireplace, and a deck. It can accommodate up to six people, with roll-aways for children.

Whether staying for a weekend, week, or longer there's plenty to keep everybody busy here. Wander down to the beach or play tennis on the inn's private court (rackets and ball are provided, lessons are available). The docks of Deer Harbor Marina are within walking distance, and from there you can arrange for a kayak tour of Orcas Island, or a wildlife watching cruise. Boaters can tie up to the inn's mooring buoy or berth their vessel at the Deer Harbor marina dock (the marina charges a fee).

How to get there: From the Orcas ferry landing head north on the Horseshoe Highway, and in 2 miles turn west on Deer Harbor Road. Follow this road as it curves around West Sound. Just before reaching the Deer Harbor Resort, turn right on Sunset Beach Road. The inn is on the left.

Orcas Hotel
P.O. Box 155; Orcas Landing; Orcas, WA 98280; phone – (360) 376-4300

Accommodations: *12 rooms and suites (some with shared bath), no TV.*
Children by arrangement, no pets, no smoking.
Extras: *Espresso bakery café (breakfast, lunch), seasonal restaurant (breakfast, lunch, dinner), lounge*
Rates: *$69 to $170. Credit cards accepted*

This gracious Victorian inn perched on a hillside within walking distance of the ferry landing is the *grande dame* of Orcas Island lodgings. The hotel, which was built between 1900 and 1904, is on the National Register of Historic Places. It was most recently refurbished in 1985, but it still boasts period furnishings throughout. Wicker furniture graces the verandah that wraps around three sides of the inn. White picket fences lined by bright flowers complete the turn-of-the-century ambiance.

All rooms have antiques and queen-size or extra-long twin beds with comfy quilts. Two spacious, romantic rooms have view balconies and private baths featuring Jacuzzis. The remaining rooms are cozier, although not cramped; three come with half baths (shower down the hall), others share baths.

How to get there: The hotel sits immediately above the Orcas Island ferry landing. Parking is on the north side of the hotel. Open year-round, except for Christmas Eve and Christmas Day

Outlook Inn on Orcas Island
P.O. Box 210; Eastsound, WA 98245; phone – (360) 376-2200;
fax – (360) 376-2256

Accommodations: *41 rooms and suites (private and shared bath, TV in some rooms). Children OK, no pets, smoking and nonsmoking*
Extras: *Restaurant (breakfast, lunch, dinner), lounge, conference/banquet room*
Rates: *Shared bath $34 to $74, private bath $44 to 120, deluxe suites $99 to $225. Credit cards accepted*

If your grandparents or great-grandparents ever visited Orcas Island, they may well have stayed at the Outlook Inn. It has a long tradition of providing lodging for island visitors. You may choose to stay in one of the 19 rooms in the historic hotel where the decor has been up-dated just enough to provide complete modern comfort with 1890s aura. Beds sport hobnail coverlets, while antiques and framed needlework fill the rooms and spill down the halls; one stairway has an old oak commode sprouting a silk caladium. All bedrooms but one have shared baths.

Visitors approach the Orcas Hotel at Orcas Landing.

Two adjacent, newer units hold additional rooms, with private baths and TV, but still with gracious antiques and flower-bedecked Victorian setting. Bayview Suites, the most recently built units, have deluxe accommodations with sunken living rooms and radiant heated floors. Each of these elegant suites provide all the pampering you'd ever desire, with whirlpool tubs, warmed towels, plush robes, bar, TV and VCR, and private balconies opening out to expansive views of the water and surrounding mountains.

The beach lies immediately across the street. Stores and restaurants of Eastsound are just steps away; however, the inn itself holds Rosies, an excellent restaurant that serves breakfast, lunch, and dinner.

How to get there: From the Orcas ferry landing, follow Horseshoe Highway north for 8½ miles to Eastsound. The inn is on the left as you enter the business district. Open year-round. For guests arriving by air, the airport is ½ mile to the north.

Rosario Resort and Spa

*1 Rosario Way; Eastsound, WA 98245; phone – (800) 562-8820
or (360) 376-2222*

Accommodations: *131 rooms (most with water views, some kitchen and fireplace suites, TV). Children OK, no pets, smoking and nonsmoking*
Extras: *Marina, moorage, marine fuel, convenience store, deli, restaurant (breakfast, lunch, and dinner), cafe open seasonally (breakfast, lunch), lounge, gift shop, boutique, beauty shop, exercise rooms, sauna, massages, indoor and outdoor pools, tennis courts, rental cars, meeting facilities, hiking, fishing, boating*
Rates: *$95 to $220, special packages available. Credit cards accepted*

For many, Rosario is an instant love affair. This elaborate facility, which graces a spectacular setting on Cascade Bay, is billed as "the premier island destination resort in the Pacific Northwest." The sumptuous Moran Mansion (on the National Register of Historic Places) that centerpieces the fascinating resort holds a restaurant, lounge, gift shop, and spa. Restaurant cuisine tends to Northwest seafood, but also includes a nice range of other dishes. The mansion's enormous plate glass windows that frame the marine view, elegant stained glass accents, exotic wood parquet flooring, and evening concerts on the historic Steinway and pipe organ are unparalleled anywhere in the Northwest. The outside swimming pool is surrounded by glass that shields sunbathers from brisk sea breezes.

Modern, hillside units contain the majority of the well-appointed hotel rooms and suites; all have view balconies. Older accommodations are above the waterfront, near the historic mansion. The friendly, helpful staff, the extensive lodging and meeting facilities, and the scenic site make it a favorite for business seminars and retreats. And, amid the bustle and up-scale ambiance, curious deer may amble up to your car in the parking lot.

How to get there: From Eastsound, drive west on the Horseshoe Highway. In 4 miles, just before entering Moran State Park, turn south (right) on Rosario Road and follow it downhill for 1¾ miles to the resort. Open year-round.

Sand Dollar Inn Bed and Breakfast

Star Route Box 10; Olga, WA 98279; phone – (360) 376-5696

Accommodations: 4 rooms (queen-size beds, private baths), no TV. No children, no pets, non-smokers only

Extras: Full breakfast, guest refrigerator and phone, water views from sun room and three bedrooms, short distance to Olga

Rates: $88 to $115. Credit cards accepted

You can well imagine this gracious home being owned by an old sea captain, with the many antiques being those that he collected on his journeys to the far corners of the world. While the home once did belong to a ferryboat captain, the present owners are Ric and Ann Sanchez. The lovely oriental furnishings were collected by Ann, who taught in Japan.

The Sand Dollar Inn sits on a slight hillside, overlooking Buck Bay. The shallow bay is a gathering spot for all sorts of waterfowl. Wander down to the shore to birdwatch, or you may be able to spot some from the inn with binoculars.

All bedrooms but one have adjoining bathrooms. Robes are provided for occupants of the Library Room, who must take a quick trek across the hall to reach their bath. Hearty breakfasts befitting a sea captain are served in the inn's sun room.

How to get there: Follow Horseshoe Highway east from Eastsound. The inn is just past the Olga intersection, on the north side of the road, 6½ miles from Eastsound. Open year-round.

Smuggler's Villa Resort

P.O. Box 79; Eastsound, WA 98245; phone – (800) 488-2097 or (360) 376-2297; fax – (360) 376-5597

Accommodations: 20 2-bedroom villas (all with private bathrooms, full kitchens, fireplaces, laundry, TV, VCR). Children OK, no pets, nonsmoking

Extras: Tennis court, hot tub, sauna, heated swimming pool, playground, basketball court, dock, moorage, beach, scenic airplane flights nearby, close to village of Eastsound

Rates: $160 to $200 up to 4 persons. Children 7 and younger free. Credit cards accepted

Families or small groups love these fully-appointed, modern, home-style units. The spacious accommodations, full kitchens, laundry facilities, and a lot of things to keep kids occupied make these lodgings a real find in the San Juans. The airport, just a clam toss away, is a transportation advantage for some; others may want to join the gulls with a scenic biplane flight.

All housing units look out to a private marina that opens to the north shore of Orcas Island. A fee is charged for moorage. The driftwood-strewn beach is fine for daytime sunning and evening strolls. Only a few miles north lie the fabled marine state park islands of Sucia, Matia, and Patos, which are quickly reached by boat or kayak. En route is Parker Reef, where seals, sea lions and a host of seabirds hang out.

How to get there: From Eastsound drive north on North Beach Road, just north of the airport a road to the left is signed as the entrance to Smuggler's Villa. Open year-round.

Spring Bay Inn
P.O. Box 97; Olga, WA 98279; phone – (360) 376-5531;
fax – (360) 376-2193

Accommodations: 4 rooms (private baths, queen-or king-size beds), no TV.
Children OK, no pets, no smoking
Extras: Full breakfast, hot tub, waterfront, guided kayak tours, forest trails
Rates: $150 to $175. Credit cards accepted

Spring Bay Inn is well off the beaten path, even for Orcas Island, but once you've arrived you will feel as if you have discovered Oz. The magnificent inn is situated on 60 acres of pristine woodland and its own tiny bay. The owners, Carl Burger and Sandy Playa, are former park rangers who have a custodial relationship with the land, keeping it in a natural state with only the clearing for the inn, road, and a few trails through the forest.

The sumptuous inn holds forth in this rustic setting. As you enter the living room, you are swept away by the 13-foot ceilings and expanse of windows framing the water view. Huge stone fireplaces anchor either end of this room, which runs nearly the width of the house. There are eight fireplaces! Although the inn is newly constructed, there are homey accents such as spacious claw-footed tubs in every bathroom (in addition to showers), and antique bed frames modified to fit the queen- and king-size beds. Bedrooms, each with its own fireplace and bath, are on the upper level. Two have private decks where, in the evening, you can watch the moon glistening on the bay. There's a hot tub at water's edge for twilight soaking.

Your stay includes a guided kayak tour and basic paddling instruction. Kayaks and all necessary gear are provided. For early risers going kayaking, a Continental breakfast is laid out. Upon your return, a full breakfast is ready.

How to get there: Follow the Horseshoe Highway east from Eastsound. After passing the Olga intersection, turn right onto Obstruction Pass Road. In about a mile take another right onto the road signed to Obstruction Pass

At Spring Bay Inn you can begin your morning with a kayak paddle.

and the Spring Bay Inn. The road immediately changes from blacktop to dirt, and in ¾ of a mile a road on the left is signed to the inn. It's another ½ mile down this driveway before the inn is reached. You can arrive at the inn by boat, too. There is good anchorage in the fjord-like cove; Spring Bay lies immediately east of Obstruction Point Campground, on Obstruction Pass. Open year-round.

Turtleback Farm Inn
Crow Valley Road; Route 1, Box 650; Eastsound, WA 98245;
phone – (800) (360) 376-4914 or (360) 376-4914

Accommodations: 7 rooms (private baths, some queen-size beds), no TV.
Children OK, no pets, no smoking indoors
Extras: Full breakfast, pastoral atmosphere, ponds, evening sherry, guest refrigerator
Rates: $80 to $160. Credit cards accepted

Turtleback Farm Inn is a meticulously restored farmhouse sitting on 80 acres of rolling pastoral land in the shadow of Turtleback Mountain. A grape-stake fence edges a country flower garden along one side of the house, while a deck that runs along the opposite side looks out to the green swale of Crow Valley. The property is actually an operating farm, raising apples, poultry, and sheep. You can spend your day wandering the farm or sunning on the deck. If you ask your hosts, Susan and Bill Fletcher, they'll suggest interesting things to do and see on Orcas Island.

The interior of the old home is awash with soft tones and floral prints. Antique-filled bedrooms range from a cozy garret-like room with a double bed, ideal for a single person or two very close friends, to a spacious light-filled room with queen-size bed and French doors opening onto a private deck. Guests share a sitting room that has a pleasant Rumford fireplace and a game table. Evening tea or a sherry will send you off to dreamland.

Breakfasts are so scrumptious that the inn has had its own cookbook published; it includes the recipe for their acclaimed granola. Your breakfast may include puffy oven pancakes with fresh berry sauce or banana pancakes with honey-nut butter.

How to get there: From the Orcas ferry landing drive north on Horseshoe Highway and turn west onto Deer Harbor Road. At the intersection with Crow Valley Road head north. The inn is on the east side of the road in 2½ miles. Open year-round; 2-night minimum during the summer season and all holidays.

Walking Horse Country Farm
Route 1, Box 27C; Eastsound, WA 98245; phone – (360) 376-5306

Accommodation: 2-bedroom home (queen-size beds, kitchen, fireplace, private bath, VCR, laundry). Children welcome, no pets, no smoking.
Extras: Carriage rides and trail rides available, nature trails, ponds, picnic area, birdwatching
Rates: $100 for 1 bedroom to $250 for entire home that accommodates four persons.

This beautiful no-host guest house on a 27-acre horse farm provides truly one-of-a-kind lodgings. Whether you just enjoy the rural ambiance, or want to join in on some of the horse-related activities, you are assured of a memorable stay. Farm owners Jeri and Doug Smart, who specialize in raising and training Tennessee Walking Horses, now offer trail rides on their horses

As a guest in the "The Little House on the Farm," you receive a 25% discount on trial rides. Horse-drawn carriage rides are available for special occasions. However, you need to make advanced reservations for all horse-related activities. The entourage of more than 20 farm animals includes Belgian draft horses and Shetland ponies, as well as the elegant Tennessee Walkers. Because of the animals on the farm, children must be supervised by an adult.

The two-bedroom home is furnished with Jeri's carefully-chosen antiques and collectibles. Various accommodation packages are available, depending on your needs. Packages range from one-bedroom with either a private or shared bath, to use of the entire two-bedroom home with its kitchen, spacious living room with stone fireplace, and laundry.

The home overlooks the farm with its barn-red outbuildings and tidy white fences. Trails on the property are open for walking, as well as riding. Picnic tables by the ponds are a nice stop on your tour of the farm. You may see deer grazing with the horses in the pastures. Ponds and woodlands attract wild birds—Doug puts out food to encourage them to stop by.

How to get there: From the ferry landing, drive north on the Horseshoe Highway for 2 miles, and turn left (west) onto Deer Harbor Road. In 1 mile, at the T-intersection with Crow Valley Road, head north on Crow Valley Road. In 3½ miles turn left (west) onto West Beach Road. The farm is on the right, just after the intersection. *See also* Transportation.

West Beach Resort
Route 1, Box 510; Eastsound, WA 98245; phone – (360) 376-2240

Accommodations: 15 cabins (1- and 2-bedroom units, kitchenettes, queen-size beds, electric heat, many with wood stoves), no TV. Children OK, pets OK (for an additional charge), smoking and nonsmoking units.
Extras: Dock, marine gas, groceries, scuba air, camping, RV hookups, laundromat, moorage, beach, kayak tours
Rates: $775 to $995 for full week, 7-day minimum July and August. Credit cards accepted

This waterfront resort is ideal for families with restless children. While parents kick back and gull-gaze on their cottage deck or on the beach, kids keep busy exploring the beach, checking out activity at the dock and store, and striking up friendships with kids in the other cottages or campground. In the evening all can gather around a beach fire to watch the sunset or take a quiet evening mini-cruise. Scuba divers favor West Beach, because several of the best dive sites in the San Juans lie north at Point Doughty and south at Lover's Cove. Scuba air is available at the store.

Cabins line the beach, just a step away from the water. Furnishings are cozy-comfortable; all have electric heat, but wood stoves add a cheery note on cool evenings.

How to get there: From the Orcas ferry landing, drive north on Horseshoe Highway West for 2 miles to the intersection with Deer Harbor Road. Turn left onto Deer Harbor Road, drive 1 mile, and at a T-intersection, go north on Crow Valley Road. In 3½ miles turn on West Beach Road which heads west, and then north. As the road makes another right turn, heading west, the signed side road to West Beach goes left. Open year-round.

West Sound Cottage Bed and Breakfast
Eastsound, WA 98245; phone – (360) 376-2172 or (360) 376-3009;
fax – (360) 376-2173

Accommodations: *3 cottage suites and a tugboat yacht suite (queen- and king-size beds, day-beds, private baths, TV). Children OK, no pets, no smoking*
Amenities: *Continental breakfast, refrigerator, coffeemaker, microwave, dishes, wood stove, private beach and dock*
Rates: *$95 for cottage, $175 for tugboat (summer only). Credit cards accepted*

These spacious, airy suites right on the water sleep up to four vacation-ers. Boaters with limited sleeping space aboard can tie up to the cottages' private dock and enjoy one of the comfortable suites. You can arrive by plane too—Kenmore Air flies into the West Sound Marina, just a short walk away. Each charming unit is nicely furnished with antiques, and beds sport cozy handmade quilts and down comforters. Guidebooks for the island are in each unit, and your hosts, who are long-time residents, can help you dis-cover the best Orcas has to offer. For breakfast, a continental breakfast bas-ket will arrive at your door. Watch boating activity on West Sound from the vantage point of the cottages' covered deck, or lean back and enjoy twi-light settling over the island.

For romantic seclusion, stay in the *The Star*, a 40-foot luxury tugbooat on East Sound. It boasts a fully-equipped galley, salon/living room, and cozy stateroom. A V-berth holds two additional berths. Outside decks are just the spot for afternoon sunbathing or evening barbeques.

How to get there: From the ferry landing, drive north on the Horse-shoe Highway, and turn left (west) onto Deer Harbor Road. The cot-tage is at the head of West Sound, by the West Sound Store. Open year-round.

WindSong Bed and Breakfast
P.O. Box 32; Orcas, WA 98280; phone – (360) 376-2500
e-mail – windsong@pacificrim.net;
web: http://www.pacficws.com/orcas/windsong.html

Accommodations: *4 rooms (private baths, queen-size beds, 1 room with addi-tional day-bed). TV in sitting room; TV in bedroom on request. Children over 12 by arrangement, no pets, no smoking*
Extras: *4-course gourmet breakfast, Jacuzzi, country atmosphere, wildlife*
Rates: *$115 to $140. Credit cards accepted*

Part of the fun of staying in a bed and breakfast inn is being surrounded by wonderful collections of objects that the owners have gathered. The interesting combinations they have put together are usually far more tastefully done than you would ever think to do, and a far cry from the ever-so-right, but usually sterile, atmosphere of a hotel or motel. This is certainly true of WindSong, where the paintings and crafts of local artists comingle with antiques and native art collected from Africa, India, and other distant locales.

You would never guess this lovely inn was once a two-room schoolhouse. The remodeling and additions have transformed it into a spacious inn. The four generously-sized bedrooms, named Concerto, Rhapsody, Symphony, and Nocturne are furnished with a comfortable blend of contemporary and antique pieces. The Harmony and Rhapsody rooms are on the upper floor; the Symphony and Nocturne rooms are on the main floor. All have private baths. You'll love the alder twig headboard (handmade in the San Juans) in the Rhapsody Room. Fireplaces in the sitting room and every bedroom warm chilly evenings, or to get really toasty, sink into the Jacuzzi, which overlooks the surrounding forest. From the deck that overhangs the former schoolyard, you may see deer, raccoons, rabbits, and other wildlife in the meadows.

How to get there: WindSong is on Deer Harbor Road, ¼ mile west of its intersection with the Horseshoe Highway. Open year-round.

VACATION HOUSE RENTALS

Private homes on Orcas Island provide a nice alternative to commercial lodgings. Brochures picturing and describing homes for short-term rental are available from several real estate firms. Call or fax the company to have theirs sent to you. By the time summer rolls around, accommodations are heavily booked, so try to reserve a home early. Rates range from $350 to $1700 a week. Summer rentals are by the week only; off-season there is a two-night minimum. The following firms list rentals on Orcas Island:

Cheri L. Lindholm Real Estate
P.O. Box 66; Eastsound, WA 98245; phone – (360) 376-2202

San Juan Property Company
*285 Blair Avenue; Friday Harbor, WA 98250; phone – (360) 378-5060;
fax – (360) 376-5579*

Windermere Real Estate/Orcas
*P.O. Box 310; Eastsound, WA 98245; phone – (800) 842-5770;
(360) 376-2262*

RESTAURANTS & CAFES

Bartholomew's Bar and Grill
Route 1, Box 1040; Eastsound, WA 98245; phone – (360) 376-2243

Dinner year-round, breakfast and lunch in summer. Beer, wine. Credit cards accepted. $$

If you want to rehash the latest Mariner's game or boast about today's fishing catch, Bartholomew's is the place to do it. This popular local watering hole is a great spot to share a brew and steak with friends. Or choose chops, ribs, or local seafood. Dine inside the newly remodeled restaurant, or on the patio overlooking the water.

Bilbo's Festivo
North Beach Road; Eastsound, WA 98245; phone – (360) 376-4728

Dinner daily year-round, lunch daily at La Taqueria in the summer. Reservations recommended. Beer, wine, cocktails. Credit cards accepted. $ to $$

A hot breath of Mexico in the San Juans! Even if it weren't for the terrific food, you'd still want to stop by Bilbo's for the charming decor. Tables in an outside courtyard surround a fire pit; grapevines trail over an arched entryway; adobe walls, cactuses, and handmade tiles accompany the wonderful aroma from the kitchen.

Start with a fresh-squeezed lime Margarita, then check out the menu for such favorites as enchiladas, burritos, tacos, and quesadillas, all done with a light, New Mexican touch. Try offerings from their mesquite grill such as *Carne* or *Pollo Asada* (grilled beef or chicken on a tortilla, topped with avocado and tomato) or *pollo y naranjas*—(chicken marinated in orange sauce), accompanied by a good Mexican beer. Even local favorites such as oysters and shrimp are given a piquant Southwestern treatment to the delight of your palate. There are soups, salads, and a tempting dessert menu, too.

The Boardwalk
Orcas Landing; Orcas, WA 98280; phone – (360) 376-2971

Breakfast, lunch, and dinner. Beer, wine. Credit cards accepted. $

The little side-by-side cottages clinging to the hillside above the Orcas ferry landing are all part of The Boardwalk. As a group they are sort of a "strolling eatery." The Boardwalk serves up hearty breakfasts, charcoal grilled hamburgers, and some of the best fish and chips on Orcas. Beer and wine as well as espresso, coffee, and soft drinks are available. Another one of the cottages offers hot pizza, and the space shared by the Boardwalk gift shop tops it all off with ice cream or frozen yogurt.

The restaurant has inside seating, but there are tables scattered outside between the cottages for a sunny day.

Cafe Olga

Orcas Island Artworks Building; Star Route Box 53; Olga, WA 98279; phone – (360) 376-5098

Brunch, lunch, and early dinner. Beer and wine. Credit cards accepted. $

Tucked into one corner of the huge building that houses the Orcas Island Artworks, Cafe Olga is a "must" stop for many visitors to Orcas. The fare includes inexpensive salads, sandwiches, quiche, baked eggs, and pasta, and includes such wonderfully inviting dishes as lemon pesto pasta, Thai seafood curry, and Mexican chili pie, all made with the freshest of ingredients. Top off your lemon pesto pasta with espresso and homemade berry pie or the most incredible cinnamon rolls you'll ever sink a tooth into.

Chimayo

Our House Mall; Eastsound, WA 98245; phone – (360) 376-6394 (376-MEXI)

Lunch and dinner daily. $

Mexican food is recognized as the new healthy fare. Chimayo does it fast and fresh with offerings such as Redemption Salad (a version of a taco salad with fresh greens) and black beans and cheese tossed in spicy vinaigrette on a warm tortilla. There's the usual tacos and burritos, and you will also find such gourmet specials as a roasted eggplant with garlic and feta cheese quesadilla topped with roasted tomato salsa. Desserts are homemade—'nuf said.

Christina's

Horseshoe Highway; Eastsound, WA 98245; phone – (360) 376-4904

Dinner daily. Beer, wine, cocktails. Reservations recommended. Credit cards accepted. $$ to $$$

Christina's, one of the most widely heralded restaurants in the Northwest, occupies the upper floor of a two-story house on Eastsound's waterfront. From such modest surroundings comes sumptuous fare such as six-lilies soup, lamb chops with wild mushroom ragu and garlic potatoes, or smoked salmon with wild rice cakes. A dish you loved last time may not be on the menu at your next visit, as chef/owner Christina Orchid regularly experiments with new creations. The seafood is the freshest the San Juans produce.

The extensive wine list includes fine domestic and imported wines. Choose a table in one of the rooms of this former home, or on the glass-enclosed porch, with water views of East Sound.

Deer Harbor Lodge and Inn
Deer Harbor, WA 98243; phone – (360) 376-4110

Dinner daily. Beer, wine. Reservations. Credit cards accepted. $$

This huge dining room in the inn above Deer Harbor has farmhouse atmosphere. A wood-burning stove sits in one corner, genteel lace table-cloths and small vases of garden flowers decorate well-used wooden tables. An outside deck has seating with a view of the harbor.

Some offerings may remind you of the wonderful meals Grandma made, others are far better than even she could have conjured up! The homemade soup is accompanied by fresh baked bread. Entrées, which are listed on the blackboard as you enter, include selections of chicken, beef, and local sea-food, as well as a vegetarian dish. The wine list includes domestic selections as well as some fine French offerings. During summer, you can take an af-ternoon break for tea and tasty finger sandwiches.

A shop in the restaurant features pottery from local artisans.

Doe Bay Cafe
Star Route Box 86; Olga, WA 98279; phone – (360) 376-2291

Breakfast and dinner Wednesday through Sunday in summer. Credit cards accepted. $

For really healthy food, head to Doe Bay. The natural foods cafe that is part of the resort serves tasty, inexpensive meals that are good for the body, too. The cafe is at the back of the lounge, in the historic building on the shore. The marine view from inside the rustic little restaurant, overlooking one of the coves of Doe Bay, is as inspiring as the food.

Doty's A-1 Cafe and Bakery
P.O. Box 138; Eastsound, WA 98245; phone – (360) 376-2593

Breakfast and lunch daily. $

You know you're going to have a great meal when you walk in the door and peruse the case full of fresh baked goodies. There are donuts, Danishes and cinnamon rolls to go with your breakfast, or pie and cake to top off your lunchtime burger. All are baked on the premises. Lunchtime meal choices include a wide range of hot and cold sandwiches.

Entrances on North Beach Road and on Prune Alley lead to two small dining rooms and an outside dining courtyard. The decor includes wild collections of knickknacks and gizmos to entertain you as you eat.

Eby's Restaurant
P.O. Box 786; Eastsound, WA 98245; phone – (360) 376-4900

Breakfast, lunch, and dinner daily. Beer, wine. $

Eby's is a local hangout featuring hearty, inexpensive meals. Nearly every night has its special: Monday is prime rib night, Thursday is Chinese, Friday is salmon. There are burgers, too. Most entrées include a choice of potatoes done several ways, vegetable, rolls, and a trip to the salad bar. Eby's is located on the hillside on the west side of Eastsound.

Garden Path
10 Prune Alley (Rear); Eastsound, WA 98245; phone – (360) 376-5177

Open 11:00 A.M. to 6:00 P.M. daily. $

Asian dishes, made from scratch with fresh ingredients, are the mainstay of this shop in the back of the bungalow occupied by Clarion gallery. Sample a flavorful curry with vegetables and rice, or a soup and traditional rice balls coated with sesame seeds. New, tasty ethnic dishes are added regularly, and there's always a daily special. Food is for take out, or in good weather you can eat it on their patio.

Hemingway's by the Sea
200 Deer Harbor Road; Deer Harbor, WA 98243; phone – (360) 376-2950 or (360) 376-4420

Dinner daily, brunch weekends, catering. Beer, wine, cocktails. Lounge, entertainment. Reservations. Closed off-season. Credit cards accepted. $$

Just a step away from the docks of Deer Harbor, this restaurant is ideal for boaters wanting a break from galley duty. Start the evening on the wide view deck by sipping a cold drink and munching a tasty appetizer of fresh local spot prawns, Westcott oysters, or smoked salmon with cream cheese and capers.

For an entrée you may want to try braised Northwest salmon, filet of beef tenderloin, medallions of pork tenderloin, or one of the inviting pasta dishes. Hazelnut cheesecake finishes the meal perfectly.

La Famiglia Ristorante
A Street and North Beach Road; Eastsound, WA 98245;
phone – (360) 376-2335

Dinner daily; lunch Monday through Saturday. Take-out pizza. Beer, wine, spirits. Reservations suggested in summer. Credit cards accepted. $$

For good food you can't go wrong with Italian—and on Orcas Island you can't go wrong with La Famiglia. It's casual enough for the family, yet special enough for your best girl. In summer you'll find this eatery crowded with local people as well as tourists, so make reservations. Seating is nearly doubled by use of an outside patio enclosed by a rustic cedar fence and cascading flowers.

The decor is warm, with candles and dark green tablecloths on the tables and lots of cedar paneling. Start out with an antipasto, fried calamari rings, local oysters or mussels, and an island-grown salad. Entrées on the extensive menu include homemade pizza, calzone, pasta, New York steak, and several seafood, veal, and chicken dishes with an Italian twist. Choose one of the fine wines or specialty beers to go with your linguini, or one of the after-dinner specialty drinks to float you off to dreamland at your B&B.

The Lower Tavern
Langell Street and Horseshoe Highway; P.O. Box 442; Eastsound, WA 98245;
phone – (360) 376-4848

Lunch and dinner daily. Beer, wine. Pool, darts, cards. $

Local people know this homey tavern in Eastsound is the place to get a really good burger. The custom is to slather on horseradish from the big jar on your table—sinuses beware! Several other hot and cold sandwiches, chili, and homemade soup round out the menu.

Grab a seat at the bar or at one of the tables and join in the casual fun, Orcas style. Challenge one of the local people to darts or pool, watch the Sonics on TV, or try out the open mike on Thursday night. The conversation will probably be local politics; you'll get a lot of insight into what makes this community work.

In case you're wondering, there used to be an Upper Tavern, too, but now it's Eby's Restaurant and Lounge.

Orcas Hotel

Orcas Landing; Orcas, WA 98280; phone – (360) 376-4300

Breakfast, lunch, and dinner daily; call for seasonal hours. Beer, wine, cocktails. Lounge. Credit cards accepted. $$

If you don't stay overnight at this historic hotel, you should still stop in for a meal and enjoy the Victorian aura. A small cafe and bakery on the west side of the building offers coffee and espresso and a mouth-watering list of home baked yummies: sticky buns, blueberry lemon muffins, raspberry orange scones, and green chili quiche are just a few. Dine inside the cheery cafe or outside at tables on the gracious verandah.

The newly-remodeled dining room and bar, on the east side of the building, has an English pub ambiance, with a large old fireplace and leaded glass windows framing the view. But old English pubs never had gustatory delights such as these! The chef will serve you dishes such as grilled king salmon with raspberry shallot butter or pan-fried chicken breast with wild mushrooms in vermouth. Select a wine from the list of fine domestic and imported wines, and top it all off with a dessert featuring some of the fresh local fruit. You'll feel as if you've dined with the queen.

Owl Bagel Shop

School Road and Prune Alley; Eastsound, WA 98245; phone – (360) 376-5854

Breakfast and lunch daily; open until 11:00 P.M. Saturday. $

Espresso and a bagel for breakfast, soup and a bagelwich for lunch— what could be more satisfying? Bagels range from the regular fare of poppy seed, sesame seed, and jalapeno to such unusual tasty offerings as date, cranberry, and chocolate chip. An ice cream cone tops off your lunch.

The two dining rooms of the shop also serve as a gallery, featuring the work of local artists and photographers. Lively Saturday evening events include performances by local musicians.

Portofino Pizzeria

A Street; Eastsound, WA 98245; phone – (360) 376-2085

Lunch and dinner daily. Beer, wine. $

Pizza by the slice, by the pie, thin crust, deep dish, country covered, to eat in, or take out—however you want your pizza, Portofino's has it. They're upstairs, above the Village Stop on A Street. Dine inside or on a large outside deck with a view of Eastsound Village and the water. Hand-tossed pizza crusts give perfect flavor and texture. There are sandwiches, subs, and fresh salads, too.

Rosario Resort

1 Rosario Way; Eastsound, WA 98245; phone – (360) 376-2222

Breakfast, lunch, and dinner daily; Friday night seafood buffet; Sunday champagne brunch; catering. Beer, wine, cocktails. Lounge. Dinner reservations required. Credit cards accepted. $$ to $$$

Rosario Resort's Orcas Room is without question the most elegant spot to dine in all the San Juans. If you want to celebrate a special event, or have a memorable "farewell to the San Juans" dinner, it's the place to go. Stroll around the grounds and inspect the historic mansion before settling in for lunch or dinner.

The varied dinner menu may include such elegant dishes as smoked salmon fettuccini, turkey and oysters Rosario, mesquite-grilled king salmon with lemon herb sauce, rib eye steak with mushroom bordelaise, and Ellensburg rack of lamb. Lunchtime fare includes terrific seafood salads as well as sandwiches, pastas, and other light dishes. The Friday night seafood buffet and Sunday champagne brunch are legendary. The resort's Vista Lounge also serves light meals.

Rose's Bakery Cafe

Eastsound Square; Eastsound, WA 98245; phone – (360) 376-4220

Breakfast and lunch daily. $

This spot was recommended to us by one of the residents, and we'll be forever grateful. You'll find the local people here hashing over the latest news and downing some of the best baked goods on the island along with their espresso. The breakfast menu is limited to eggs and fresh baked pastry, lunch is a range of soups and sandwiches. Eat at one of several small tables with brightly painted tops that are works of art in themselves. There're baked goods to go, too. You won't be able to resist carting off a bag full of goodies for a snack later.

Rosies at the Outlook Inn

P.O. Box 210; Eastsound, WA 98245; phone – (360) 376-2200

*Breakfast, lunch, and dinner daily. Espresso, beer, wine, cocktails. Lounge.
Credit cards accepted. $$*

Settle down to Chicken Calypso with fresh fruit salsa or Starlite
Salmon with strawberry butter as you enjoy the view of East Sound from
the etched glass windows of this gracious old inn. If you're not from the
West Coast, discover cioppino—our version of bouillabaisse (the North-
west version is a bit different than the San Francisco style). Whether
you're having breakfast, lunch, or dinner, the menu is sure to have some-
thing to please every member of the family. A good selection of vegetar-
ian dishes is included.

If you have a large group, a party room can be reserved. Take-out and
catering also available.

Ship Bay Oyster House

Horseshoe Highway; Eastsound, WA 98245; phone – (360) 376-5886

*Dinner daily. Closed in winter. Beer, wine, cocktails. Lounge. Credit cards
accepted. $$$*

The tidy farmhouse surrounded by an old apple orchard could well be
the home of a retired sea captain. You can just imagine him sitting in the
front yard, spyglass to his eye, scanning the bay for incoming ships.

The restaurant's decor befits a sea captain's home too, with trim white
and gray color scheme and nautical prints on the walls. You'll find oysters
fixed nearly a dozen different ways as appetizers and entrées. There are scallops, mussels, shrimp, and fish as well. Daily specials include what's freshly
caught that morning. If there's someone in your party who doesn't feel like
eating seafood at the moment (hard to imagine!), the menu includes New
York steak, grilled chicken, or baby back ribs.

The list of excellent wines includes fine local and California vintages,
as well as some imported ones. Try an espresso or one of several apéritifs to
go with your dessert. This restaurant may close after the 1996 tourist season, so check first before planning to dine here.

Teezer's Cookies, Etc.
A Street and North Beach Road; Eastsound, WA 98245;
phone – (360) 376-2913

Light breakfast, snacks. $

Not just cookies, although they're so great that would probably be enough. Have a homemade muffin and juice with your morning Starbuck's espresso. For an afternoon snack dig into some scrumptious Haagen Dazs ice cream.

Vern's Bayside Restaurant & Lounge
Horseshoe Highway, P.O. Box 27; Eastsound, WA 98245;
phone – (360) 376-2231

Breakfast, lunch, and dinner daily; pizza to go. Beer, wine, cocktails. Lounge, coffee shop. Credit cards accepted. $ to $$

The setting is right on the water, with huge windows in their spacious dining room offering a sweeping view the length of East Sound and surrounding forested hillsides. An outside patio puts you within the sound of lapping waves and mewing gulls.

Breakfasts are the old standbys—steak, egg, hotcakes, omelets. All good, hearty fare to start the day. Lunchtime offerings include hamburgers, fish and chips, sandwiches, salads, and some Mexican offerings. Or you can build your own pizza to eat here or to go. For dinner try blackened prime rib, barbequed ribs, chicken, or some of their excellent, always fresh, seafood choices. Or sample Italian or Chinese inspired dishes. All meals have vegetarian options.

GROCERIES, DELIS, TAKE OUT & LIQUOR
●

The Bounty at Deer Harbor
P.O. Box 200; Deer Harbor, WA 98243; phone – (360) 376-4420

Here's the spot to stop if you're looking for grub after bicycling to Deer Harbor or if your boat's supplies are low. You'll find a good assortment of packaged, fresh, and frozen foods, as well as beer, wine, and soft drinks.

The adjacent deli offers a great menu of gourmet pastas and sauces. Try ravioli stuffed with smoked salmon or fresh fettuccini with any of a number of sauces. There are homemade bread, homemade pizzas,excellent wines, and espresso. A hand-dipped ice cream cone will top it off.

Island Market

*P.O. Box 186; Eastsound, WA 98245; phone – (360) 376-6000;
fax – (360) 376-6001*

Island Market, the largest, best-stocked grocery store on the island, has everything you'll need to replenish your boat's larder, including fresh meat, fresh bakery goods, beer, and wine. Video rentals, too.

Stop by the deli for picnic makings to enjoy at Moran State Park. Don't miss the armadillo eggs (jalapeños stuffed with cream cheese, dipped in batter, and deep fried), or if you're new to the Northwest, discover the ecstasy of Nanaimo bars, a calorie-loaded dessert delicacy.

Boaters wanting to pick up ship's stores can tie up to the public dock at Madrona Point or drop anchor just off it and take their dinghy to the dock. From there it's just a two-block walk to the market.

Olga Store

Olga, WA 98279; phone – (360) 376-5862; fax – (360) 376-5070

This small grocery store at Olga is generally open only during the summer. After the long trip down island, bicyclists find it a welcome spot to pick up sandwich makings and a cold soda.

Orcas Home Grown Market and Deli

North Beach Road; Eastsound, WA 98245; phone – (360) 376-2009

This oasis of natural and organic foods in the heart of Eastsound provides friendly, personal service, with an emphasis on environmental consciousness. Fresh local produce and seafood are its forte. Hikers, bikers, and boaters delight in the bulk food section with its variety of trail mixes, nuts, and dried fruits. Homeopathic and herbal medications are also sold. The natural foods deli specializes in alternative baking and vegin cooking.

Orcas Store

Orcas Ferry Landing; Orcas, WA 98280; phone – (360) 376-4384

This small store right next to the ferry landing has been a long-time standby for supplying fresh coffee, ice cream treats, and snacks to ferry-bound travelers. Its size belies the range of merchandise you'll find inside. There are groceries, deli sandwiches, hot dogs, smoked salmon, fresh meat, fresh produce, beer, wine, fishing tackle, hardware, magazines, newspapers, candy, toys, and souvenir items. It's fun to stop in here just to see what you'll discover. Boaters making a fuel stop at Russell's can dash up to replenish supplies.

Rose's Breads and Specialties
Eastsound Square, #D3; Eastsound, WA, 98245: (360) 376-5805

You may have sampled some of the terrific baked goods at the nearby Rose's Cafe. Here's your opportunity to take some home. This shop sells specialty breads, pastry, fine wines, pastas, and gourmet deli meats and cheeses. It's just the place to put together a picnic lunch for your excursion to Mount Constitution.

West Sound Store and Deli
Crow Valley Road and Deer Harbor Road; Eastsound, WA 98245;
phone – (360) 376-4440

Whether you're bicycling by, boating, or are out for a casual car tour of Orcas, this delightful little store, sitting on a slight hill overlooking the bay, is the perfect spot to stop for lunch. Select your soup, salad, or sandwich from the delectable array in the deli case, then settle down at a table in a sunny corner. If the weather's nice you'll surely choose a spot on their outside deck, overlooking the water. You can pick up a "loaf of bread and jug of wine" for a picnic to enjoy at Deer Harbor or down on the public boat dock just below.

In the morning, there's a full breakfast or fresh pastry and steaming espresso. Lunch specials may be steamed clams (local, of course), fish and chips, or grilled sandwiches. Don't miss their excellent selection of wines and beer. You're sure to find a special one for a friend back home.

Washington State Liquor Store—Eastsound
P.O. Box 925; Eastsound, WA 98245; phone – (360) 376-2616

The Eastsound liquor store, which for many years was in the waterfront in the Porter Station, is now on the south side of A Street, in the same building as the Village Stop.

Washington State Liquor Store—Orcas
P.O. Box 196; Orcas, WA 98280; phone – (360) 376-4389

In Orcas you'll find the liquor store in the lower level of Russells' Store, immediately to the west of the ferry landing.

SHOPPING

Autumn's

East Sound Square; Eastsound, WA 98245; phone – (360) 376-4630

Autumn's is a women's clothing store, and an eclectic little gift shop as well. You'll discover lovely imported garments and lots of natural fibers, as well as hats, jewelry, and even some shoes to accessorize them. You'll never know what trinkets you'll find tucked in some corner—a few choice books, fancy soaps, a handmade doll, or a pretty teapot.

Bella International, Ltd.

P.O. Box 1557; 100 Prune Alley; Eastsound, WA 98245;
phone – (360) 376-6360 or (800) 32-BELLA

This Eastsound gallery carries prints and original paintings by such renowned artists as Margaret Keane (those adorable big-eyed waifs) and Robert Lyn Nelson. You'll find a nice selection of art with nautical or natural themes. The shop also frames art, whether you purchase it there, or bring in. It shares a building with Vern's Cafe on the north side of Eastsound.

The Boardwalk

Orcas Ferry Landing; Orcas, WA 98280; phone – (360) 376-2971

Browse here for that last-minute gift while waiting for the ferry. The store stocks a supply of nice tourist souvenirs, posters, original serigraphs, jewelry, postcards, and greeting cards. Find a book of regional interest to take home as a reminder of your visit, or a novel to while away your time on the boat ride. In another of their gift shops you'll discover wine and related gifts as well.

Clarion

North Beach Road; Eastsound, WA 98245; phone – (360) 376-6040

Island artists are the specialty of this gallery, housed in a tidy little bungalow across from the historical museum. Even if you're not looking to buy, stop in to see paintings, sculpture, and pottery by the islands' finest artists. Shows change monthly. You'll be so impressed you'll simply have to own one.

Cottage Gift Shop
Orcas Ferry Landing; P.O. Box 234; Orcas, WA 98280;
phone – (360) 376-4374

You wouldn't want to leave the island without a pair of slug earrings or a gnome wearing an Orcas Island souvenir shirt! Here's the place to hit for that last-minute souvenir or gift before hopping on the ferry. There're games and toys to keep the kids busy if the boat is delayed; postcards, books, and posters to remind you of your visit; pretty little knickknacks to take back to Aunt Edith; and jewelry, bags, and tons of other stuff you'll want for yourself. Their T-shirts, sweatshirts, and jackets are exceptionally nice. The post office shares the same building, so you can mail your cards and gifts to friends back home right there.

Crow Valley Pottery
Route 1, Box 83B; Eastsound, WA 98245; phone – (360) 376-4260

A historic log cabin in a natural setting on Horseshoe Highway houses a nifty little gallery. Its location, on the west side of the road, across from the golf course, makes it a perfect place for a first stop after leaving the ferry. Pottery and tiles made from native clays are the main feature; however there are other selections from the gifted hands of local artists. You can choose from sterling silver jewelry, hand-woven mats and rugs, metalwork, masks, fine black and white photo prints, and stunning glass creations made from fused and slumped glass.

Crow Valley Pottery is open from 10 A.M. to 5 P.M., seven days a week from Memorial Day through September. From October through Christmas and mid-April to Memorial Day you'll find them open weekends, or by appointment.

Darvill's Rare Print Shop and Bookstore
P.O. Box 47; Eastsound, WA 98245; print shop phone – (360) 376-2351,
bookstore phone – (360) 376-2135

Many vacationers who really know the San Juans always make a point of checking to find out what Darvill's has that's new. For the dedicated reader there's sure to be a great mystery, a boating book, or something of local interest. The knowledgeable clerks can help you find the latest book to slake your literary thirst, or you can skim their monthly newsletter to see what's been a best seller. You'll also find greeting cards, calendars, and Books on Tape.

But that's only half the story. Don't miss Darvill's outstanding collection of fine antique maps and prints, both framed and unframed. You're sure to find a lovely little botanical or wildlife print that will look absolutely perfect in your home. Or do as some people do, and start a collection of engravings, etchings, or hand-colored prints, buying a new one as a remembrance each time you visit the island.

Deer Harbor Gift Shop

P.O. Box 200; Deer Harbor, WA 98243; phone – (360) 376-4480

This small shop that shares space with the resort's registration desk offers a nice assortment of things you may need to make your vacation complete, or items to bring friends at home. In addition to the de rigueur T-shirts, you'll find swimming suits, local guide books, cassette tapes, jewelry, antiques, and nautical gifts.

Eastsound Sporting Goods

Templin's Center: Eastsound, WA 98245; (360) 376-5588

Just about everything you need, whatever your favorite sport is will be found in this shop in the corner of Templin's Center. If they don't have an item in stock, they should be able to order it for you. The emphasis is on fishing, with gear for both fresh and saltwater, and a spool winding machine where you can custom wind your own reel from bulk stock line. There's lots of camping gear, too.

When these folks took over the space of the variety store that was formerly here, they kept the charming model trail that puffs its way around the perimeter of the shop at head level. Bring the kids in to see it.

Evergreen Gallery

North Beach Road; P.O. Box 1772; Eastsound, WA 98245;
phone – (360) 376-2801

A quaint cottage on North Beach Road houses the unique gallery that sells owner Michele deLong's handmade jewelry and the work of several other island craftspeople. You'll be swept away by the pottery, homespun yarn, weaving, sweaters, beads from around the world, and museum-quality Alaskan art. Don't miss the fossils—there are trilobites, ammonites, and other reminders of ancient life, both polished and in their natural state.

Gulls and Buoys Gifts
P.O. Box 23; Eastsound, WA 98245; phone – (360) 376-2199

Don't miss this boutique if you're looking for gifts. Chances are good that you'll walk away with a couple of "gifts" for yourself, too. The selection is almost limitless: dishes, pottery, glassware, rugs, afghans, place mats, toys, dolls (including those wonderful Nan's Dolls), candles, Christmas collectibles, candy (Aplets and Cotlets—yummm!), jellies, stationary, soap, and even more. Whether you end up with a funny refrigerator magnet or a beautiful Mikasa glass plate, you'll be delighted with your selection. You'll also find maps, nautical charts, and videos of local interest.

Howe Art
Horseshoe Highway, Eastsound, WA 98245; phone – (360) 376-2945

Spectacular is the only word to describe the Captain Nemo-like creations of artist Tony Howe. You can't avoid being amazed and delighted by his work. As you head down Horseshoe Highway, just ¼ mile before you arrive at Eastsound, you'll see some of them beside the road. They hang from tree limbs, twirling in the air like huge, silvery aliens or Brobdingnagian cocoons. Howe's combined studio and gallery is just up the side road, off the highway. The artist works primarily in various metals; however some his works incorporate other materials such as fiberglass or painted mylar stretched over metal frames. Although large, fanciful, sculptures that twirl in the wind and make interesting sounds are his delight, he also creates chairs, tables, fountains, and even chess sets.

Kay's Accents
Our House Mall; Eastsound, WA 98245; phone – (360) 376-4538

Here's one of our very favorite shops on Orcas Island. It's mostly antiques, mixed with contemporary jewelry and other gift items. You'll find really unusual antique jewelry, porcelain, dishes, glassware, linens, and some furniture. Prices range from quite inexpensive upwards; all are reasonably priced for their fine quality.

Leapin' Lizards
Number 2 Eastsound Square; Eastsound, WA 98245; phone – (360) 376-5790

You may expect to find Orphan Annie just around the corner in this terrific kids' toy store, engrossed in a puzzle or glow-in-the-dark star chart. You'll enjoy giving a child one of the excellent selections of educational toys and art supplies as much as they'll enjoy receiving it. There's also a colorful and unusual selection of kids' T-shirts and 100% cotton clothing.

Lighthouse Christian Bookstore
Eastsound Square; Eastsound, WA 98245; phone – (360) 376-2153

This tidy little shop facing on the Eastsound Square boardwalk carries religious books, bibles, cards, posters, and (yes, even here) T-shirts.

The Naked Lamb Spinning and Weaving
*Route 1, Box 511; West Beach Road; Eastsound, WA 98245;
phone – (360) 376-4606*

If you knit or weave, or are looking for wonderful handmade sweaters, shawls, hats, and vests, don't miss this shop. It's off the beaten path, in one of the prettiest corners of the island, and definitely worth the trip. Jewel-bright skeins of wool hang from racks and tumble out of displays in this tiny, rustic shop. Some yarns are locally raised, spun, and dyed. (That sheep

Orcas Island sheep provide the wool for many island handcrafts.

you drive by in one of the pastures may have fostered your sweater.) There are also needles and patterns for the knitters, as well as buttons, porcelain jewelry, and other fun stuff.

To reach the shop from Eastsound, turn off Lover's Lane onto Enchanted Forest Road. Drive for a little over two miles and continue straight ahead when the road turns sharply left. Follow the road past the signed entrance to West Beach Resort, and in a few hundred feet watch for a dirt road on the left signed for The Naked Lamb and The Right Place Pottery.

Nature's Art
P.O. Box 185; Eastsound, WA 98245; phone – (360) 376-4343

This Northwest-inspired shop creates custom-embroidered shirts, bags, and other items. You'll also find nature oriented note cards, casual apparel, CD's, and cassettes, with a few select, mouth-watering gourmet food items such as jams and herb vinegars tucked around them.

Once Upon a Time
Templin's Center; Eastsound, WA 98245; phone – (360) 376-4223

Truly something out of a fairy tale, Once Upon a Time is stuffed with enchanting gift items and home furnishings. Enjoy antique jewelry, potpourri, decorative accessories for home and self, greeting cards, and locally made gift items.

Orcas Arts and Gifts By Suzanne
Horseshoe Highway; Eastsound, WA 98245; phone – (360) 376-5915

At Orcas Arts and Gifts you'll discover bolo ties, hair barrettes, pendants, rings, and other locally made jewelry of silver, turquoise, and semi-precious stones. There are pottery and knickknacks that will fit right in with your Western lifestyle. The apparel is ruggedly Western too, featuring Woolrich knit sweaters, raingear, jackets, bandannas, caps, muck boots, and rubber sandals.

Orcas Everlasting
Our House Mall; Eastsound WA 98245; (360) 376-5991

Who can resist a teddy bear? There's lots of them at Orcas Everlasting, along with dried flower arrangements, herbal mixes, and other decorative items for the home. The shop also has antique and custom produced furniture, local pottery, and crafts. Lots of great stuff!

Orcas Island Artworks

Orcas Island Artworks Building; P.O. Box 125; Olga, WA 98279;
phone – (360) 376-4408

Back in the 1930s the huge old building at the Olga road intersection was a strawberry processing plant. Today it holds Orcas Island Artworks, a local artists' cooperative, representing the work of over 70 artists and craftspeople who work in a wide range of materials and mediums. Everything on display is crafted by local artists, exclusively.

It's a treasure trove! There's no end to the beautiful fine art and functional things. You'll find handmade quilts, quilted wall hangings, tapestries, soft sculptures, wearable art such as fanciful wool hats, ceramics, pottery, porcelain, handmade tiles, sculpture, note cards, jewelry, chess sets, handcrafted wooden toys, paintings…the list goes on. You won't be able to pry yourself away.

Orcas Island Jewelry

A Street and North Beach Road; Eastsound, WA 98245;
phone – (360) 376-2858

Whether it's the redesign of an old piece of jewelry or the creation of a new one especially for you, you'll love the work of Orcas Island Jewelry. Among the unique rings, pins, and pendants in 14 and 18 karat gold, platinum, and silver, some containing precious or semiprecious stones, you're sure to find that super-special gift or remembrance of the islands—perhaps a starfish for your charm bracelet collection or an orca-inspired pendant or earrings.

Orcas Island Pottery

Route 1, Box 23; Eastsound, WA 98245; phone – (360) 376-2813

One of the greatest spots on Orcas Island! It's not just a place to shop—it's an experience in itself. The studio hold forth in several little log cabins scattered in the woods, with views out to President Channel. After leaving your car in the small parking area, stroll down a woodland path past a trickling, pottery-crafted fountain. Ferns trail over garden sculptures, platters and pottery sculptures decorate outside walls, and wind chimes hang from cabin eaves. Expect a gnome to pop out at any minute!

Browse through the little shops discovering a new pottery or porcelain treasure for your home or garden in every corner. There're unique mugs, pots, platters, soup tureens, and casseroles. Look for garlic pots, butter dishes, and spoon rests. The owner/artist's whimsical sense of humor touches many of her works.

To reach Orcas Island Pottery, drive north from West Sound or south from Eastsound on Crow Valley Road, and turn west onto West Beach Road. About 1 mile later a road to the left is signed to the studio.

Orcas Leather Works
#1 East Sound Square; P.O. Box 2; Eastsound, WA 98245;
phone – (360) 376-2900

You'll love caressing the elegant, supple leather of the purses, backpacks, and luggage in this fine store. You'll also discover sheepskin moccasins, belts,

The shops of Eastsound Square face on a pretty boardwalk.

scabbards, and non-leather items such as jewelry, beads, buckles, and knives. Some of the leather goods are made on the premises. Even if you're just browsing, stop in for the wonderful aroma of leather.

Orcas Northwest
East Sound Square; Eastsound, WA 98245; phone – (360) 376-4630

This men's clothing shop is strong on casual wear and beach clothes, although there are also plenty of nice sweaters and pants, along with the sweats and shorts. It's the place to go for the real Northwest look of rugged and warm. They carry a selection of CD's and guitar strings (so you can make your own music).

Orcas Wine Company
Porter Station; P.O. Box 34; Eastsound, WA 98245; phone – (360) 376-6244

Sample a chardonnay here, and then carry away several bottles or a case of fine Washington wine to enjoy later. The Orcas Wine Company sells their own Madrona Cellars label. As you taste the various wines, you can browse through the shop's selection of gift items—books on wine, wine accessories, and locally produced gourmet jams, sauces, herb vinegars and specialty foods. Watercolors and prints on sale are by Orcas artist Caroline Buchanan and well-known Alaskan artist Rie Muñoz.

The Orcas Wine Company is in the Porter Station Building, below Christina's restaurant. Just follow the brick walkway to a gorgeous view of East Sound.

Pat's Outback and Gifts
Templin's Center; Eastsound, WA 98245; phone – (360) 376-5915

You've probably never thought of it, but Australia and Orcas Island are a natural combination. The island's earthy, outdoorsy attitude is straight out of The Man from Snowy River. This store stocks the clothes you'll need to herd sheep or horses—or to just be comfortable in Northwest weather. Try on a great Australian drover's coat and a jaunty Aussie hat. Clothes from Outback Trading Company Limited come from Down Under, but there are also rugged Northwest brands such as Patagonia and Woolrich. For really soggy weather, pick out some oilskins and duck boots.

Penny Lane Antiques & Fashionables
Eastsound, WA 98245; phone – (360) 376-2995

You'll find Penny Lane just across from The Orcas Island Wine Company, behind Darvills Print Shop. Into this nook is tucked a delightful array of antique dishes, jewelry, vintage clothing, and other accessories. You may find a whalebone corset, a lacy chemise, or silver candelabra.

Poppies
A Street; Eastsound, WA 98245; phone – (360) 376-2686

Many needleworkers relax best with a pretty project underway. This store has just about everything you'll need to keep your fingers busy while your mind lazes away: yarns, color coordinated quilting squares, needlework canvas, thread, and pattern books, as well as bolt fabrics for more ambitious works. Their stock of quilting supplies is exceptionally good.

Pyewacket Books, Etc.
Templin's Center; Eastsound, WA 98245; phone – (360) 376-2043

Bring in those paperbacks you've read on the boat trip up, and take away an armload of different ones for the ride back. Pyewacket carries used books (mostly paperback), as well as a good selection of new ones of regional interest. You'll also find maps, some very nice note cards, out-of-town newspapers such as the New York Times, and a friendly staff who'll be glad to suggest places to eat and stay, or to just tell you about the islands.

Ray's Pharmacy
P.O. Box 230; Eastsound, WA 98245; phone – (360) 376-2230

Ray's is a full-service pharmacy, well stocked with drugs and sundries. It carries a nice selection of souvenirs and gifts with a San Juan flair. You'll find inexpensive toys and games to keep the kids happy while waiting in the ferry line. Drop your film off for quick processing, and pick up several more rolls to take those priceless island photos.

The Right Place Pottery
Route 1, Box 511; Eastsound, WA 98245; phone – (360) 376-4023

The Right Place Pottery sits on the west side of Orcas Island, next door to the Naked Lamb Wool Shop. Wonderful pots, platters, garden sculptures, and plates are displayed both outside and in the shop. You'll also delight in the hand-blown glass and large and small silk screened paper cuts. All pottery and glass is made here in this tiny studio; you may be able to watch owner, Trudy Erwin, at work.

To reach The Right Place Pottery from Eastsound, drive out Enchanted Forest Road and go to the end of the road. Turn left just before you reach the water.

Russell's at Orcas
P.O. Box 196; Orcas, WA 98280; phone – (360) 376-4389

This shop, handily located at Orcas Landing, is bound to have just that special gift you're looking for. You'll find books, pottery, porcelain figurines, prints, handcrafts…and oodles more. There's some very nice women's apparel, too. Select a Christmas ornament (they have them year-round) to remind you of your summer San Juan holiday for many winters to come.

Schoolhouse Herbs, Teas, and Gifts
Our House Building, Suite D; Eastsound WA 98245; phone – (360) 376-5404

Now, we bet you don't know what a Victorian tussie-mussie is, but the folks at this shop have them for you, along with a selection of things such as herbs, teas, spiced vinegars, soap, candles, teapots, dried flowers, books, CD's, and other things to make your life more pleasant. All are creatively displayed on old school desks and other antique furniture. Oh yes, a tussie-mussie? It's a garland of flowers.

Shearwater Kayaks Adventure Store
A Street; Eastsound, WA 98245; phone – (360) 376-4699

Paddlers and campers can find needed outdoor gear at the Eastsound store operated by Shearwater kayak tours. The shop carries paddles, dry bags, PFD's, spray skirts, wet suits, books, and instructional videos along with such essentials as sunscreen, water bottles, and hats. You'll also find a selection of new and used kayaks. You can find some great buys on used gear that's on sale from their tour fleet.

Shinola Jewelry
P.O. Box 84; North Beach Road; Eastsound, WA 98245;
phone – (360) 376-4508

The exterior design of this shop, with its fanciful mosaic of cedar shakes, is enough to make you want to stop in. Once there, the merchandise will entrance you. Goldsmith and jeweler Vance Stephens, the shop's owner, specializes in custom designed fine jewelry with precious and unusual semi-precious stones. Select a unique pendant for the love of your life, or a one-of-a-kind wedding set.

Smuggler's Wife
Templin's Center; Eastsound, WA 98245; phone – (360) 376-4879

Why pack a bag to come to the San Juans on vacation when you can buy such terrific women's clothes right here? Although the Smuggler's Wife specializes in sweaters (remember those cool Orcas evenings!), there are also separates, pants, blouses, lingerie, handbags, and costume jewelry. For cool evenings there're jean and sweatshirt jackets.

Starfire
Our House Building; Eastsound, WA 98245; phone – (360) 376-3699

When Elizabeth Star recently moved her shop from the little bungalow on North Beach Road to the new space in Our House Building, it gave her all the more space to display her unusual treasures. The array of merchandise includes blown glass vases and ornamental art glass, jewelry, handmade candles, copies of ancient art, and argillite carvings. Eye-catching crystals and geodes include specimens of quartz, amethyst, and pyrite.

For extra fun, the store also offers handwriting analysis by Angeline Welk, author and teacher.

Temenos Books and Music
Orcas Island Artworks Building; P.O. Box 154; Olga, WA 98279;
phone – (360) 376-5645

This shop on a balcony nook above the Orcas Island Artworks and Cafe Olga is your source on Orcas Island for cassette tapes and CD's. For children there are music and story-telling tapes as well as a great selection of books. Browse through fascinating volumes on mysticism, health, philosophy, psychology, poetry, earth studies, and Native Americans. You'll love the selection of unusual musical instruments, masks, incense, and gift items.

The Waterfront Gallery
Our House Mall, P.O. Box 367; Eastsound, WA 98245;
phone – (360) 376-5949

This prestigious gallery displays the work of a number of Orcas Island's best artists, as well as other well known wildlife artists such as Robert Bateman. View paintings, signed limited edition wildlife prints, hand-colored etchings and engravings, limited edition graphics, and fine photography.

The knowledgeable staff will help you select and custom frame something just right for your home, office, or boat. If you've purchased an unframed antique print from Darvill's, take it to these folks for the perfect frame.

Wolf Lodge
10 Prune Alley; Eastsound, WA 98245; (360) 376-6081

You won't want to miss this unusual shop in a small cottage on Prune Alley. It features Native American ceremonial objects and jewelry, metaphysical and Native American books, healing tapes, and items by local craftsman. Some of the pieces were created by practicing medicine people of various cultures. Included are beautiful dream catchers, kachina dolls, jewelry, and drums.

EVENTS & ATTRACTIONS

Fourth of July Parade

Orcas Island people really know how to have fun. Join them in their community Fourth of July Parade at Eastsound to see them really kick up their heels with good old-fashioned festivities. It's a family event with zany costumes, bands, and that Fourth of July standby—piles of food. Concerts, boat races, and other fun events, underway all day long, are capped off by an evening fireworks display. It's a grand small town American celebration you'll always remember.

Orcas Theater and Community Center
Mount Baker Road; P.O. Box 567; Eastsound, WA 98245;
phone – (360) 376-ARTS or (360) 376-ACT 1

Whether it's a solo recital by a renowned flutist, a presentation of one-act plays by the local theater group, a barbershop quartet concert, or a children's marionette show, you never know what will be going on next at the Orcas Center. The presentations are always first rate, whether the artists are local folks, or come from off-island. The Orcas Island theatrical and choral groups are loaded with talent, and work hard at their craft. The center also serves as an art gallery for the works of local artists and mounts regular art shows.

Check the local newspaper to find out what's currently going on, or you may find it posted on the bulletin board at Templin's Center. The theater is on the south side of Mount Baker Road, just east of its intersection with North Beach Road. You can't miss it—there's an enormous orca whale sculpture on the grounds in front of the building.

Orcas Island Historical Museum
Eastsound, WA 98245; phone – (360) 376-4849

Hours: *1 P.M. to 4 P.M. From Memorial Day through Labor Day, it is open Monday through Saturday; May 1 to Memorial Day and Labor Day through October 15, open Friday and Saturday only; other times by appointment*

Here's a real time-travel adventure. These six linked log cabins were moved to their centrally-located site in Eastsound from their original locations on the island. Inside you'll discover what it was like to live on the island in the "good old days." There are household goods, tools, weapons, arrowheads, and all manner of other pioneer memorabilia, as well as photographs of early times on the island.

The collection of Native American artifacts is exceptionally fine. Some are from the collections of Ethan Allen, who lived on Blakely Island in the early 1900s. One wall is covered with Chinese "coolie" hats collected during the time when Asians were illegally smuggled through San Juan waters. An outside shed houses machinery that was used to farm the island long ago.

How to get there: The Museum is in Eastsound, on the west side of North Beach Road, ½ block north of the Horseshoe Highway

School House Museum
Crow Valley Road, Eastsound, WA ; phone – (360) 376-4260

Hours: 1:00 P.M. to 4:00 P.M., Thursday through Saturday, from Memorial Day to September 15. Tours by appointment.

Your kids will find it hard to picture themselves in this setting. The Crow Valley School, built in 1888, was for 20 years the place where Orcas

The Orcas Island Historical Museum is housed in several log cabins.

youngsters learned their three R's. On display are photographs and other memorabilia from school days on Orcas Island.

You'll find it on the west side of Crow Valley Road, about 5 miles north of the intersection with Deer Harbor Road.

ON-ISLAND TRANSPORTATION

Alternative Transportation Systems
P.O. Box 325; Eastsound, WA 98245; phone – (800) 967-1892

The "Orcas Tortas," a privately operated bus, carries passengers between Orcas Landing and Olga Junction with stops en route at Eastsound, Rosario, and Moran State Park. An optional side tour to the top of Mount Constitution, scenic tours, and special charters are also offered. They will haul your camping gear and bicycles, too. The service operates on weekends from late May through July 1 and daily from then through Labor Day.

The bus connects with all scheduled ferries at Orcas Landing. Reservations are requested for groups of six or more. Call for current schedules and fares.

Dolphin Bay Bicycles
Orcas Landing; Orcas Island, WA 98245; phone – (360) 376-4157 or (360) 376-3093

Avoid the cost and frustrating waits of auto travel to Orcas Island; just leave your car in Anacortes and pick up a bicycle two blocks from the Orcas ferry landing. It's a pedal of 3½ miles to West Sound, 8 miles to Deer Harbor or Eastsound, 16 miles to the entrance of Moran State Park, and 18 miles to Olga. Rates vary by duration of rental; helmets are provided free. Racks and touring packs may also be rented. Phone reservations accepted 48 hours in advance.

Key Moped Rentals
Prune Alley; Eastsound, WA 98245; phone – (360) 376-2474

Although bicycle tours of Orcas Island are nice, the shape of the island makes trips between various locations quite long, and the road to the top of Mount Constitution is a real bear on a bike. For those who enjoy the open air and scenic views provided by a two-wheeled vehicle, but are not into the more extreme athletics of bicycling, a moped is the answer. Call for information and reservations.

Orcas Island Taxi and Car Rental
P.O. Box 1251; Eastsound, WA 98245; phone – (360) 376-8294.

Taxi service is on call 24 hours per day to take you to and from any location on Orcas Island. The company also has two rental cars available for on-island use.

San Juan Transit, Inc.
P.O. Box 2809; Friday Harbor, WA, 98250; phone – (800) 887-8387 or (360) 376-8887

During summer months this company runs a scheduled bus service to major points of interest and resorts on Orcas Island. Locations served include Orcas Landing, West Sound, Deer Harbor, Eastsound, Moran State Park, Mount Constitution, Olga, Obstruction Pass, the golf course, and the airport. Among the resorts served are West Beach, Smugglers Villa, Bartwood, Rosario, and Doe Bay. Point-to-point fares range from $3 to $8, and round trip from $5 to $8, depending on destinations. One-day, multi-day, and commuter passes are available. Call for latest schedules, routes, and rates.

Walking Horse Country Farm
Route 1, Box 27C; Eastsound, WA 98245; phone – (360) 376-5306

Trail rides and horse-drawn carriage rides may not be your usual means of getting around Orcas Island, but they certainly are a great way to enjoy yourself. Jeri and Doug Smart at Walking Horse Country Farm will take you on guided rides on their 27-acres of bridle trail. Consider hiring one of their carriages to leave your wedding in romantic style. You'll feel like fairy-tale royalty. They're also available for other special occasions. *See also* Lodging.

Wildlife Cycles
P.O. Box 1048; Eastsound, WA 98245; phone – (360) 376-4708

Start your bicycle tour of Orcas Island from Eastsound, the hub of the island. This bicycle rental shop is on North Beach Road, north of A Street in Eastsound. It's open daily during summer months. Hours are reduced off-season.

BOAT & KAYAK TOURS, CRUISES & CHARTERS

Amante Sail Tours
P.O. Box 51; Deer Harbor, WA 98243; phone – (360) 376-4231

You can either assist as crew, or just relax and enjoy a sail aboard the 33-foot sloop *Amante*. Skippered half-day or overnight trips leave from Deer Harbor on Orcas Island. Overnight sails for four to six guests include dinner and a Continental breakfast.

Brisa Charters, Ltd.
P.O. Box 172; Olga WA 98279; phone – (Orcas Island) (360) 376-3264
(Port Townsend) 385-2309 ; e-mail – pikenw@olympus.net

For those who prefer an elegant rather than a vigorous sailing experience, the 45-foot, classic Lapworth-designed sloop *Annie Too* is the perfect answer. She sails twice daily out of Lieberhaven Resort, on Obstruction Pass, for a three-hour tour of local waters. Gourmet snacks and beverages add to the enjoyment of the trip. The boat, which holds six, may also be chartered for special occasions such as corporate seminars, weddings, and anniversaries. No overnight cruises are available; however, a lodging package is available with Obstruction Pass Vacation Homes.

Choice Marine Charters
P.O. Box 555; Eastsound, WA 98245; phone – (360) 376-4416

Enjoy a multi-day boating adventure for sightseeing, fishing, or inter-island transportation. Sail out of any port on Orcas Island for overnight or more extended cruises. The 52-foot *Good Times* can accommodate parties of up to 6 persons on personalized charters. Call to discuss how they can provide you with your dream vacation.

Crescent Beach Kayaks
P.O. Box 543; Eastsound, WA 98245; phone – (360) 376-2464

Both double and single kayaks are available for rent from this business at the head of East Sound, immediately across the road from Crescent Beach.

One of the historic buildings at Deer Harbor Resort houses a grocery and deli.

If you don't have kayaking experience they will provide basic instructions before you set out. Paddle along the safe, protected shoreline of East Sound to view a startling variety of underwater life, marine mammals, and birds.

Deer Harbor Charters
P.O. Box 303; Deer Harbor, WA 98243; phone – (800) 544-5758 or (360) 376-5989

Deer Harbor Resort offers a whole spectrum of water-oriented adventure. Small 14- and 15-foot boats with outboards can be rented by the hour or day for fishing or exploring nearby island state parks. Fishing trips, with rental gear, are led by guides whose local knowledge will increase your odds of landing the big ones. Enjoy skippered day-sailing trips and dramatic sunset cruises. Both skippered and bareboat yacht charters are available for a day, a week, or longer. Whale watch cruises take you into channels between the San Juan Islands to spot eagles perched in shoreline snags, seals and sea lions hauled out on rocky beaches, or with luck, orca whales, porpoises, and minke whales.

Island Kayak Guides
Star Route Box 86; Olga, WA 98279; phone Orcas: (360) 376-4755 or (360) 376-2291; Lopez: (360) 468-4755

Guided kayak tours, based at Doe Bay Resort on Orcas Island, explore the rocks and reefs on the east side of Orcas Island. A 2½ hour introduction to sea kayaking skirts the protected waters of Doe Bay and the nearby channel west of Doe Island. The trip, in two- or three-person kayaks is open to individuals or families with children three years or older. A more advanced course in kayak skills is available.

Take a half-day kayak trip to explore Peapod Islands Wildlife Refuge (north of Doe Bay) or head south to Gorilla Rock (along the shore of Doe Island). You'll see marine birds, eagles, and marine life. Trips beginning just before sunset are offered on cloudless nights, when the moon is full. You can take longer and more strenuous full-day trips, overnight, and customized multi-day trips that include camping at the marine state parks.

Orcas Island Eclipse Charters
P.O. Box 290; Orcas, WA 98290; phone – (800) (360) 376-6566; (360) 376-4663

Come aboard the 36-foot M.V. *Eclipse* for four-hour cruises among the San Juan Islands. Depart from Orcas Landing, stop at marine state parks for a picnic lunch, spot marine mammals and birds, drop a line for bottom-fish, or just sightsee. The boat carries up to six passengers; four persons are the minimum. All gear and bait provided.

Osprey Tours
Eastsound, WA 98245; phone – (360) 376-3677

Here's a tour where you'll enjoy native traditions along with the fun of kayaking. Kayak excursions out of West Beach Resort use unique, traditionally built Aleutian style canoes for half-day and full day trips in the waters off the northwest side of Orcas Island. Paddlers wear pointed-brimmed, woven native hats, to bring the spirit of Native American culture to tour participants (and ward off sunburn). Sorry, you don't get to keep the hat when the tour is over.

Kayak tours give visitors the opportunity to see the more remote parts of the San Juan Islands.

Shearwater Adventures, Inc.

P.O. Box 787; Eastsound, WA 98245: phone – (360) 376-4699'
e-mail – Paddlenw@aol.com; web – http://www.pacificrim.net/-kayak

Shearwater Adventures has offered kayak trips in the San Juan Islands for over 15 years. Whatever your level of experience or interest you should find one of their offerings of interest to you. They have half-day, full-day, or multi-day tours in the islands. No experience necessary; all kayaks are safe stable two-person models. You'll be trained in basic paddling techniques and safety before the trip begins. Overnight trips include camping on remote islands. Some trips and classes are for women, and are led and taught by women.

If you want to sharpen your skills, classes in basic and intermediate level kayaking are offered. Their three-day advanced first aid class is geared specifically to people who spend a lot of time out of doors and around the water. Natural history kayak seminars, some of which are offered through the North Cascades Institute, are focused on the unique environment. Knowledgeable tour leaders take you to the best places to see the amazing variety of marine birds, wildlife, and wildflowers.

Valkyrie Sailing Charters

P.O. Box 716; Eastsound, WA 98245; phone – (360) 376-4018

The 32-foot blue water sloop Valkyrie, located in Orcas Island's West Sound, takes up to four guests for half- and full-day sails anywhere in the San Juans. Be part of the crew, or just sit back and enjoy yourself and let the skipper handle the boat. Overnight trips can be arranged for up to two guests, once compatibility has been established on a shorter cruise.

West Beach Resort

Route 1, Box 510; Eastsound, WA 98245; phone – (360) 376-2240

President Channel, between Orcas and Waldron islands, is popular for its wealth of marine recreation: fishing, kayaking, whale watching, and scuba diving. West Beach Resort, on the northwest side of Orcas Island, gives ready access to the channel. In addition to the resort's cabins and campground, facilities for boaters include a launch ramp, dock and float, fuel (gas, propane), ice, groceries, and dive air. *See also* Lodging.

MARINAS & LAUNCH RAMPS

Deer Harbor Resort and Marina
*P.O. Box 200; Deer Harbor, WA 98243; phone – (360) 376-4420;
VHF channel 9 and 16*

Deer Harbor Marina, located near the head of Deer Harbor, offers 75 guest slips and a fuel dock (gas, diesel, kerosene, butane, propane, premix, alcohol). You'll find restrooms and showers, and bait and tackle sales on the dock; a grocery store, restaurant, and post office sit across the street. *See also* Lodging.

Rosario Resort
1 Rosario Way; Eastsound, WA 98245-2222; phone – (360) 376-2222

Rosario Resort, on East Sound's Cascade Bay, has a small marina with 22 guest slips with power and water, a launch ramp, and numerous mooring buoys offshore. A water taxi is available to transport guests from boats on buoys to shore-side facilities. On shore you'll find a fuel dock, restrooms, showers, laundry facilities, groceries, restaurants, and the full amenities of the resort. There is a charge for overnight use of mooring buoys. *See also* Lodging.

Russell's at Orcas
P.O. Box 196; Orcas, WA 98280; phone – (360) 376-4389

This marina sits on Harney Channel at Orcas, just west of the ferry landing. Floats adjacent to the fuel dock (gas, diesel, kerosene, premix, alcohol) provide some limited transient moorage. In the village at the head of the dock are a post office, general store, grocery store, restaurants, and a hotel. Other nearby stores sell hardware, bait and tackle, beverages, gifts, liquor, and drugs.

Tim's Mobile Marine
*P.O. Box 63; Orcas, WA 98280; phone – (360) 376-2332;
cellular phone: 739-2285; VHF channel 16*

Boating is usually a pleasant and memorable experience—unless your boat runs into mechanical problems, or worse. Then it becomes just memorable. However, assistance is but a call away, no matter where you are in the

San Juans. Tim's speedy repair boat will come to you with parts and a marine technician experienced in mechanical and electrical repairs. They also assist in recovery from groundings, light salvage and rescue, or provide tows for boats up to 65 feet.

West Sound Marina

P.O. Box 19; Orcas WA 98280; phone – (360) 376-2314; VHF channel 16

This full-service marina is midway up the west shore of Orcas Island's West Sound. It provides permanent moorage plus a limited amount of guest moorage on a float with power and water. Marine facilities include a fuel dock (gas, diesel, kerosene, alcohol), marine chandlery, haulouts to 30 tons and a complete line of maintenance and repair services. Additional facilities are a pumpout station, restrooms, and showers. West Sound Store and Deli, which is within walking distance of the marina, features sandwiches, soups, salads, beer, and wine.

Obstruction Pass Launch Ramp

The Obstruction Pass launch ramp provides quick access to kayakers' favorite waters around the south and east side of Orcas Island. To reach the ramp, take the Horseshoe Highway southeast from Eastsound through Moran State Park to Olga. Turn north on Point Lawrence Road, and in ½ mile turn south on Obstruction Pass Road. Follow this road for 2 miles to a parking lot sitting above a county dock and single-lane launch ramp.

PARKS, CAMPGROUNDS & CAMPS

Doe Bay Village Resort and Retreat

Star Route Box 86; Olga, WA 98279; phone – (360) 376-2291 or (360) 376-4755

For those willing to bypass more civilized cabins for a simple pitched tent, Doe Bay Resort provides camping on a large lawn with picnic benches. A multitude of smaller campsites are atop the wooded rocky bluff on the east side of the small cove jutting into the main resort area. Campsites are spartan—most are just a flat spot in the brush, possibly with a fire ring. Views overlook the cove and the main portion of the resort.

Another camping area uphill from the spa offers a few sites in the woods with an occasional picnic table and another broad open field for pick-your-spot camping. Restrooms in this area have showers and a bathtub. The campsite fee permits you to use the showers, mineral baths, and sauna (swimsuits optional in the tubs and sauna.).

The company store carries some basic groceries. *See also* Lodging.

Four Winds * Westward Ho
P.O. Box 140; Deer Harbor, WA 98243; phone – (360) 376-2277

Age: *Boys and girls age 6 to 18*
Fees: *1 week, $485; 4 weeks, $2,550; scholarships available*
Facilities: *Lodging in 4-6 person cabins or wall-tents with counselor, restrooms and showers, dining lodge, stables with 26 horses, crafts cabins, dance court, dock and boathouse, amphitheater, infirmary, archery range, tennis courts, basketball court, badminton court, sports field, beach*
Activities: *Rowing, sailing, canoeing, bicycling, hiking, fishing, tide-pool exploration, horse riding (English and Western, trail riding, cart driving), tennis, archery, soccer, lacrosse, volleyball, basketball, crafts (woodcarving, weaving, photography, painting, more), drama, music, folk dancing, campfires, out-of-camp trips*

Four Winds Camp was founded for girls in 1927, and its boys' counterpart, Westward Ho, opened three years later. Today they are joined as a single, large, co-ed camp on the west shore of Orcas Island's West Sound. The camp's several dozen rustic buildings are casually scattered around 150 wooded acres that encircle Four Winds Bay.

Mid-June to late-August camp sessions are divided by age group. A low-key, one-week session offers beginning campers, aged six to nine, a chance to live together and gain outdoor knowledge. Close staff supervision ensures these youngsters a positive camp experience. For more seasoned campers, four-week sessions for ages 8 to 16 provide greater freedom and individual growth. A counselor training program is offered for 16- to 18-year-old experienced campers.

Moran State Park
Star Route 22; Eastsound, WA 98245; phone – (360) 376-2326

Facilities: *151 standard campsites, 15 primitive campsites, 54 picnic sites, 5 kitchen shelters, restrooms, vault toilets, trailer dump station, interpretive displays, 2 bathhouses, 2 boat launch ramps (on lakes), 2 docks with boat* *rentals, swimming areas, children's play equipment, 31 miles of trail, 8¾ miles of unimproved road, nature trail, Environmental Learning Center.*

Moran, Washington's fourth largest state park, is a veritable cornucopia overflowing with outdoor recreational activities: camping, picnicking, boating, paddling, sailing, swimming, fishing, bicycling, hiking, and bird-watching. It is one of the most popular destinations in the San Juan Islands, and the park's 151 campsites are nearly always full throughout the summer. Campsite reservations are required between Memorial Day and Labor Day.

The park tops out at 2,407-foot-high Mount Constitution, the highest point in the San Juan Islands. You can reach the mountain summit via a steep, winding (but well-paved) road that affords spectacular viewpoints en route. RV trailers are not recommended for the climb, but other vehicles will have no problems.

From the top of Mount Constitution views stretch from Canada to Mount Rainier.

At the summit, near the edge of a sheer cliff that breaks from the east face, are incomparable views across Rosario Strait and the Strait of Georgia to the massive ice cone of Mount Baker and the mountains of the Canadian Coastal Range. Climb the stairs of the picturesque stone tower atop the mountain, built by the CCC in 1936 to mimic fortifications found in the Russian Caucuses Mountains. It offers even broader views of all of the waterways and the many islands of the archipelago. A display in the tower identifies surrounding points of interest.

Moran contains five crystal-clear lakes. The second largest is Cascade Lake (with adjoining Rosario Lagoon). The lake, originally much smaller and more shallow, grew to its present size with the damming of its outlet to create a hydroelectric power source for Robert Moran's estate, Rosario, now Rosario Resort. Three of the island's four campgrounds and its primary day-use area are along the shore of the lake. Here also are a swimming beach, paddle boat rentals, and an Environmental Learning Center.

The largest lake in the park, Mountain Lake, lies upstream in a forested pocket between Mounts Constitution and Picket. It too has camping and boat rentals. Cascade Creek, which connects the two lakes, boasts several delightful waterfalls that can be reached by trail. The largest of these, Cascade Falls, is spectacular in spring and early summer. The park's other three lakes, Summit and the pair of Twin Lakes, are smaller, and require short to moderate hikes to reach.

The heavily wooded park has nearly 40 miles of trails and unimproved roads that offer hikes through beautiful, quiet forests, some of magnificent old cedar, some of tall stately hemlock, others of densely packed lodgepole pine. Portions of these trails are open to mountain bicycle use, and cyclists may use other sections only during certain periods of the year. Check with the park for current restrictions.

How to get there: From the Orcas ferry landing, follow the Horseshoe Highway north to Eastsound, then south to the park, a total distance of 13 miles.

West Beach Resort
Route 1, Box 510; Eastsound, WA 98245; phone – (360) 376-2240

This popular resort on a broad bay facing President Channel offers camping as part of its extensive recreation package. A large, open lawn atop a bluff holds a series of staked-out campsites, each with power, water, and sewer hookups. Nearby are additional utility sites without hookups for either RV or tent camping. A building at the edge of the camping area contains restrooms, showers, and laundry facilities.

For kids, there's an assortment of playground equipment and the wonderful sandy beach below. The resort has a small grocery store, cabins, and a variety of marine rentals and supplies. *See also* Lodging.

YMCA Camp Orkila

P.O. Box 1149, Eastsound, WA 98245. Offices: 909 Fourth Avenue; Seattle, WA 98104; phone – Eastsound: (360) 376-2678; Seattle: 382-5009

Age: Boys and girls age 11 to 18; families

Fees: Sessions vary from 10 to 24 days; fees range from $325 to $480 for YMCA members, $30 additional for limited members. Short-term, family sessions also available

Facilities: Lodging in rustic open-air cabins with counselor, restrooms, dining hall, swimming pool, playing fields, archery range, rifle and B-B range, nature trails, beach, basketball court, volleyball court, climbing wall, dock, craft center, chapel, animal farm, riding facilities, 40-ft. cruiser

Activities: Swimming, fishing, nature study, crafts, music, drama, hiking, rock climbing, camping, bicycling, horse riding and care, farming, gardening, sailing, kayaking, canoeing, basketball, volleyball, soccer, campfires, out-of-camp trips

Several generations of Northwest campers fondly recall their sun-drenched summers at Camp Orkila. The YMCA camp, based on Orcas Island's northwest shore, has been holding forth since 1906. Youngsters acquire new skills and develop positive values—and all the time they think they're just having fun!

Sessions ranging from 10 to 24 days for youngsters from sixth through twelfth grades offer a broad range of experiences. Programs include Seekers and Explorers (the traditional camping program), Pioneer Camp (farming, gardening, and animal care), Horsemasters (equine care and riding techniques), and Adventure Trips (wilderness skills for teens). Special sessions are offered for children with diabetes; four- and six-day camps are available for entire families.

SAN JUAN

Whales, History, & All That Jazz

S AN JUAN ISLAND IS the Big Apple—Where It's Happening—in the San Juans. OK, so that's a relative thing here in the islands, where the pace rarely quickens beyond a casual mosey. But it's big enough. It boasts a town with diversified stores and gourmet restaurants, it has fascinating historical parks and museums, and it has fun and excitement with the jazz festival, golf tournament, boat races, and other events.

Canadians are most familiar with San Juan Island because the Washington State ferry from Sidney stops here, and the two US customs check-in sites are at Friday Harbor and Roche Harbor. During Dominion Day and other Canadian holidays you'll see an exceptional number of maple leaf ensigns at the docks. Some Canadian and Yankee friends schedule boat rendezvous here.

Friday Harbor, on the west side of San Juan Island, is the major center of commerce. It's the county seat and the only incorporated town in the county. (All of the San Juan Islands constitute San Juan County.) The handsome group of buildings on your right as the ferry enters the harbor are the University of Washington Friday Harbor labs, a marine research center where faculty and students from the UW and other universities take part in studies of San Juan marine life.

The Friday Harbor business district covers about eight square blocks

Opposite: *California poppies decorate the Westside Road on San Juan Island. The view is out to Haro Strait.*

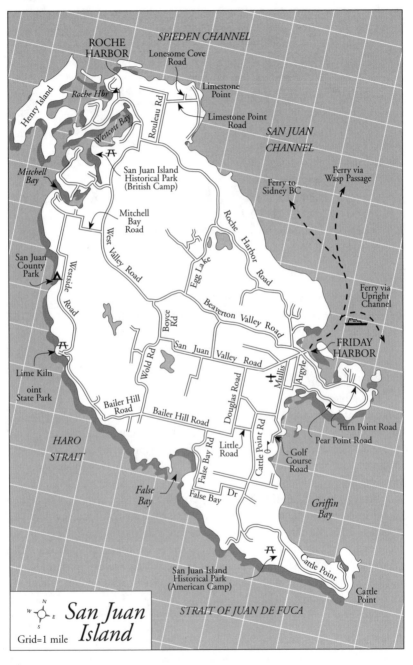

SPIEDEN CHANNEL

ROCHE HARBOR

Lonesome Cove Road

Roche Hbr

Henry Island

Westcott Bay

Limestone Point

Limestone Point Road

SAN JUAN CHANNEL

Rouleau Rd

San Juan Island Historical Park (British Camp)

Mitchell Bay

Mitchell Bay Road

Ferry via Wasp Passage

Ferry to Sidney BC

West Valley Road

Roche Harbor Road

San Juan County Park

Wesside Road

Egg Lake

Ferry via Upright Channel

Beaverton Valley Road

Boyce Rd

Lime Kiln oint State Park

San Juan Valley Road

Wold Rd

FRIDAY HARBOR

Mullis

Argyle

HARO STRAIT

Bailer Hill Road

Bailer Hill Road

Douglas Road

Cattle Point Rd

Turn Point Road

Pear Point Road

Golf Course Road

False Bay Rd

Little Road

False Bay

False Bay Dr

Griffin Bay

San Juan Island Historical Park (American Camp)

Cattle Point

Cattle Point

STRAIT OF JUAN DE FUCA

N
W E
S

San Juan Island

Grid=1 mile

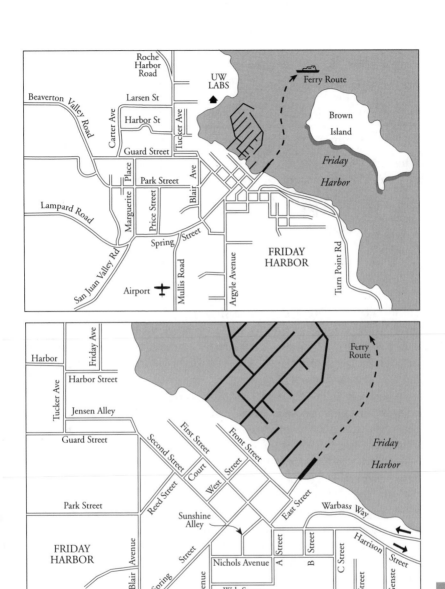

spreading out from the ferry landing. It's easy to cover it all on foot. If you arrive by car, the attendant will direct you to take a right turn off the ferry, and then another quick left turn. You'll be on Spring Street, the main drag. It's only three blocks long, so be careful, or before you know it you'll be out of town.

There's no hokey, planned, "Olde Tyme" ambiance to Friday Harbor; it just grew, and it's terrific! The street layout is haphazard, but that's part of the fun. Little alleys and backstreets lead to great stores tucked in the lower level or backside of others. Many businesses are found in remodeled store-fronts or old historic homes. Cannery Landing, adjacent to the ferry land-ing, once housed a fish cannery; in its current reincarnation it holds small shops and offices.

If you're in Friday Harbor and are startled by the sound of a trumpet blasting out "Alexander's Rag Time Band," you'll know it's the time of the annual Jazz Festival. This is the biggest event of the year—yachts are jammed rail-to-rail in the harbor, shoppers sashay around stores, keeping time to the beat wafting through the doors, and everyone joins in the fun with crazy hats and old-time hoopla. There are other grand celebrations here too, throughout the summer—the Pig War Barbecue, the county fair, and a number of boat races and festivals.

Once you leave Friday Harbor, there is rolling farmland and forested hills. In spring, wildflowers paint roadsides with an exuberance of color. Sheep, cattle, and horses graze in velvet pastures, and if you're watchful you'll spot hawks and eagles soaring overhead or perched in trees. For spectacular beauty, drive or bicycle along West Side Road, south of Lime Kiln State Park. It's the most scenically splendid road in all the islands, as it winds along the cliffs above Haro Strait.

Other than at Friday Harbor, the only gathering of stores and services on San Juan Island is at Roche Harbor, where there are a small general store, a couple of shops, and gas pump—all part of the large resort that is cen-tered on the bay. Numerous resorts and bed and breakfast inns are scattered around the island.

San Juan Island is a cradle of Northwest history, for it was here that the United States and Great Britain very nearly became embroiled in an all-out war. It all began in 1859. The Treaty of 1846 was negotiated to set the bound-ary between British Canada and the US; however the line through the San Juans was not clearly described, and both countries laid claim to them. An American settler, Lyman Cutlar, had scratched out a farm in the middle of a British Hudson's Bay Company sheep pasture on the south end of San

Juan Island. One of the Hudson's Bay's pigs persisted in rooting up Cutlar's potatoes, and in desperation he finally settled his problem by shooting the pig. When Cutlar, a US citizen, was threatened with arrest by the British, the question of sovereignty came to a head.

Troops from both sides were dispatched to the islands. The Americans set up camp on the south end, near the home of the recently-deceased pig, while the British chose a site on the west shore, on Garrison Bay. Cooler heads prevailed, and Germany's Kaiser Wilhelm I was asked

A park ranger in a dashing period costume conducts tours at American Camp of the San Juan Island National Historical Park.

to arbitrate. Eventually he determined the boundary should be down Haro Strait, making the San Juans property of the US (little did the pig care, by this point).

A simple enough story—except it took 13 years to resolve. During this time the detachments from both sides set up housekeeping at their camps, and life went on. There still remains interesting evidence of their life on the island. Today the two camps make up San Juan Island National Historical Park on Garrison Bay on the west side of the island, and Griffin Bay on the southeast.

You can't visit the San Juans without realizing orca whales are a very big deal here. Although these whales (also known as killer whales) range throughout the northern hemisphere, islanders consider this their home. Three "pods" or family groups of orca spend their summers in the waters off the islands. Because of this, in 1976 the Orca Survey, a research activity sponsored by the Moclips Cetological Society, began a study of their food-gathering habits, communication, and social behavior in the San Juans.

By 1980, public interest in whales in general, and orcas in particular, triggered the expansion of the survey beyond its research mission. The organization acquired a building in Friday Harbor, and volunteers set about converting the top floor into a museum—the only one of its kind in the world.

As a complement to the museum, Lime Kiln State Park, on the west side of San Juan Island, has a whale watching site with displays describing the various whales you might see. A number of cruise boats will take you out to search for whales or other wildlife. Most of these cruise captains are hooked up to the Whale Hotline, so they receive reports of the latest sightings, increasing your chance of really seeing these thrilling mammals.

LODGING

●

Prices quoted for accommodations are summer rates, double occupancy, as of 1996, unless otherwise indicated, and are subject to change. Lower rates are usually offered off-season. A tax of 7.6% is added.

Argyle House Bed and Breakfast

685 Argyle Avenue; P.O. Box 2569; Friday Harbor, WA 98250; phone – (360) 378-4084

Accommodations: 3 guest rooms and cottage (private baths, queen-size beds) TV. No children, no pets, smoking outside.
Extras: Full breakfast, deck, hot tub, garden; boat charters available
Rates: rooms $95, cottage $125. Credit cards accepted

The gardens surrounding this 1910-vintage Craftsman house provide a lovely accent to the home itself. Even the names of the guest rooms, Robin's Nest, The Fountain, and Garden View reflect the focus on the landscaping. Innkeepers Bill and Chris Carli have created gracious accommodations within a few blocks walk of Friday Harbor. Each room is a variation of a fresh color scheme of burgundy and green, with crisp white walls, and charming touches such as lace curtains, and an antique doll and knickknacks tucked into a corner. The beautifully decorated separate cottage is spacious and airy, with skylight and a large deck. It has a microwave and a small refrigerator for quick snacks.

The Carlis serve a full, hearty breakfast of fresh fruit, eggs, strata or pancakes, or non-egg dishes. Bill Carli is a charter boat captain whose spent years sailing in the islands; inquire about charters he may be offering.

Blair House Bed and Breakfast

345 Blair Avenue; Friday Harbor, WA 98250 ; phone – (360) 378-5907; fax – (360) 378-3300

Accommodations: 6 rooms (shared and private baths), cottage (queen-size bed and private bath, kitchenette, TV). Children and pets by arrangement, no smoking
Extras: Full breakfast, swimming pool, hot tub, in Friday Harbor
Rates: $75 to $95; cottage $125. Credit cards accepted

Here's country living within strolling distance of the shops and restaurants of Friday Harbor. Blair House combines the best of both worlds: gracious, relaxed accommodations in a wooded setting, along with a convenient location. Pamper yourself with a swim in the swimming pool or a soak in the hot tub. Tall Douglas firs and a garden of colorful rhododendrons surround the tidy inn. Sip iced tea on the porch that stretches across the front of the inn, or enjoy it in the sun by the pool.

Furnishings are tastefully charming, with just enough antiques so you don't feel as if you've moved in with your maiden aunt. Bedrooms in the main home have shared baths. Families will find the adjoining one-bedroom cottage equipped with a kitchenette and queen-size bed and hide-a-bed ideal for a relaxed vacation.

How to get there: From the ferry terminal drive north on Spring for three blocks and turn right on Blair Avenue. The inn is on the left. Open year-round.

The Duffy House Bed and Breakfast
760 Pear Point Road; Friday Harbor, WA 98250; phone – (800) 972-2089; (360) 378-5604; fax – (360) 378-6535

Accommodations: *5 rooms with queen-size beds, one room with 2 beds, private baths, no TV. Children over 8 OK, no pets, no smoking*
Extras: *Full breakfast, guest refrigerator, views of Griffin Bay, orchard, garden, private beach in front of house*
Rates: *$80 to $95. Credit cards accepted*

Part of the fun of staying at a bed and breakfast inn is the opportunity to share someone's home. Duffy House is a bit different than the usual Victorian-era lodgings—it's a 1920s Tudor with gabled roof, coved ceilings, mahogany woodwork, and leaded glass windows. An apple orchard and cheery flower garden add to the 20s aura. The view from the home's hillside perch looks south across the blue waters of Griffin Bay and over American Camp to the Olympic Mountains. Each beautifully appointed room is named for its view: Orchard, Garden, Panorama, Sunset, and Eagle's Nest. The Eagle's Nest is especially aptly named, as there are two trees with bald eagle nests on the property. You're almost guaranteed to see one soaring overhead.

Although the inn sits across the road from the water, a short path leads down to the shore. The gradually tapering sand and gravel beach holds lots of driftwood for afternoon lazing, picnicking, and eagle watching. Boating guests can moor offshore, or kayakers can beach their boats, and trot up the path to a cozy night's lodging at the home of Mary and Arthur Miller.

How to get there: From the ferry landing drive north on Spring for 2 blocks and angle left on Argyle Avenue. In about 1 mile turn left on Pear Point Road. Duffy House is on the left in about ¾ mile. Open year-round.

Friday Harbor House

130 West Street, P.O. Box 1385; Friday Harbor, WA 98250;
phone – (360) 378-8455, fax – (360) 378-8453

Accommodations: *20 rooms (queen-size beds, gas fireplace, refrigerator, coffee-maker, Jacuzzi, TV. Disabled access. Children OK, pets permitted in first floor rooms, with advanced deposit, smoking on decks only*
Extras: *Continental breakfast, robes, restaurant, swimming pool, spa, sauna, exercise room, game room, beauty salon. Meeting rooms available for groups of 20 to 50*
Rates: *$165 to $185. Suite $300. Credit cards accepted*

This elegant hotel on the bluff above the harbor offers the finest modern accommodations in the San Juans. You can luxuriate in pampered living in your beautifully appointed room with its two-person Jacuzzi and gas fireplace. Bedrooms have one or two European queen-size beds; guest often compliment the hotel on these longer, fuller beds. Rooms facing on the water enjoy what is probably the best view of Friday Harbor from their balconies, with ferries and boats of the marina just below. The room decor brings the tones and textures of the outside in with slate floors and soft wood tones.

Guests receive a complimentary Continental breakfast, served in the restaurant or at one of the tiny bistro tables on the adjoining patio. End your evening with one of the restaurant's gourmet dinners. Hotel guests have preferred seating, however reservations are recommended.

How to get there: From the ferry landing, turn northwest off Spring Street onto First Street. Go 1 block to West Street and turn right. The hotel is at the end of the street, overlooking the harbor.

Friday's Historical Inn

35 First Street; P.O. Box 2023; Friday Harbor, WA 98250;
phone – (800) 352-2632 or (360) 378-5848; fax – (360) 378-2881;
web: http://www.fhsji.com/~fridays

Accommodations: *9 rooms and suites (some with shared bath, some with TV), honeymoon package. Children OK, no pets, no smoking*
Extras: *Continental breakfast, some rooms with Jacuzzis, restaurant (lunch and dinner), marine views*
Rates: *$90 to $160. Credit cards accepted*

Whether you're here for whale watching, kayaking, or to tour the island, Friday's will put you right in the heart of Friday Harbor doings. The hotel has seen several lives since it originally opened in 1891 to serve San

Juan visitors; most recently it was the Elite Hotel, an economy-rate youth hostel. In 1992 the building was handsomely renovated; it now offers upscale lodgings with the gracious atmosphere of yesteryear. A nature theme carries throughout the inn, from the lovely limited-edition wildlife prints on the wall to names of the accommodations such as Osprey Room, Eagle Cove, and Tulip Room. Each room is furnished with a tasteful blend of modern and period pieces.

The Bistro Restaurant is on the building's main level. The hotel occupies the upper two floors. Moderately priced rooms on the second floor have double beds, with shared baths just a step across the hall. Enjoy a generous Continental breakfast of gourmet coffee, juice, fresh fruit, hot and cold cereal, and fresh baked scones.

Some of the rooms can be combined to form suites for families. The Orca Room, with a king-size bed and Jacuzzi, is a luxurious honeymoon retreat. Or reserve the Eagle Cove with its king-size bed, kitchen, Jacuzzi, TV, shower for two, and private deck offering a bird's eye view of the harbor.

How to get there: Friday's is on First Street, 2 blocks from the ferry landing. Open year-round.

Harrison House Suites
235 C Street; Friday Harbor, WA 98250; phone – (800) 407-7933;
(360) 378-3587

Accommodations: 4 suites (1- and 2-bedrooms, sleep from 2 to 8, private baths, decks, TV, VCR, kitchens). Children OK, pets by arrangement, no smoking
Extras: Complimentary continental breakfast (full breakfast available), gourmet dinner by arrangement, Jacuzzis, laundry
Rates: $100 to $165 a night (2 guests), $600 to $1000 a week (4 guests). Credit cards accepted

These spacious suites right in Friday Harbor are ideal for a weekend or for more long-term stays. Three of the suites share a 1905 Craftsman-style home; one suite is on the main floor, two are on the upper level. The entire home can be rented for a family or group gathering. A fourth suite in a nearby cottage sleeps up to four. All have kitchens.

The suites are tastefully decorated with a nice blend of modern furnishings and period pieces. Hardwood floors, a formal dining room, piano, sun deck, and a Jacuzzi make the main floor suite a true home away from home. Extra sleeping space is on pull outs in the living room and sun room.

Farhad Ghatan, your enthusiastic host, is an outstanding chef. He uses fresh local seafood and vegetables he grows. His special omelet, bursting with smoked salmon and at least six different vegetables always brings rave reviews. By advanced reservation, he'll cook evening meals for you, too.

How to get there: From Spring Street in Friday Harbor go southeast on First Street which becomes Harrison in one block as it turns uphill. The lodgings are on the corner of Harrison and C Street; parking is just before C Street or by the office on C Street.

Hillside House Bed and Breakfast
365 Carter Avenue; Friday Harbor, WA 98250; phone – (800) 232-4730; (360) 378-4730; fax – (360) 378-4715

Accommodations: 7 rooms (private or designated baths, some with queen-size beds), honeymoon suite (king-size bed, private bath, Jacuzzi, TV, private phone, wet bar). Children under 10 by arrangement, no pets, no smoking
Extras: Full breakfast, guest refrigerator, aviary, walking distance to Friday Harbor
Rates: $85 to $155. Credit cards accepted

Joe and Anne, a pair of standard poodles, may announce your arrival at this spacious modern home, embraced by native firs and rhododendrons. Its hillside perch affords the best views of any Friday Harbor lodging, with the town and bay spread below, and the mountains rising above. The large deck on the main floor is the perfect spot to soak up the view with a cool drink in hand. Some bedrooms have harbor vistas. Others that face the hillside have an equally interesting view—a stunning full-flight aviary that stretches across the back of the house and serves as the garden's focal point. An exotic pheasant with brilliant plumage or unique, quiet ducks may parade right outside your window. A covey of adorable little quail live in the yard.

One of the inn's beautifully decorated rooms is sure to be exactly to your liking: Captain's Quarters contains fascinating mementos from the owners' three-year odyssey on their 46-foot boat; Sherwood will delight young and old with its twin beds, woodsy tones, and the curious pheasant that loves to peer in the window. Grandest of all is the secluded Eagle's Nest on the top floor. It makes the perfect honeymoon hideaway with its comfy king-size bed, Jacuzzi, wet bar, TV, and aerie-like balcony.

How to get there: From Spring Street in Friday Harbor turn northwest onto Second Street, which angles left and becomes Guard Street. In two more blocks turn right on Carter Street. The inn is on the left in ½ block. Open year-round.

The Inn at Friday Harbor
410 Spring West, P.O. Box 339, Friday Harbor, WA 98250;
phone – (800) 752-5752 or (360) 378-4000; fax – (360) 378-5800

Accommodations: 72 rooms and suites (queen-size beds, some with kitchenettes,
cable TV), disabled access. Children OK, no pets, smoking and nonsmoking
Extras: In-room coffee makers, restaurant (breakfast, lunch, and dinner), indoor
heated swimming pool, spa and exercise room, game room, car rental service,
meeting space, tour bus, ferry and airport pickup, conference facilities, gift shop
Rates: $90 to $213. Credit cards accepted

Enjoy the San Juan Islands in comfort at this first-class inn. Accommodations range from standard hotel rooms to spacious two-bedroom, two-bath suites. Each of the nicely appointed rooms include coffee makers and cable TV. All suites have kitchenettes and private decks or patios. Schedule a conference or business retreat here; the full range of facilities makes it ideal for your function.

The Inn's unique, bright red double-decker bus will take you on a narrated tour of English Camp, the Whale Watch Park, and other San Juan Island points of interest. After seeing the island, relax in the heated swimming pool and curl up with a bottle of suntan lotion in the adjoining patio, or the helpful staff will suggest some afternoon recreation.

How to get there: The inn is 4 blocks from the ferry terminal on Spring Street. Open year-round.

The Inn at Friday Harbor Suites
680 Spring Street; Friday Harbor, WA 98250; phone – (360) 378-3031;
fax – (360) 378-4228

Accommodations: 60 condominium-style suites (1- and 2-bedroom units with
queen-size beds, living rooms, kitchens, cable TV), disabled access. Children
OK, no pets, smoking and nonsmoking
Extras: Restaurant (breakfast lunch, and dinner), indoor heated swimming pool,
spa and exercise room, game room, car rental service, meeting space, tour bus,
ferry and airport pickup, conference facilities, gift shop
Rates: $104 to $213. Credit cards accepted.

These condominium-style suites, run in conjunction with the Inn at Friday Harbor, are the answer for family groups or people staying a week or longer on the island, and wanting home-like conveniences such as a living room and fully equipped kitchen. The suites share the swimming pool, spa, and other facilities with the Inn at Friday Harbor.

How to get there: The suites are 6 blocks from the ferry terminal, at 680 Spring Street. Open year-round.

Island Lodge at Friday Harbor

1016 Guard Street; Friday Harbor, WA 98250; phone – (800) 822-4753 or (360) 378-2000

Accommodations: *20 rooms and 8 suites (queen-size beds, some with kitchen-ettes, TV). Children OK, no pets, smoking and nonsmoking*
Extras: *In-room coffeemaker, outdoor hot tub, sauna, barbecue, sundeck, pond, meeting room, tennis courts nearby*
Rates: *$85 to $140. Credit cards accepted*

Where else can you have your afternoon coffee on a sundeck overlooking a llama pasture? This motel on the outskirts of Friday Harbor offers standard, nicely furnished motel rooms in a laid-back setting. The adjoining garden has a pond, sundeck, barbecues, and a hot tub. Tennis courts are just down the street, at the high school. The innkeepers keep a file of menus from local restaurants that you can check to see where you want might want to eat.

How to get there: From Spring Street in Friday Harbor turn right on Second Street which becomes Guard Street. The lodge is reached in about ½ mile. Open year-round.

Jensen Bay Bed and Breakfast

300 Jensen Bay Road; Friday Harbor, WA 98250; phone – (360) 378-5318

Accommodations: *1-bedroom cottage (queen-size bed, futons, private bath, fireplace). Children OK, pets by arrangement, no smoking*
Extras: *Continental breakfast, basic cooking staples in kitchen, barbeque*
Rates: *$165. No credit cards*

This is like having your own summer home in the country. It's a great base of operations for island exploring, or it can be a peaceful retreat for absolute solitude. The charming, beautifully decorated home, which is tucked away on five sunny acres south of Friday Harbor, is ideal for a couple or family of four. In addition to the bedroom, two futon seats in the living room fold out to double beds.

A continental breakfast of fruit and baked goods is provided, or you can whip up a complete meal in the fully equipped kitchen (staples and main breakfast ingredients such as cereal and eggs are on hand—you bring in the main groceries). There's a back yard barbeque too, for grilling a steak or burgers. Then spend the evening on the porch, enjoying the sunset and mists settling in the surrounding forest.

Owner Manya Pickard is an artist who creates exquisite handmade jewelry of silver and semi-precious stones. Her studio is nearby on the property. If you ask, she will show you her work; once you see it you undoubtedly will want to purchase some. It's also for sale in Friday Harbor at The Garuda and I.

How to get there: From the Friday Harbor ferry landing follow Spring Street to Mullis Road and turn left (south). This becomes Cattle Point Road. 4¼ miles from the ferry landing turn left on Jensen Bay Road. The bed and breakfast is the first house on the left.

Lonesome Cove Resort
5810-A Lonesome Cove Road; Friday Harbor, WA 98250;
phone – (360) 378-4477

Accommodations: *6 cabin suites (kitchens, fireplaces, no TV). Children OK, no pets, no smoking*
Extras: *Beach, dock with float, trout pond, library*
Rates: *$95 to $150. Credit cards accepted*

The cove may be lonesome because of its isolation, but you'll never be lonesome with so much to do in such beautiful surroundings. The resort's six cabins face on Spieden Channel. You can bring your boat up to the 100-foot-long dock and use the resort as a base for island exploration. Lonesome Cove is centered smack dab in one of the best scuba diving areas in the San Juans. The steep walls of Limestone Point are within swimming distance of the resort beach. Underwater rock formations and offshore reefs around the point are teeming with marine life that attracts divers.

For those souls seeking quieter pastimes, there's the beach to stroll, a small library stocked with books, lush grassy lawns to sunbathe on, and lots of wildlife to watch.

The newly remodeled cabins are exceptionally nice. All have full kitchens, fireplaces, and electric heat. The largest accommodates six. They are well spaced for privacy so you don't feel you're living in your neighbor's hip pocket. The six acres of deep forest that encloses the resort assures solitude.

How to get there: Drive northwest from Friday Harbor on Roche Harbor Road. In 7½ miles, just before reaching Roche Harbor, turn north on Roluleau Road, and in a mile angle right on Limestone Point Road. Lonesome Cove Road, which leads to the resort, is on the left in another ½ mile. Open year-round. 5-day minimum in summer, 2-day minimum other times.

Mariella Inn and Cottages

630 Turn Point Road; Friday Harbor, WA 98250; phone – (360) 378-6868; fax – (360) 378-6822

Accommodations: *11 rooms (private baths), 10 waterfront cottages (1- to 3-bedroom, kitchenettes, private baths), no TV. Children OK, no pets, no smoking.*

Extras: *Full breakfast with rooms, picnic basket continental breakfast in cottages, water views, moorage, dock, kayak and bicycle rentals and tours, hot tub, dinner available (by reservation), 65-foot classic wooden motor yacht available for charter*

Rates: *Rooms $140 and $160, cottages $195 to $235. Credit cards accepted*

You can almost see little girls in pinafores and sausage curls and boys in kneepants playing on the lawn of this historic Victorian inn. Unlike many bed and breakfast inns that were formerly homes, this truly extraordinary inn has served vacationers since 1902. It sits majestically on a point of land facing the town of Friday Harbor. A grand lawn sweeps down to the water, and gardens embrace the entrance. The gracious setting makes it a favorite for weddings. Boaters with cabin fever will find Mariella Inn an ideal layover; boats up to 60 feet can tie up at the dock, or there's ample anchorage space offshore. Or you can charter the inn's 65-foot classic wooden motor yacht, built in 1927.

Bedrooms are all grandly furnished with antiques and decorated with lace and delicately flowered wallpaper. Chose a sunny room to lift the spirit or a more shaded one to soothe the soul. The ten waterfront cottages, recently renovated and redecorated, offer comfortable lodging for families, couples, or others who want a bit more seclusion.

Friday Harbor is within walking distance of the inn, or you can rent one of their bicycles for a peddling tour. Kayaks are available for rent if you want to explore the protected waters of Friday Harbor and around Brown Island. Turn Point State Park is about a mile to the east, around Pear Point.

Mariella carries on its long tradition of hospitality with its mouth-watering breakfasts. Tea, coffee, and pastries are on hand any time of day. In the summer enjoy gourmet dinners in the waterfront dining room. If you plan to dine here (and you won't be able to resist, once you catch the aroma from the kitchen), reservations are necessary.

How to get there: From Spring Street in Friday Harbor turn left on First Street, which merges into Harrison Street and then becomes Turn Point Road. The inn is on the left, about ½ mile from Friday Harbor. Open year-round.

Mar Vista Resort

2005 False Bay Drive; Friday Harbor, WA 98250; phone – (360) 378-4448

Accommodations: *8 cottages (1- to 3-bedroom, private baths, kitchenettes, 1 cottage with fireplace, no TV). Children OK, no pets, smoking and non-smoking*

Extras: *Children's play equipment, picnic tables, pond, beach, trails, whale watching*

Rates: *$80 (2-person cabin) to $125 (6-person cabin). Credit cards accepted*

Pack up the kids and head for Mar Vista! This resort has "family fun" written all over it. The cottages are simply furnished, but comfortable—just the thing for carefree relaxation. Mom can settle down with a book and let Dad and the kids take over the cooking and dish washing; who cares if you have hot dogs for five days? A spacious lawn holds a slide, jungle gym

The Washington State ferry arrives at Friday Harbor.

and merry-go-round. Trails lead down to the beach where kids can spend hours building driftwood castles, collecting rocks, or playing in the water. As evening settles in, Mom and Dad can sneak in some romantic stargazing as the kids play games with new-found buddies from neighboring cabins.

Spectacular scenery is part of the resort's package; views from the high bluff are out to Haro Strait and the Strait of Juan de Fuca. Bring binoculars and watch for whales that pass by offshore. The cabins are nicely separated so you're not forced to enjoy someone else's kids. One-bedroom cottages have kitchenettes, two-bedroom cottages offer living rooms and kitchens. The three-bedroom cabin has a working fireplace.

How to get there: Drive south from Friday Harbor on Argyle which joins Cattle Point Road. Follow Cattle Point Road to False Bay Drive and turn west. In 1¾ miles False Bay Drive turns north. The signed driveway to Mar Vista Resort is at this road bend. Open Mid-April to mid-October; two-night minimum.

The Meadows Bed and Breakfast
1980 Cattle Point Road; Friday Harbor, WA 98250; phone – (360) 378-4004

Accommodations: 2 units (twin and queen-size beds, shared bath), no TV.
Children over 10 by arrangement, no pets, no smoking
Extras: Full breakfast, mountain and water views, country setting
Rates: $80. 2-night minimum may apply. Cash or checks preferred, credit cards accepted

Although your hosts are there when needed, you won't feel as if you've moved in with them, as you do in some bed and breakfast inns, because these accommodations are in a unit separate from the main home. The two spacious, side-by-side bedrooms share a bath between them. The quarters are ideal for a family or two couples. Furnishings are attractive, cheerful, and quite comfortable.

Bicyclers heading out for a day's ride can carbo-load on the generous breakfast served in the 1892 farmhouse. If you're not feeling that energetic, stroll around the grounds, relax on the deck or in the sun room, drinking in the view of Griffin Bay, or settle into a hammock underneath the oak trees with a good book.

How to get there: From Spring Street in Friday Harbor turn south on Mullis Road, which merges into Argyle. When Argyle turns west it becomes Cattle Point Road. Shortly after Cattle Point Road turns south, the sign for the inn is on the left. Open year-round.

Moon & Sixpence

3021 Beaverton Valley Road; Friday Harbor, WA 98250;
phone – (360) 378-4138

Accommodations: *Tower suite (queen-size bed, private bath, refrigerator,*
toaster, electric teapot), TV. No children, no pets, no smoking
Extras: *Pastoral setting, resident weaver, flower garden*
Rates: *$90. 2 night minimum. No credit cards*

If you're an artist, writer, or merely have the soul of a poet, you'll thrive at the Moon & Sixpence. Named for Somerset Maugham's novel based on the life of Paul Gauguin, the farm evokes feelings of the "special place" to which the artist was drawn. The Water Tower, a unique vacation rental, is a three-level, remodeled real watertower. The private bath is on the entry level; from there stairs lead up to the romantic bedroom with a queen-size bed. Up yet another level is a sunny sitting room with eagle's-eye views of Mount Dallas and the green swale of Beaverton Valley. Breakfast is not provided; however a refrigerator, toaster, and teapot are provided so you can make your own.

The property is the home of Charles and Evelyn Tuller. Evelyn is a weaver, and if you ask, she'll welcome you to her studio where she creates blankets, shawls, rugs, and fine religious vestments.

When you publish your novel, remember to dedicate it to the Moon & Sixpence.

How to get there: From Spring Street in Friday Harbor, turn right onto Second Street, which becomes Guard Street and in 4 blocks angles right as Beaverton Valley Road. Moon & Sixpence is 3 miles from Friday Harbor. Open year-round.

Old English Roses Manor

3161 Beaverton Valley Road; Friday Harbor, WA 98250;
phone – (360) 378-6484

Accommodations: *4 units (double and king-size beds, some with shared bath) no*
TV. Children by arrangement, no pets, no smoking
Extras: *Full breakfast, games and music available, sitting room with fireplace, coun-*
try setting
Rates: *$75 to $95. Credit cards accepted*

Quaint English bed and breakfast inns were the inspiration for this getaway in the heart of San Juan Island. The two-story Tudor-style home, surrounded by masses of roses sets the tone. Inside, innkeepers Lane and Janka

Cameron have used charming touches borrowed from England, such as wash basins enclosed in antique sideboards and pretty baskets to hold soaps and other bath essentials. All bathrooms have large, claw-foot tubs, ideal for an evening's relaxing soak.

Three of the rooms have full-size beds. The king-size bed in the fourth room can be split into two twins, if guests desire. Down comforters provide pampered luxury. In the evening, gather around the fireplace for spirited conversation or games with other guests or wander the rose garden and watch the stars come out.

The three-course hearty breakfast is enough to last you all through your day of exploring the island. Homemade blueberry pancakes and Canadian bacon always brings raves. Afternoon tea is standard here from 3:00 P.M. to 4:00 P.M. It's served with homemade shortbread, or strawberry shortcake, in season.

How to get there: From Friday Harbor, turn northwest on Second Street, which becomes Guard Street, and then Beaverton Valley Road. Continue west on Beaverton Valley Road for 3 miles to the inn.

Olympic Lights Bed and Breakfast

4531A Cattle Point Road; Friday Harbor, WA 98250; phone – (360) 378-3186

Accommodations: *5 rooms (private and shared baths), no TV. Children by arrangement, no pets, no smoking*
Extras: *Full breakfast, country setting, farm*
Rates: *$70 to $105. No credit cards*

Leave your stress at the gate! This sunny 1895 Victorian farmhouse is sure to lift your spirits. The inn sits in grandeur on a bluff at the south end of San Juan Island, seeming to rise as high as the Olympic Mountains it looks out to. The bright yellow clapboard exterior hints at the white wicker furnishings and soft pastels of the cheerful country interior. The second floor is carpeted completely in white. Guests are asked to remove their shoes before going upstairs—who cannot be relaxed while padding across a cushy carpet in stocking feet?

The Garden Room on the first floor holds a comfy king-size bed and private bath. Four guest rooms on the second floor share two full-size baths. Fluffy feather comforters that warm the beds hold the sweet scent of salt air and fresh grass. In the morning, innkeepers Christian and Lea Andrade serve a hearty farm breakfast on elegant china in the parlor or in the spacious kitchen.

The setting is as open and airy as the house itself. Rolling grassland spreads south to the tip of the island, with few trees to obstruct the panoramic view. The wide lawn is a perfect spot for a genteel round of croquet in the afternoon or a more energetic game of horseshoes. Evenings bring salty breezes rising off the straits and a sky with more stars than you ever knew existed.

How to get there: From Spring Street in Friday Harbor, angle left on Argyle Avenue. Follow the road as it heads south and becomes Cattle Point Road. The lane leading to the inn is on the right in 5½ miles, just before reaching American Camp. Open year-round.

Orcinus Inn

3580 Beaverton Valley Road; Friday Harbor, WA 98250;
phone – (360) 378-4060

Accommodations: 5 bedrooms (king-size and double beds, private and shared baths), 1 dormitory-style room (bunk beds, shared bath). Children OK, pets by arrangement, no smoking
Extras: Coffee, tea, scuba gear washing area
Rates: $25 (dorm room) to $65 (bedroom with private bath). Credit cards accepted

Orcinus Inn is just the ticket for comfortable, reasonably-priced accommodations in the San Juans. The rustic farmhouse is a favorite with divers and cyclists. It's also a grand place to stage a family gathering, with a variety of sleeping arrangements, and lots of room to kick back and have fun. The cabin kitchen can be available to groups, by arrangement. The living room with its large stone fireplace is just the spot for sharing a big bowl of popcorn in the evening and discussing the days adventures.

One room has a king-size bed and private bath. The dormitory room, which sleeps six in bunk beds, has a shared shower. Three rooms designed for two or three persons have unique A-frame bunk beds that have a comfortable double bed below and a single bed above. One room has a private bath, two share a bath.

How to get there: From Friday Harbor head northwest on Second Street, which becomes Guard Street. At a T-intersection turn right (north) on Beaverton Valley Road and follow it for 4 miles. The marked driveway to the inn is on the right.

Panacea Bed and Breakfast

595 Park Street; P.O. Box 2023; Friday Harbor, WA 98250;
phone – (800) 352-2632; (360) 378-5858; fax 387-2881;
web: http://www.fhsji.com/~fridays

Accommodations: *4 rooms (all with private entry, private baths, cable TV),*
kitchen. No children, no pets, no smoking
Extras: *Continental breakfast, two rooms with Jacuzzis, kitchen and outdoor*
barbeque. Running track and tennis courts nearby
Rates: *$120 to $145. Credit cards accepted*

At the turn of the century, the small town of Friday Harbor boasted few prosperous residents or fancy homes. One exception was Peter Kirk, the founder of Kirkland, who retired in style in a now-classic 1907 Craftsman home. The granite rock used in the foundation, pillared entry, and fireplaces was barged over from Mount Baker. The spacious parlor has twelve-foot ceilings, arched doorways, wainscotting, and leaded glass accent windows. This elegant home now serves as a bed and breakfast inn, offering relaxation and renewal from the stresses of everyday life. Hence the name, Panacea: "the cure for all that ails."

Each of the four large bedrooms of Panacea feature entries from the parlor, as well as an outside entry for maximum privacy. The Garden and Courtyard rooms have queen beds and showers; the extra-spacious Sunset and Mount Baker rooms each have king-size beds and Jacuzzis for two. Mount Baker room also boasts a fireplace. Both of these rooms have private, covered verandahs with views. A continental breakfast is provided, and the home's fully equipped kitchen is available for you to prepare quick meals.

At the Panacea, the focus of owner Steve Demarest is on creating a place that is a destination in itself, not just a great place to stay when visiting San Juan Island. The nearness of the public running track and tennis courts at the high school makes this a place for a complete vacation getaway.

How to get there: Panacea is in Friday Harbor on Park Street, five blocks from the ferry land. Open year-round.

Roche Harbor Resort

4950 Rueben Tarte Memorial Drive; Roche Harbor, WA 98250;
phone – (800) 451-8910 or (360) 378-2155

Accommodations: 58 units (hotel rooms, cottages, and condominiums; some
   shared baths in the hotel; kitchenettes in cabins and condos; TV in condos),
   honeymoon and Presidential suite in hotel. Children OK, no pets, smoking
   and nonsmoking rooms available

Extras: 107-year old Hotel de Haro, marina, convenience store, restaurant, lounge,
   entertainment, swimming pool, tennis courts, formal gardens, air strip, small
   boat rentals, laundry

Rates: $70 to $140. Credit cards accepted

You won't want to miss Roche Harbor when you visit San Juan Island—
it's the premier destination. Boaters flock here to rendezvous with their friends,
or just to revel in the marine atmosphere. But even if you're not a boater, the
history and scenery make it a fascinating spot to visit.

Roche Harbor is the legacy of John S. McMillin, who built a lime quarry

The historic Hotel de Haro is the centerpiece of Roche Harbor Resort.

empire here more than 100 years ago. The limestone eventually played out, and in the 1950s the business closed. Since that time the once-deteriorating buildings have been restored and the property developed as a first class destination resort.

The hotel was built to house McMillin's business customers and friends. Its proudest moment was in 1906, when President Theodore Roosevelt stayed here. Although the hotel has been renovated, it still maintains much of its historic character. If you want to be right in the heart of harbor activity, you can choose a room in the hotel—perhaps it will be the very one that Roosevelt used. Decks that stretch the width of the two upper stories afford supreme views of the harbor.

A number of the historic cottages used by workers in the lime kiln business have been recently renovated and converted to overnight lodgings. They are close to the swimming pool; some have views of the marina. All are two-bedroom and have kitchens and bathrooms. The large cottages sleep six, the smaller ones sleep four.

However, if you want something more modern, you may opt for one of the condominium-style lodgings a short walk away, around the bay. They come as 1-, 2-, or 3-bedroom units. All have fireplaces, TV, kitchens, and view decks. Guests have use of the resort's swimming pool and tennis courts.

How to get there: From Friday Harbor, follow Roche Harbor Road northwest to the resort. The resort has an adjacent airstrip for guests who fly in. Open May to November; 4-night minimum for cottages in July and August

Sandpiper Condominiums
570 Jensen Alley; Friday Harbor, WA 98250; phone – (360) 378-5610 or (360) 378-8155

Accommodations: Studio apartments with kitchenettes
Extras: Walking distance to Friday Harbor, tennis courts nearby
Rates: $65 to 85 per day, $250 to $350 per week. No credit cards

If what you're looking for is a moderately-priced base of operations, Sandpiper exactly fills the bill, offering daily and weekly fully furnished studio rentals within walking distance of downtown Friday Harbor. All units are fully furnished and equipped with kitchenettes and cooking equipment. Rollaways are available for added sleeping space.

How to get there: From Spring Street in Friday Harbor, head northwest on Second Street, which becomes Guard. Turn right on Tucker; Sandpiper Condominiums are immediately on the right. Open year-round; daily or weekly.

San Juan Inn
*50 Spring Street West; P.O. Box 776 ; Friday Harbor, WA 98250;
phone – (800) 742-8210 or (360) 378-2070*

Accommodations: *10 rooms (private and shared baths), no TV. Children by
arrangement, pets by arrangement, no smoking*
Extras: *Continental-plus breakfast, parlor, garden, 7-person Jacuzzi in garden,
bicycle storage*
Rates: *Rooms $70 to $100, suites $135 to $175. Credit cards accepted*

Let nostalgia reign as you enjoy your generous breakfast of coffee, juice,
fruit, muffins, and bagels in the second-floor parlor and watch the town
awaken to greet a new day. For lunch, one of the nearby delis will pack you
a picnic to spread out under the ornamental cherry tree in the garden.

Boaters who want a day's break from the confines of their bunks, or
who have more crew than they can sleep, will find the inn's location, just a
short stroll from the docks, perfect for their needs.

Since 1873 San Juan Inn has been hosting travelers to the islands. It's
been completely modernized since that time, of course, but it still beautifully continues the comfort and elegance of Victorian times. Brass and wicker
beds and other antique pieces fill the bedrooms, and delicate lace curtains
frame the Friday Harbor view. Some rooms look out to the private flower
garden that supplies fresh flowers for the inn.

How to get there: The inn is on Spring Street, ½ block from the ferry.
Open year-round.

Snug Harbor Marina Resort
2371 Mitchell Bay Road; Friday Harbor, WA 98250; phone – (360) 378-4762

Accommodations: *10 waterfront bungalows (studio and 2-bedroom, queen-size
beds, kitchenettes); treehouse cabin, 2-bedroom cottage with hot tub. Some
units have TVs and fireplaces. Children OK, pets OK, smoking and
nonsmoking units*
Extras: *Marina, boat launch, kayak and boat rentals, fishing gear and crabpot rentals, fuel (gas), propane, scuba air refills, store, RV sites, campground, evening
bonfires. Vacation packages available*
Rates: *$80 (deluxe trailers in camp setting with view of bay) to $245 (4-person
cottage). Sneakaway Packages available. Credit cards accepted*

You'll want to return time after time to this friendly little resort on San
Juan Island's west side. Everything you need for a great island vacation is
right here. It is the closest resort to prime kayaking, scuba diving, salmon

fishing, and whale watching. The resort's bungalows line the waterfront, with the docks just a few steps away. The nicely furnished accommodations have wood paneling and vaulted ceilings. All couches are hide-a-beds, so there is space to add an extra person or two (for an added charge). If you like extra pampering, reserve the cottage with the hot tub. Check out the Treehouse, with its fireplace and huge bay window overlooking the harbor; it's secluded, and ideal for a romantic retreat.

Try one of the resort's Sneakaway Vacation Packages, which include lodging of your choice, use of a either a sailboat or outboard boat, with a scuba tank refill or use of fishing poles and a crabpot. Imagine bringing back fresh crab to steam for your dinner!

How to get there: From Friday Harbor follow Beaverton Valley Road, which becomes West Valley Road, for 6 miles to Mitchell Bay Road, and turn left. The signed road to Snug Harbor Resort is on the right in ¾ mile. Open year-round.

States Inn Bed and Breakfast
2039 West Valley Road; Friday Harbor, WA 98250; phone – (360) 378-6240; ranch: (360) 378-4243; fax – (360) 378-6241

Accommodations: 9 rooms and 2-bedroom suites (private baths, some queen- and king-size beds, 1 unit with fireplace), disabled access, no TV. Children by arrangement, no pets, no smoking
Extras: Full breakfast, working ranch, pastoral setting. Hiking nearby
Rates: $80 to $175. Credit cards accepted

Did you ever imagine you could enjoy the splendor of a Louisiana plantation or the laid-back comfort of a Montana ranch right here in the San Juans? At States Inn you can. Each of the inn's nine bedrooms are uniquely decorated with authentic touches from different states around the US. The Louisiana bedroom has cool white wicker furniture and soft eyelet curtains; the Arizona-New Mexico suite boasts warm southwest tones and Mexican blankets. All bedrooms have adjoining baths except for the Rhode Island room—its bath is just a step down the hall. The Arizona-New Mexico suite, with its two separate bedrooms and shared bathroom and sitting room, is perfect for a family or two couples.

The core of the historic house was a dance hall, dating back to 1910. It's been remodeled and expanded to become the modern two-story San Juan ranchhouse you see today. Getting acquainted with the horses, chickens, and sheep that live on the farm will be a thrill for city kids. The English

Camp section of the San Juan Island Historic Park is just a mile down the road. Guests wanting to stretch their legs can hike down to the park's buildings, or climb to the top of Mount Young for grand views out to Haro Strait.

How to get there: From Friday Harbor drive northwest on Second Street, and follow it as it becomes Guard Street, and then Beaverton Valley Road. Continue on this road for approximately 7 miles. The sign for the inn is ½ mile north of the Mitchell Bay Road intersection. Open year-round.

Tower House Bed and Breakfast

1230 Little Road; Friday Harbor, WA 98250; phone – (360) 378-5464;
e-mail – 71157.1441@compuserve.com;
web: http://ourworld.com/homepages/Joe_Luma

Accommodations: *2 bedrooms (private baths, queen-size beds, sitting rooms), TV in living room. No children, no pets, no smoking*
Extras: *Full breakfast, guest use of refrigerator, pond, country setting*
Rates: *$95 to $115. Credit cards accepted*

When we first saw this fabulous inn in the country overlooking San Juan Valley, we knew it was a place we wanted to stay. We returned several weeks later, and it fulfilled our dreams. The unique Queen Anne style home has a round two-story tower with leaded glass windows and decorative shingling on the exterior. A romantic sitting room inside the tower adjoins a bedroom. Sun streaming through the stained glass windows casts soft colors across the suite. The sitting room for the second bedroom is a cozy library with windows opening out to the garden behind the inn.

Antique furniture blends beautifully with fascinating pieces such as a lacquered Oriental screen and carved animals from Africa collected by Chris and Joe Luma, the inn's owners. They will tell you how the house itself traveled from afar! It was originally built on Vancouver Island and was barged to the San Juans.

Feast on the sumptuous breakfast, elegantly presented on fine china, crystal, and silver, in the dining room.

How to get there: From Spring Street in Friday Harbor turn south on Argyle and follow it as it becomes Cattle Point Road. When Cattle Point Road turns south, Little Road is on the right in about ½ mile. The Tower House is on the right in a short ½ mile, just before the intersection with Douglas Road. Open year-round.

Opposite: *A sunny sitting room at Tower House Bed and Breakfast invites an afternoon of relaxed reading.*

Trumpeter Inn Bed and Breakfast
420 Trumpeter Way; Friday Harbor, WA 98250;
phone – (800) 826-7926 (reservations) or (360) 378-3884

Accommodations: *5 rooms (private baths, queen- or king-size beds), TV.*
Children by arrangement, no pets, no smoking
Extras: *Full breakfast, country atmosphere*
Rates: *$90 to $105. Credit cards accepted*

With guest rooms named for rosemary, yarrow, and other sweet-scented herbs, you will know this is an inn designed to appeal to your senses. Trumpeter Inn proves that a house doesn't have to be old to be charming and comfortable; it's a modern country home with spacious, sunny bedrooms, and lovely accents of flowers throughout. All bedrooms are beautifully decorated, and have either king- or queen-size beds and full bathrooms. A handicap accessible room has twin beds, a sitting room, and private bath.

The B&B, hosted by innkeepers Don and Bobbie Wiesner, sits on a hillside overlooking rolling, bucolic pastures, with the distant peaks of the Olympic Mountains rising above. Spend a quiet evening on the deck listening to the gentle sounds of the country. Graceful trumpeter swans (the namesake of the inn) winter in the area. You may see them on neighboring ponds and pastures.

How to get there: Follow Spring Street out of Friday Harbor; at a Y-intersection stay left on San Juan Valley Road. The signed lane leading to the inn is on the north in about 2 miles. Open year-round.

Tucker House Bed and Breakfast
260 B Street; Friday Harbor, WA 98250; phone – (800) 965-0123
or (360) 378-2783; fax – (360) 378-6437

Accommodations: *2 rooms (shared bath, queen-size beds, TV, VCR), 3 cottages*
(private baths, queen-size beds, some kitchenettes, woodstoves, TV). Chil-
dren OK, no pets, no smoking
Extras: *Full breakfast, hot tub, 2-blocks walking distance from ferry and Friday*
Harbor
Rates: *$65 to $135. Credit cards accepted*

You can enjoy the quaint setting of a Victorian Bed and Breakfast right in Friday Harbor. Soak up the full turn-of-the-century flavor from one of the two rooms in the circa-1898 home. Or if you prefer more privacy, opt for one of the three private cottages. All accommodations are comfortably furnished. The cottages have cozy wood-burning stoves, and two have kitchenettes. The in-deck Jacuzzi may not be vintage Victorian, but it certainly adds to the pleasure of your stay.

Breakfast on homemade cinnamon bread, eggs, fruit, orange juice, and gourmet coffee or tea served in the home's solarium. Then it's off to do the walking tour of Friday Harbor with all its interesting shops, marinas, and restaurants.

Gift certificates are available for birthdays, anniversaries, or other special occasions.

How to get there: From Spring Street in Friday Harbor head east on First Street. In one block angle left on Harrison and in one more block turn right on B Street. Tucker House is on the left at the end of the block. Open year-round.

Westwinds Bed and Breakfast

4909-H Hannah Highland Road; Friday Harbor, WA 98250;
phone – (360) 378-5283

Accommodations: *1200 square-foot home (2 bedrooms, 2 private baths, kitchen, TV). Children and pets by arrangement, no smoking*
Extras: *Hearty continental breakfast, privacy, spectacular water view*
Rates: *$245. Credit cards accepted*

You'll feel as if you are on your own private island in this exquisite retreat, rated the "ultimate place to kiss in the Northwest." The lodgings accommodate only one couple or a family of four at a time, but therein lies much of its charm: you can be assured of absolute solitude for your honeymoon or vacation getaway. From its hillside perch, the home's huge glass windows look out to a panoramic vista of rolling grasslands with miniature horses that the owner raises, Haro Strait, and the Straits of Juan de Fuca. Bring binoculars to watch passing boat traffic or possibly even whales offshore (the island's whale watching park is just up the road a mile).

The beautifully decorated suite boasts a cathedral-ceilinged bedroom, a large soaking tub in the bathroom, and French doors opening onto the view deck where you can enjoy your morning repast.

How to get there: From Friday Harbor follow Spring Street to a Y-intersection at the outskirts of town. Stay left on San Juan Valley Road. In about 1 mile head south (left) on Douglas Road, which curves west in about 1¾ miles and becomes Bailer Hill Road. As Bailer Road reaches the water and heads north as West Side Road, Hannah Road is on the right. Open year-round.

Wharfside Bed and Breakfast – Aboard the *Jacquelyn*
Port of Friday Harbor, K Dock; P.O. Box 1212;
Friday Harbor, WA 98250; phone – (360) 378-5661

Accommodations: *2 staterooms on a 60-foot sailboat, (queen-size bed and double bed plus 2 bunks, shared and private baths), TV. Children OK, pets by arrangement, no smoking*
Extras: *Full breakfast, nautical atmosphere, rowing dinghy. Fishing, shrimping, and crabbing gear available. 3-block walk to town and ferry*
Rates: *$80 to $85. 2-night minimum in summer. Credit cards accepted*

How can you vacation in the San Juans without getting boating fever? A stay on the *Jacquelyn* will satisfy that fever. However, beware—you may become so enamored that you'll want to rush out to buy your own boat! Clyde and Bette Rice and their friendly keeshound will welcome you aboard

Mount Baker can be seen from the docks at Friday Harbor.

their 24-year old motorsailor. The boat has the warmth and elegance of an old-time sailing ship, with teak and tapestry settees, carved wood, skylights, and a wood-burning stove in the main saloon.

Guests rave about the world-class breakfast that is created in the boat's tidy galley. Some claim it's the best they've ever had. When the weather's nice, your breakfast is served on the spacious outside deck. It's so pleasant here you'll want to linger for an afternoon of sunbathing. You can stay tied up to the dock and bask in the salty bustle of the docks.

The aft stateroom, which is ideal for an unforgettable honeymoon retreat, has a private entrance, queen-size bed, and private toilet and sink. The forward stateroom has a double bed and two bunks; the bath is shared. Boaters who arrive at Friday Harbor with a full party will find the *Jacquelyn* ideal for added sleeping space—but make reservations as it's heavily booked in summer.

How to get there: The *Jacquelyn* is tied up in slip K13 of the Port of Friday Harbor docks. Open year-round.

VACATION HOUSE RENTALS

For more personalized lodgings, try one of the two realtors in the San Juans listed below. The firms manage year-round vacation rental properties. The majority of these private homes are on San Juan Island, although a few are on Orcas and other nearby islands. Offerings range from cabins to condos to homes. Weekly rates start at $500.

Most rentals are for one or two weeks, but some properties are available for longer stays; occasionally two- or three-night rentals may be secured. You can call the companies to request their brochure that pictures each of the lodgings, describes them, and quotes rates.

Lighthouse Properties, Inc.
P.O. Box 457; Friday Harbor, WA 98250; phone – (360) 378-4663

San Juan Property Company
285 Blair Avenue; P.O. Box 1459; Friday Harbor, WA 98250;
phone – (800) 992-1904; (360) 378-5060; fax – (360) 378-5171

RESTAURANTS & CAFES

Amigos

40 B Spring Street; Friday Harbor, WA 98250; phone – (360) 378-5908

Lunch and dinner daily. Beer, wine, margaritas. Credit cards accepted. $

Step off Spring Street and land south of the border. This cantina at the top of a narrow boardwalk features Mexican favorites such as tacos, enchiladas, flautas, and chimachungas washed down with imported or domestic beer or a Margarita. Eat inside the bright restaurant or outside on their patio. Amigos makes up orders to go, too, for you to share with your crew down on the docks.

The Bistro

35 First Street; Friday Harbor, WA 98250; phone – (360) 378-3076

Lunch and dinner daily. Beer, wine. Orders to go. Credit cards accepted. $$

Back in 1891 when this hotel was built, who could have imagined that it would one day be dispensing pizza pies! The Bistro shares a historic hotel with Friday's Bed and Breakfast Inn. This lively eatery offers sandwiches, salads, and pastas along with beer, wine, and espresso. Split one of their specialty deep dish pizza with your sweetheart in their enclosed outdoor courtyard. Pizzas are made from scratch daily, with the freshest of ingredients.

The Blue Dolphin Cafe

185 First Street; Friday Harbor, WA 98250; phone – (360) 378-616

Breakfast and lunch daily. Orders to go. $

Here's your best chance for grabbing a quick breakfast or lunch while waiting for the ferry. The Blue Dolphin is right next to the end of the ferry lanes on First Street. They open at 5:00 A.M. for those catching the early boat. It's not just hamburgers—they fix great eggs and delicious deli sandwiches.

Opposite: *Jazz festival-goers swarm off the ferry at Friday Harbor.*

Cannery House Restaurant
174 North First; Friday Harbor, WA 98250; phone – (360) 378-2500

Lunch and dinner daily, except no dinner on Sunday or in winter. Beer, wine. Orders to go. Reservations. Credit cards accepted. $$

The Cannery House is a long-time Friday Harbor standby, purveying fresh local seafood, homemade clam chowder, hot sandwiches, Mexican specialties, and other family favorites. The dining is casual, the view spectacular. Enjoy a bird's eye view of the yacht harbor from either the dining room or the spacious outside deck.

They'll fix you burgers and other orders to go, too.

China Pearl
*51 Spring Street; P.O. Box 3299; Friday Harbor, WA 98250;
phone – (360) 378-5254*

Lunch and dinner daily. Orders to go. Beer, wine, cocktails. Lounge, card room. Reservations. Credit cards accepted. $$

Whether you've mastered chopsticks or not, Chinese food is always a favorite. China Pearl offers Mandarin, Cantonese, and spicy hot Szechwan cuisines, as well as Thai and Korean. Select from a wide range of dishes and combinations, or if you want a really gala dinner, order Peking duck.

For an evening of fun, there's a card room, and live music on weekends.

The Doctor's Office
85 Front Street; Friday Harbor, WA 98250; phone – (360) 378-8865

Of course ice cream is just what the doctor ordered, as well as espresso and healthy juice drinks. This terrific shop in a Victorian home at the head of the ferry landing dispenses delectable homemade ice cream, in cones or hand-packed pints and quarts. Seating is inside or outside on the front porch so you can watch ferry activity and catch your boat on time.

Downrigger's
*On the Waterfront; P.O. Box 1337; Friday Harbor, WA 98250;
phone – (360) 378-2700*

Lunch and dinner daily; breakfast weekends. Beer, wine, cocktails. Reservations. Credit cards accepted. $$

The decor is ship-shape nautical, with lots of blue and brass. The view, especially from the outside deck, is smack dab above the harbor comings and goings. The food is good old seafood standbys—and that's hard to beat in the San Juans. The menu also includes steak, ribs, and chicken dishes and an extensive array of appetizers, beverages, and desserts. A "Daily Fresh Sheet" tells you which seafood is fresh off the boats.

A children's menu features kid-sized burgers and that all-American favorite, grilled cheese sandwiches.

Duck Soup Inn

3090 Roche Harbor Road; Friday Harbor, WA 98250; phone – (360) 378-4878

Dinners daily; closed in winter. Beer, wine. Reservations. Credit cards accepted.
$$$

We can't think of a better way to spend a summer evening than to take a short drive in the country and stop for a gourmet dinner in a rustic setting. Duck Soup Inn is a scenic six mile drive from Friday Harbor, on Roche Harbor Road. The restaurant's interior reflects the surrounding forest, with lots of natural wood, dark green accents, and a field stone fireplace.

The wide-ranging menu features dishes from such varied cuisines as Northwest, French, Cajun, or Thai; fresh ingredients and inventive seasonings are the common thread. Entrées include game, as well as a range of seafood, poultry, and beef selections. The excellent wine list features both domestic and imported fine wines.

The Electric Company

175 First Street South; Friday Harbor, WA 98250; phone – (360) 378-4118

Breakfast, lunch, and dinner daily. Beer, wine, cocktails. Reservations. Credit
cards accepted. $ to $$

The Electric Company offers burgers and steaks in a lively pub atmosphere. But that's not the only thing on the menu. For dinner you can chose from such all-time favorites as pizza, barbecued salmon, crab cakes, pasta, fettucine, surf and turf, or ribs. There's also a nightly fish special. Lunch selections are soups, salads, and a great variety of burgers—"the best in town," it's claimed.

The Electric Company is a popular spot with local people (who are more interested in good food than waterfront views) and in-the-know tourists, so reservations are recommended in summer.

The Fat Cat Cafe

275 A Street; Friday Harbor, WA 98250; phone – (360) 378-8646

Breakfast and lunch daily. $

This airy cafe in a bungalow at the corner of Nichols and A streets serves light, healthy breakfasts and lunches. Soups, sandwiches, and salads, including a variety of great pasta salads, are all on the menu. Espresso too.

Ford's Bar and Grille

Spring and Second; Friday Harbor, WA 98250; phone – (360) 378-4747

Breakfast, lunch, and dinner daily. Beer, wine, cocktails. Lounge, entertainment. Credit cards accepted. $ to $$

Ford's promises you "enjoyable dining, friendly atmosphere and *absolutely* no view at all." What it also promises (and delivers), is the liveliest entertainment in Friday Harbor. Weekends bring live rock music or R&B

Friday's Crabhouse in the boardwalk plaza by the ferry terminal offers fresh seafood and a casual atmosphere.

for dancing. Wednesday is open mike night, and often there's a chance for musicians to step up and jam with the best bands on the island. If you're a sports fan, join the gang cheering or jeering events on satellite TV.

The restaurant portion of the bar specializes in fine Italian cuisine such as pizza and pasta, as well as chops, steak, prime rib, and filet mignon.

Friday Harbor House
130 West Street; Friday Harbor, WA; phone – (360) 378-8455

Dinner daily, from 5:30 P.M.; winter hours vary. Reservations. Credit cards accepted. $$ to $$$

You are guaranteed superb dining and one of the finest views in the San Juans at the Friday Harbor House. The restaurant has been awarded the prestigious AAA Four Diamond Award, as well as receiving the highest of ratings from other *"Best"* publications.

The varied menu features gourmet selections of local Westcott Bay oysters, Shoal Bay mussels and other seafood, along with unique offerings such as Thai-style satay with dipping sauces or rosemary-rubbed lamb chops with white beans and sage. Vegetarian and vegan selections are always offered. Locally grown vegetables ensure a fresh taste of the Northwest. You won't be able to pass up delectable dessert selections that include handmade ice creams and sorbets, fresh fruit tart, and Gianduia crème brûlée.

Friday's Crabhouse
65 Front Street; Friday Harbor, WA; phone – (360) 378-8801

Lunch and dinner daily. Beer, wine. Credit cards accepted. $$

You can't leave the San Juans without filling up on local seafood, and Friday's Crabhouse is just the place to do it. In summer you'll find this open air cafe in the boardwalk plaza above the ferry terminal. Settle down to a brimming plate of fresh cracked crab, prawns, scallops, fish, oysters, or calamari. You can also get shrimp and crab cocktails.

Front Street Cafe
101 Spring Street; Friday Harbor, WA 98250; phone – (360) 378-2245

Breakfast and lunch daily. $

This little cafe overlooking the ferry terminal is just the spot to have breakfast while waiting for an early boat or to pick up a sandwich before heading off on a moped tour of the island. Choose a full breakfast or some of their bakery goodies and an espresso. Lunch offerings include homemade soup, sandwiches, and a hot entrée such as pizza or spinach feta pie. Tables inside the cafe or on the covered deck provide seating with a close-up view of ferry goings-on.

Garden Path Cafe (Marilyn's)
232 A Street, Churchill Square; Friday Harbor, WA 98250;
phone – (360) 378-6255

10:30 A.M. to 5:00 P.M. daily except Sunday. Orders to go. Credit cards accepted.
$ to $$

Tempting fresh salads (Greek salad is a specialty), an assortment of sandwiches, and soups are on the varied menu offered by this charming eatery. For a late breakfast or early lunch, sample their Belgian waffles, cinnamon rolls, or other homemade pastries. They will also pack up a picnic lunch to your specifications for your tour of the island.

For a very special treat, high tea is served the second Thursday of every month. Reservations are required for this popular affair.

Herb's Tavern
80 First Street South; Friday Harbor, WA 98250; phone – (360) 378-7076

Beer, wine. $

For over 30 years Herb's Tavern was a local watering hole at the corner of Spring and First Street. The recently remodeled saloon now offers live music and dancing in its spiffy, all-new digs. You'll want to have one of their great burgers to go with your cold beer. They offer seafood and appetizers, too. Stop in for lunch of hearty soup and a sandwich topped off with your favorite microbrew.

The Hungry Clam
130 First Street; Friday Harbor, WA 98250;
phone – (360) 378-FISH ((360) 378-3474)

Lunch and dinner daily. Orders to go. Beer, wine $

When their phone number says FISH, it's pretty clear what you'll get here. The decor is fast-food plain; however the fish, shrimp, clams, and oysters are heartily endorsed by locals and tourists alike. Hamburgers round out the menu. There's inside seating, or take your order back to the ravenous gang waiting in the car at the nearby ferry landing

Katrina's
65-B Nichols Street; Friday Harbor, WA 98250; phone – (360) 378-7290

Lunch. $

Whether it's a mouth-watering lunch or a take-away picnic, Katrina's will fix it for you. Located on Nichols Street, behind Funk and Junk, this casual cafe specializes in wholesome, homemade foods. A different kind of handmade bread is featured each day. Katrina's also handles special baking orders for cakes, tarts, crisps, and pies. Surprise your birthday-person with a custom-baked cake.

La Ceiba
395 Spring Street, P.O. Box 885; Friday Harbor, WA 98250:
phone – (360) 378-8666

11:00 A.M. to 7:00 P.M. daily, except Sunday. Beer, wine. Credit cards accepted. $

Great food doesn't have to come loaded with guilt to be good. At La Cieba the ingredients are fresh, healthy, and low-fat. You'll find a tasty selection of burritos, tacos, and quesadillas—all large and filling. Tortillas and fresh salsas are made right here. Seating is inside in two rooms decorated with Mayan paintings and artifacts, or in a sunny outside courtyard.

Madelyn's Bagels
A Street; Friday Harbor, WA 98250; phone – (360) 378-4545

Homemade bagels in a variety of flavors (including jalapeño cheddar!) are the mainstay at Madelyn's. You can also get bagel sandwiches and bags of crispy bagel chips. But that's not all. This sunny little shop on A Street also offers huge muffins, cookies, homemade soup, coffee, espresso, and ice cream bars. Eat at one of the inside tables, on the outside deck with a view of the harbor and ferry landing, or take your lunch away to munch as you cruise Friday Harbor.

Maloula Restaurant
Town Square; Spring and Front streets; Friday Harbor, WA 98250;
phone – (360) 378-8485

Lunch and dinner daily. Beer, wine. Reservations. Credit cards accepted. $ to $$

Ethnic food is always a nice change of pace. Maloula features savory Mediterranean, Middle Eastern, and American cuisines. The food is so good you'll probably become a regular. Lunch features gyros with an assortment of meats, hamburgers, and several choices of green salads, rices, lentils, and hummus. Dinners include more elaborate offerings such as marinated salmon steak, kabob, seafood, or Cornish game hen. In the mood for a whole leg of lamb? Order it a day ahead and the restaurant will prepare it for six persons or more. The beverage list includes interesting imported wines and beers as well as domestic ones that go well with the exotic flavorings of the cuisine. Don't neglect dessert! Choose from incredible Greek pastries, including *six* different kinds of baklava.

In summer, dine outside in a roof garden on tall chairs and tables that improve the view of the harbor.

Mariella Inn

630 Turn Point Road; Friday Harbor, WA 98250; phone – (360) 378-6868

Dinner, Wednesday through Sunday. Beer wine. Reservations (one seating). Credit cards accepted. $$$

Gourmet dining in classic Victorian elegance—what could be more romantic? Mariella Inn is primarily a fine bed and breakfast inn on the waterfront east of Friday Harbor. However, the dining room is open to all, offering sumptuous, three- and four-course dinners. Call for reservations.

The menu, which changes frequently, is usually printed in their ad in the weekly Friday Harbor newspaper, or you can call to find out what is offered. Whatever it is, your mouth will water. The entrée might be a choice of wild king salmon grilled with sun-dried tomatoes or roasted duckling with forest mushrooms. Choices of appetizers and desserts are equally tempting. The inn also does catering for weddings and other special events.

Niccolo's

95 Nichols Street; The Victorian House; Friday Harbor, WA 98250; phone – (360) 378-6682

Lunch and dinner. Beer, wine. Orders to go. Credit cards accepted. $ to $$

With a name like "Niccolo's," it's Italian food, naturally! Pizzas, subs, and pasta are all on the menu at Niccolo's, but there's also chicken, chicken wings, ribs, and shrimp—all the choices you'll want for a hearty, casual dinner. For lunch, chow down on one of their 11 different kinds of sub sandwiches. Niccolo's fixes food to go, or if you can't tear yourself away from a swinging party in Friday Harbor (or down on the docks), they'll deliver it to you.

Papa Joe's Restaurant & Lounge
(The Inn at Friday Harbor Suites)

680 Spring Street West; Friday Harbor, WA 98250; phone – (360) 378-6955

Breakfast, lunch, and dinner daily from 7:00 A.M. to 2:00 P.M. and 5:00 P.M. to 9:00 P.M. Closed Sunday evening and Monday until 5:00 P.M.; reservations. Beer, wine. Lounge, banquet facilities. Reservations. Credit cards accepted. $$ to $$$

Papa Joe's offers fine dining in gracious surroundings. The all-you-can eat soup and salad bar is a good place to start. Then try one of their excellent seafood dishes, featuring only the best fresh fish, or order pasta, fajitas, or steak. Chicken is prepared a number of innovative ways, and vegetarian dishes are offered. Lunches are lighter, but equally varied, with sandwiches, a number of pasta and seafood dishes, steak, and stir fry.

Roberto Paolo, Cucina Italiana

205 A Street; Friday Harbor, WA 98250; phone – (360) 378-6333

Dinner daily. Beer, wine. Reservations. Credit cards accepted. $$ to $$$

How can you resist a restaurant with a dish called Pasta from Hell, Prawns from Heaven? Roberto's takes Italian food to a new height with interesting combinations and creative (and sometimes very hot) spicing. For appetizers, try antipasti, raw oysters on the half shell, or "killer" Margarita prawns in very hot chili sauce. Entrées might include yellowfin tuna, chicken mushroom marsala, veal picata, garlic prawns, or a selection of pasta dishes.

Roche Harbor Restaurant

*4950 Tarte Memorial Drive; Roche Harbor, WA 98250;
phone – (360) 378-5757 or (360) 378-2155*

Breakfast, lunch, and dinner daily in full season (May to October). Beer, wine, cocktails. Lounge, entertainment, banquet rooms. Reservations. Credit cards accepted. $$ to $$$

Roche Harbor is one of our favorite places in the San Juans. We love the fascinating history, the natural setting, and the relaxed, yet lively marine surroundings. Before you settle in for dinner at the restaurant, stroll through the gardens with your date; it's a very romantic spot. If you didn't arrive by boat, wander down the docks and soak in all the fiberglass, teak, and salty atmosphere.

The restaurant is in the former home of John S. McMillin, who founded the Roche Harbor Lime and Cement Company. The home has a welcoming elegance, with lots of richly polished wood. The deck that stretches across the front of the house and adjoins the bar is a recent addition.

From your window seat in the restaurant you can enjoy all the harbor bustle. If you've made your reservation for sunset, you can enjoy "afterglow" as it paints the harbor and islands with a rosy hue. The menu is typically Northwest—lots of fresh seafood, some chicken and steak—done with interesting sauces and accompaniments. Oysters come from Westcott Bay, just a stone's throw away. How could they be fresher? The new management and chef assure you that the quality and consistency of your dining experience will be the best it has ever been. The lounge on the main floor serves light meals and snacks. If you're rendezvousing here with boating friends, reserve a banquet room in advance.

San Juan Brewing Company
1 Front Street; Friday Harbor, WA 98250;
phone – (360) 378-BEER (378-2337)

Breakfast, lunch and dinner daily. Beer, wine. Credit cards accepted. $

The multi-page menu alone is worth a stop at the Front Street Ale House. Decorated with hilarious cartoon characters, it will keep you chuckling as you try to decide among the many terrific offerings. The ambiance is British pub, and the menu follows suit, with such favorites as porridge and bangers. Page after page of the menu reveals more eclectic choices: "angels on horseback," calamari, nachos, "ass-kicking" chili, San Juan clam chowder, seafood Caesar salad, homecut French fries, ⅓-lb beef burgers, and a variety of hot sandwiches. Seafood? Try fish and chips, salmon and chips, oysters and chips, scampi and chips, or scallops and chips.

Featured beers come from San Juan Brewing Company, a micro-brewery, right next door. As of last count, 11 different unique ales, lagers, and stouts were home brewed on the premises. Other domestic and imported beers are available, too.

San Juan Donut Shop Restaurant & Bakery
209 Spring Street; Friday Harbor, WA 98250; phone – (360) 378-2271

Breakfast and lunch daily. $

When you see the local people here, downing their coffee and donuts and sharing the daily news, you'll know this casual cafe is one of the best places in town for breakfast. You can get a full hearty breakfast, or choose from their homebaked muffins, danishes, or other pastries. Lunches feature hamburgers, sandwiches, and the soup of the day. You won't want to leave without a bag full of homemade cookies for mid-afternoon carbo-loading.

Seating is at tables or booths; however the long bar that runs down the middle of the shop is the best place to join in the local gossip.

Springtree Café
310 Spring Street; Friday Harbor, WA 98250; phone – (360) 378-4848

Lunch and dinner daily; Sunday brunch. Beer, wine. Reservations. Credit cards accepted. $$ to $$$

You may feel like Alice in Wonderland as you wander through the white picket fence, duck under the ancient camperdown elm that arches over the

Many of Friday Harbor's businesses line Spring Street.

entry, and enter the little courtyard. Springtree Café is widely lauded in *"Best"* publications, and justifiably so. The cuisine is European bistro at its finest—fresh ingredients, imaginative seasonings, and meticulous preparation. Nootka Rose Farm on Waldron Island produces many of the salad greens, herbs, and vegetables served. Entrées are largely seafood and chicken, with a few selections of beef. Steamed local spot prawns (live until cooked) come complete with a hot towel for cleaning fingers, and, if necessary, the waitress will give you directions for handling the prawns.

The atmosphere is light and airy; sunlight floods the room through windows opening onto the courtyard. There's outside seating in the courtyard and on a heated deck, too.

Vic's Driftwood Drive Inn
25 Second Street; Friday Harbor, WA 98250; phone – (360) 378-2120

Breakfast, lunch, and dinner daily. Orders to go. $

You won't find any McDonalds or Burger Kings in the San Juan Islands, but when the gang is clamoring for good old burgers and fries, Vic's will deliciously fill the bill. It's just a block east of the high school. Sit inside, or take your cheeseburger the traditional way—to go.

GROCERIES, DELIS, TAKE OUT & LIQUOR

Entertainment Tonight
420 Argyle Avenue; Friday Harbor, WA 98250; phone – (360) 378-2424,
pizza and deli (360) 378-3700

This convenience store is open early and late hours, making it the spot to dash out to for a late night pizza, deli snacks, or a video. At 7 A.M. you can grab some hot coffee and homemade pastries to fortify you for that early morning ferry wait.

Friday Harbor Grocery
100 First Street; Friday Harbor, WA 98250; phone – (360) 378-2887

Friday Harbor Grocery is the closest grocery store to the docks, making it a favorite with boaters needing to resupply their ship's larder. The grocery carries all the fresh, frozen, and packaged foods you'll need, including fresh meat, produce, beer, wine, and a great selection of deli items. Top

Friday Harbor Seafoods sells fresh oysters, crabs, and other seafood right at the dock.

it off with a few bags of ice and you're ready to go. If you buy too much to carry, they'll deliver to the dock for you.

Friday Harbor Seafoods

Port Dock Main Pier; P.O. Box 1656; Friday Harbor, WA 98250; phone – (360) 378-5779

For the freshest seafood, go right to the source. You can buy cooked Dungeness crab, clams, and shrimp right out of steaming pots at this little houseboat on the Friday Harbor docks. Spirit your purchases back to your boat, break out the tartar sauce, and be prepared for paradise! Pick out fresh oysters, salmon and other seafood too; grill it on your hibachi or have it packed in ice to take home. It's the best you'll find in the San Juans.

King's Market and Marine Center

160 Spring Street West; Friday Harbor, WA 98250; phone – (360) 378-4505,
deli: (360) 378-4522, marine center: (360) 378-4593,
meat dept: (360) 378-4537, variety: (360) 378-4591

A grocery store as a tourist attraction? It's certainly true of King's. We never go to the San Juans without taking a whirl down its aisles. Besides the usual Cheerios and Pampers, you'll find selections of locally made foods—jams, jellies, sauces, wine—that provide a sampling of the San Juans' bounty. Stop by the deli and pick up everything you need for a picnic lunch or an evening barbecue on the boat. King's will deliver your bags of grub to the dock for you, too. There're also clothing, marine, and variety departments.

The Little Store

285 Spring Street; Friday Harbor, WA 98250; phone – (360) 378-4422

If you want to fête a bunch of your friends down on your boat, give these folks a call, and they'll whip up an extravagant party tray in their deli. For cyclists wanting to get an early start in the cool of the morning, The Little Store is open at 6:30 A.M., ready with all the carbohydrates you'll need for a long day. The deli is open 7 A.M. to 5 P.M. daily.

Roche Harbor Grocery Store

P.O. Box 948; Friday Harbor, WA 98250; phone – (360) 378-5562

Boaters needing to replenish their larders will find what they need at this store on the dock at Roche Harbor. You'll find fresh produce and meat, and other things to spice up tiresome galley meals. Also for sale are fishing gear, bait, some kitchenware, books, magazines, and all sorts of odds and ends.

San Juan Coffee Roasting Co.

18 Cannery Landing; Friday Harbor, WA 98250; phone – (360) 378-4443

This shop right next to the ferry landing has become a San Juan tradition in our family, as I'm sure it has in many others. We always make a point to park in the ferry line in time to saunter down to Cannery Landing and get one of their luscious Haagen Dazs ice cream cones. It's also a wonderful place to pick up a last minute gift. Who wouldn't love to receive a package of specially roasted Caffé San Juan, select teas, or some gourmet chocolates? If you're not in the mood for ice cream, try some fresh pastry and an espresso.

At Roche Harbor you can buy groceries, as well as fuel and other supplies for your boat.

The Waterfront Deli & Market
5 Front Street; Friday Harbor, WA 98250; phone – (360) 378-8444

There's so much to see on San Juan Island that you'll want to just grab some food and go. The folks at the Waterfront Deli will fix you up with everything you'll need for a gourmet picnic at one of the down-island parks, or to toss into your kayak as you head out to explore off-shore islands. Your mouth will water at the selection of pastas, salads, and meats. For drinks, choose from beer, wine, soda, or espresso. It's right next to the Front Street Ale House.

Washington State Liquor Store
365 Spring Street; Friday Harbor, WA 98250; phone – (360) 378-2956

You'll locate the liquor store in Friday Harbor in the group of shops known as Harbor Village at the Y-intersection of Spring Street and Argyle Avenue.

SHOPPING

Annikin

165 First Street; Friday Harbor, WA 98250; phone – (360) 378-7286

For really high quality arts and crafts, this is *the* place. Annikin represents the work of over 60 artists and craftspeople, both local and national. The emphasis is more on crafts than on paintings or prints. Depending on which artists' works are on display, you'll find furniture exquisitely crafted from natural wood, swirling forms of handblown glass, pottery that moves beyond mere function to true fine art, wind chimes that emit soothing musical tones, and pieces of handmade jewelry that are tiny pieces of fine sculpture. There're things for children too—whimsical wooden toys and puzzles and precious little finger puppets.

Arctic Raven Gallery

Town Square Building, 2nd floor; Friday Harbor, WA 98250;
phone – (360) 378-3433; fax – (360) 378-3963

This gallery on the upper level of the Town Square building specializes in fine art from Inuit, Northwest Coast, and Plains Indians. Sculptures, masks, and wood carvings are featured, as well as water colors by Lisa Fifield.

Atelier Gallerie

232 A Street, Churchill Square Building; Friday Harbor, WA 98250;
phone – (360) 378-2918

The Churchill Square Building is a remodeled historic home at the corner of Harrison and A streets. Atelier Gallerie, which occupies one portion of this interesting old building, shows paintings by local artists, limited edition prints, etchings, and pottery. You won't want to miss the exceptional selections of scrimshaw and handmade jewelry. If you choose an unframed print, these folks can help you select a perfect frame and frame it for you, too.

Banana Belt

1 Spring Street, Friday Harbor, WA 98250; phone – (360) 378-2722

You'll find the perfect outfit for lounging around your resort, or dining out at one of Friday Harbor's fine restaurant at this shop. The racks are loaded with great women's clothes, including all kinds of colorful separates for really chic combinations. Accessorize with some of their interesting jewelry.

Big Daddy's
21 Spring Street West; Friday Harbor, WA 98250 ; phone – (360) 378-2200

Men and women's apparel, with an accent on casual, is featured at this trendy shop on Spring Street. If you find you didn't pack enough sports clothes for your trip, or are looking for a special gift for a relative back home, here's the place to stop.

Boardwalk Bookstore
5 Spring Street West; P.O. Box 283; Friday Harbor, WA 98250;
phone – (360) 378-2787

A wonderland of books lies just up the stairs leading from a little court-yard on Spring Street. There's all the latest fiction, along with a wide selection of guide books, books of regional interest, beautiful coffeetable volumes, children's books, or something covering your special interest. You're sure to find the ideal book to curl up with on the beach at your resort or the deck of your boat. Store owner Dorothea Augusztiny will special order books for you, or mail them to wherever you wish.

Books are not all the store carries. You'll find maps and nautical charts too, as well as postcards and nice greeting cards to go along with that book selection.

Chris P's Herbs and Oils
180 First Street, Friday Harbor, WA 98250; phone – (360) 378-2939

You'll find this nice shop on the lower level, between Spring Street, and East Street, next door to the laundromat. They carry a wide selection of herbs, vitamins, bulk herbs, essential oils, natural hair coloring, bath products, health-oriented books, dried flowers, and gifts.

Dan Levin Originals
50 First Street; P.O. Box 1309; Friday Harbor, WA 98250;
phone – (360) 378-2051

Fine jewelry created by goldsmiths Dan and Diane Levin is known throughout the Northwest. Each stunning piece is hand signed and sure to appreciate in value over time, as well as bring joy to the wearer. At the artists' studio gallery you may select a pendant of a tiny, exquisitely detailed gold crab with ruby eyes and a diamond clutched in one claw, or a ring with pearls wrapped in a froth of free-form gold.

Dolphin Arts
28 Cannery Landing; Friday Harbor, WA 98250; phone – (360) 378-3531

Clothing was never before so much fun! This shop features the work of artist Vivien Burnett. You'll find her beautiful designs silk screened on T-shirts, shirts, and jackets. There are clothes for women, men, and absolutely irresistible items for kids. Posters, note cards, and wall hangings also feature her art. Jewelry comes from the creative hands of local artist Deborah Johnsen.

Dominique's
20 First Street; Friday Harbor, WA 98250; phone – (360) 378-6454

You'll find this shop in a remodeled farm home at the end of Spring Street, near the Inn at Friday Harbor. Wandering through the interesting rooms is half the fun of shopping here. Dominique is there nearly every day to assist you in putting together a really great outfit from her selection of dresses, separates, accessories, and shoes. The store is definitely an unexpected attitude in dressing.

The English Country House
Spring Street at Harbor Village; Friday Harbor, WA 98250;
phone – (360) 378-3101

If you're a tourist, the beautiful furniture this store carries may be hard to pack in your suitcase (although you'll probably want to); however, you will find lots of smaller treasures that will make perfect accents for your home. Select a beautiful piece of glassware, china, or a charming little knickknack. They also carry some exceptionally fine antiques.

Feats of Clay
260 Spring Street; Friday Harbor, WA 98250; phone – (360) 378-2227

Shop owner Lois Longley creates charming little knicknacks and custom-made quilts. You may discover a unique Christmas ornament as a remembrance of your San Juan trip, or a doll-sized tea set.

Friday Harbor Drug Company
210 Spring Street; Friday Harbor, WA 98250; phone – (360) 378-4421

In the San Juans even an ordinary drug store has a different twist. Friday Harbor Drug Co. tucks nautical paraphernalia in with the lipstick and toothpaste. You'll find nautical instruments, log books, charts, maps, tide tables, and boating publications. The store also carries a nice line of gift items, many of which are nautically oriented (of course).

Friday Harbor Souvenirs and Gifts
150 First Street; Friday Harbor, WA 98250; phone – (360) 378-5304

The name certainly says it all. From T-shirts to tea towels this store is sure to have something for everyone on your gift list. Shelves are stacked with great merchandise ranging from functional things such as high quality jackets and sweatshirts to toys and outrageously funny gag gifts.

Friday Harbor Trading Company
180 First Street; Friday Harbor, WA 98250; phone – (360) 378-6660

Authentically detailed Native American figurines, exquisite carvings of whales, and framed limited edition prints of wildlife are but a few of the extraordinary works of art displayed in this gallery that specializes in art based on wildlife and Native American themes. Handcrafted bird houses, Northwest Indian carvings, clocks, scrimshaw, brass and silver nautical pieces, and an array of smaller gift items are available. You'll marvel at all the unique offerings.

Every year artist Mark Hopkins creates a new limited edition bronze sculpture of a different jazz musician. These sculptures, which are sold by the Trading Company, are sure to become collectors' items for those fortunate enough to purchase them.

Friday's Marketplace
65 Front Street; Friday Harbor; phone – (360) 378-8300

Friday's Market place is an open air plaza right at the head of the ferry lines. In summer various businesses set up their booths and carts. Whoever is there varies from year to year, and even from week to week, but there is usually an espresso stand, hot dogs, ice cream, and a number of arts and crafts offerings. It's all grand fun.

Funk and Junk
65 Nichols Street; Friday Harbor, WA 98250; phone – (360) 378-2638

Gizmos, gimcracks, and whatcha-ma-callits! Squeeze through the aisles of this little cottage crammed with everything from treasures to "the kitchen sink." You'll delight in old postcards, books, musical instruments, shoes, quilts, costume jewelry, cookwares, used furniture, and on and on. If it's old, it's probably here. There are some true antiques, some wonderful collectibles, and some things that will make you puzzle what they're supposed to be. Spring and summer auctions by Funk and Junk are now a part of island events.

The Garuda and I
60 First Street; Friday Harbor, WA 98250; phone – (360) 378-3733

This shop is many things rolled into one: There are imports from Africa, India, Thailand, the Philippines, and other mid- and far-eastern places; there are crafts supplies with bins full of gorgeous beads, findings, tools, books, and other supplies to create your own jewelry; and finally, it's a gallery selling the work of local artists and featuring the magnificent tapestries of islander Whitney Peckman. The fine imports include pillows, baskets, and pottery; you're sure to find the perfect accents or conversation pieces for your home.

Giannangelo Farms
5500 Limestone Point Road; San Juan Island, WA 98250; phone – (360) 378-4218

Whether you're a dedicated gardener, gourmet cook, or you just like a nice ride in the country, Giannangelo Farms is the place to head. This charming farm sells garden plants, flowers, fresh salad greens, and dried herbs. All plants are certified organic—raised without chemicals or pesticides. You'll marvel at the many varieties of thyme, sage, parsley, onion, and other herbs on display—many so beautiful you'll want them just for their decorative appeal. Select some fresh or dried catnip for Tom or Tabby back at home (they'll love you for it). The tiny, heavenly scented shop also sells herbed vinegars, mixed spices, potpourri, and bunches of dried flowers.

Forest of cedar, fir, and hemlock surround the farm, which flows down a terraced hillside. Gravel paths trace their way through the three levels of gardens. You will delight at the two aviaries, built around cedar trees, that house a number of white doves and zebra finches.

How to get there: Drive west out of Friday Harbor on Roche Harbor Road for 9 miles. Turn right on Rouleau Road, continue 1 mile, then turn right again on Limestone Point Road and follow the signs.

You'll be fascinated by the variety of herbs, flowers, and other plants at Giannangelo Farms.

The Gourmet's Galley
9 Spring Street West; Friday Harbor, WA 98250; phone – (360) 378-2251

Who doesn't love to cook—or at least to eat. The Gourmet's Galley is overflowing with good stuff for either cooks or gastronomes, featuring fresh ground coffees, fine wine, beer, teas, spices, cookware, cookbooks, unique teapots, kitchen gadgets, and candy. Many are local brands. We purchased a gorgeous laminated hardwood cutting board shaped like an apple as a Washington remembrance for a relative in Iowa.

For the health-conscious part of you there are hypoallergenic cosmetics, and nutritional foods and supplements.

Griffin Bay Bookstore
40 First Street; Friday Harbor, WA 98250; phone – (360) 378-5511

This nook isn't much wider than a good-sized book itself, but its packed with great literary finds. The store claims over 10,000 volumes, and it's easy to believe. There's a good selection of regional books, as well as all the latest fiction and best sellers. And if they don't have the book you're looking for, they'll order it for you. The store also carries music cassettes and CD's, Books on Tape, note cards, and maps.

Harbor Bookstore

24 Cannery Landing; Friday Harbor, WA 98250; phone – (360) 378-7222

Wander up to the upper level of Cannery Landing and you'll discover this newly opened bookstore. It stocks plenty of good fiction, mysteries, and regional paperbacks. Their excellent selection of children's books also have a regional flair, with tales of ferry boats, whales, seals, and other wildlife. There are cassettes for your tape deck and a nice line of cards, too.

Images

First and West streets; Friday Harbor, WA 98250; phone – (360) 378-5566

You'll be able to put together a perfect outfit in this up-scale women's shop. When I last visited, I discovered a stunning beaded vest to layer over a soft top. A few dresses are stocked, but it's mostly separates and accessories—denim skirts and pants, shirts, sweaters, jackets, jewelry, belts, scarves, and bags. There is hosiery, lingerie, some selected china and crystal gift items, and charming knickknacks. Their adorable "Teddly Bears" are sure to steal your heart.

Island Flower Works

80 Nichols Street, P.O. Box 1699; Friday Harbor ,WA 98250;
phone – (800) 443-7461 or (360) 378-3010, fax – (360) 378-3552

A small cottage with a white picket fence houses one of the San Juans' most unique businesses. The talented folks at Island Flower Works create gifts and treasured keepsakes with pressed flowers. They have framed calligraphy sentiments, pictures, candles, handmade sachets, potpourris, handpainted floral lampshades, and baskets. For a very special remembrance, have them frame a wedding or birth announcement or other personal memento and custom decorate it with blossoms. Everything is made with flowers grown locally, most of them in the gardens that surround the shop, and created by artisans, one blossom at a time.

Island Lady Antiques

55 Second Street; Friday Harbor, WA 98250; phone – (360) 378-2890

This shop in a remodeled historic home displays exceptionally beautiful antiques. A wing recently added to the home holds commercial offices, but the front portion, which Island Lady occupies, still retains its original, Victorian character. Owner Joan Johnson has filled the gracious rooms with just the things that were originally used to furnish them, ranging from furniture, period candelabras, paintings, needlepoint and vintage pillows, crystal, porcelain, and sterling silver, to a child's once-cherished teddy bear. Antique linens are Island Lady's specialty; when we visited we saw an exquisite antique wedding dress.

Island Needlepoint and Cross stitch

232 A Street; Churchill Square Building; Friday Harbor, WA 98250;
phone – (360) 378-6130

To a needleworker there's nothing as enticing as piles of rainbow-hued yarn just waiting for a magic touch to turn it into a treasured work of art. Island Needlepoint sells hand painted canvases, yarns, embroidery floss, and novelty threads just waiting for your magic fingers. The shop's owner also provides all the supplies and instruction to help you get started.

Island Wine Company

Cannery Landing Building; P.O. Box 1895; Friday Harbor, WA 98250 ;
phone – (800) 248-9463; (360) 378-3229; fax – (360) 378-6229

The Island Wine Company is just a few steps from the end of the ferry ramp, making it a convenient place to begin, or complete, your visit to Friday Harbor. Several select French, Italian, and Australian wines are available, and some of the lesser known, but highly rated California wines also show up in the racks. However, the store concentrates on the quality Washington and Oregon wines that make up the bulk of their stock. The company bottles a limited supply of seven different wines from Yakima grapes under its own label, San Juan Cellars, which you can sample in a tasting room at the store. This is the only place the label is sold retail. Purchase a bottle of fine wine and the store will ship it for you to anywhere in the US.

Island Wools and Weaving

30 First Street South; Friday Harbor, WA 98250; phone – (360) 378-2148

Knitters rejoice! Heaven is at hand, and it's right here in Friday Harbor. You'll find piles of luscious yarns for knitting, weaving, needlepoint, or all your other handicraft projects. Some yarns are grown, spun, and dyed on the island, while others are imported. There are unique hand-cast pewter buttons too, as well as all the needles, instruction books, and other supplies you'll need.

Hanging baskets and planters filled with flowers brighten the Friday Harbor waterfront.

Island's Own
Cannery Landing; Friday Harbor, WA 98250; phone – (360) 378-4013

Here's a perfect spot to browse while waiting for the ferry. You'll discover loads of trinkets to take back to friends at home, or to keep as souvenirs of your island visit, including T-shirts, coffee mugs, and games for the kids to play in the car or on the ferry. The shop also features art by local artists Lewis and Nancy Spaulding.

Kitchen Corner
300 Spring Street, P.O. Box 1640; Friday Harbor, WA 98250;
phone – (360) 378-3931

This nook on Spring Street is brimming with marvelous items for the kitchen. You're sure to find some gadget to make life easier in the ship's galley, or perhaps some pretty napkins to brighten a picnic basket. Cookbooks, linens, glassware, candles and candlesticks — the list of great finds goes on and on.

Mellowoods and Music Store
85 Nichols Street; Friday Harbor, WA 98250; phone – (360) 378-5151

Stop in at Mellowoods whether you're a musician or not; it's the only store of its kind in the islands, and we found it fascinating. Instruments ranging from tin whistles and kazoos to dulcimers and violins hang from the walls. There're ethnic instruments and percussion galore. Maybe you've always wanted to play the harmonica? Mellowoods has instruments and instruction books to get you started. The store is a dealer for C. F. Martin guitars, the finest made in America.

Mellowoods stocks music books, CD's, and cassettes and offers lessons, repairs, and musical research. And you'll find they're always ready to jam! The back of the shop is a recording studio and sound production lab where musicians and singers can make demos.

Moonlight Studio and Gallery
42B First Street North; Friday Harbor, WA 98250; phone – (360) 378-6817

Look for this charming gallery in a cottage tucked behind Raven House Realty on First Street. It carries a nice selection of framed and unframed art, as well as paintings, carvings, and jewelry, all by local artists, and very reasonably priced.

Moyer's Jewelry
165 Spring Street; Friday Harbor, WA 98250; phone – (360) 378-2486 or (360) 378-5999

The gorgeous items in the window will surely draw you in to this fine jewelry store. Select a piece of fine crystal as a gift for the hostess you've been visiting here on the island—she's sure to invite you back again. You'll also find delightful porcelain dishes and figurines, and quality souvenirs of the island. Some 250 gold and silver charms await your selection for your remembrance bracelet.

Mystical Mermaid
65 Spring Street West; Friday Harbor, WA 98250; phone – (360) 378-2617

The lavender and shocking green building just down the alley off Spring Street is sure to catch you attention. Once inside you'll be glad you stopped. The Mystical Mermaid has lots of fun, inexpensive items—it's the perfect place for kids to select something to keep themselves occupied in the camper or boat, or for you to choose gifts for friends back home. Shelves and racks offer books, games, knickknacks, and no end of unusual souvenir items.

Nature's Images
225 A Street; Friday Harbor, WA 98250; phone – (360) 378-6545

This gift shop, which focuses on environmental awareness, stocks a wide selection of items made from recycled materials. You'll find rain forest bath products, hand-blown glass hummingbird feeders, greeting cards and stationery, handmade jewelry, handwoven rugs, glass suncatchers, and educational toys and posters for children and adults. They carry their own line of T-shirts with terrific wolf, llama, orca, and other nature-inspired designs. Be sure to notice the T-shirts made from recycled plastic bottles—you'll swear they're fine quality cotton.

The Olde Mades
First Street; Friday Harbor, WA 98250; phone – (360) 378-6151

Antique stores always are a step back into history, as well as a fascinating place to browse. Every one-of-a-kind item cries to be examined and marveled at. There's lots to marvel at the Old Mades—old books, dishes, housewares, pictures, sterling silver. The store also carries a selection of antique linens and lingerie. What could be more elegant than dressing in an old lace camisole?

Osito's

310 Spring Street; P.O. Box 395; Friday Harbor, WA 98250;
phone – (360) 378-4320

From Brio trains to Breyer horses, Osito's will delight the child in your life. This shop in an old home at the top of Spring Street is filled with fantastic toys for the young and young at heart. It also carries a nice selection of children's clothes and sleepwear, a few books, puzzles, and cards. We were intrigued by the tiny "paper dolls" made out of wood, with clothes that attach by Velcro.

El Picaflor (The Hummingbird)

Spring Street and Front Street, B-2; Friday Harbor, WA 98250;
phone – (360) 378-3051

This is one of our favorite haunts in Friday Harbor. It's filled with terrific, inexpensive handicraft imports from Latin America. Don't miss their delightful fabric wall hangings, filled with handmade, two-inch tall people. Select from rugs, tapestries, blouses, sweaters, pottery, leather goods, jewelry (both inexpensive and high quality), toys, dolls, wicker dollhouse furniture—the treasures are limitless. There are also several kinds of lovely hummingbirds, the shop's motif.

Sandpebble

245 Spring Street; Friday Harbor, WA 98250; phone – (360) 378-2788

If you love Victoriana, you won't be able to drag yourself away from this shop. It's a diverse mix embellished by lace, lace, and more lace. You'll ohh and ahh over whimsical teapots, gracious china and crystal, beautiful lamps, decorative pillows, brass candlesticks (and candles to go with them), potpourri by the scoop, pretty greeting cards, and charming stuffed animals. There's women's clothing too: dresses, peignoirs, and lingerie—all lace, flowers, and flounces, of course.

San Juan Jewels

Jeri's Spring Street Center; 260 Spring Street; Friday Harbor, WA 98250;
phone – (360) 378-5877

San Juan Jewels, located at the end of a little indoor mall on Spring Street, stocks some really unique items, in addition to regular crystal, timepieces, and fine jewelry. Their selection of sterling silver and turquoise Native American jewelry is excellent. They also carry collectible Melody in Motion handpainted porcelain figurines. Original paintings, etchings, woodcuts, and engravings by local artists that are displayed in the store and on walls in the mall are sold on consignment.

The Second Act
450 Spring Street, P.O. Box 2673; Friday Harbor, WA 98250;
phone – (360) 378-3828

Often the best part of shopping if finding a really terrific buy. This exclusive resale shop is the place to find new and used clothing for men, women and children at the very best prices.

Serendipity
Suite 2, Churchill Square, 232 A Street, Friday Harbor, WA 98250;
phone – (360) 378-2665

Wander up the stairs at Churchill Square to discover this dandy used book shop. Owners Carol Jackson and Betty Stewart are former librarians who have a great sense for the kinds of books that will please their customers. Bring in your used paperbacks and swap them two-for-one. There're nautical books for the boat cap'n and lots of fiction for the crew.

Software for the Body
260 Spring Street, Friday Harbor, WA 98250; phone – (360) 378-3077

You're sure to find a spot in your wardrobe for some of the terrific clothes in this shop. It's all casual, all comfortable. There's all kinds of separate— sweaters, shirts, pants, and skirts as well as jackets, and a nice line of accessories to top it all off. Some kids' wear too.

The Sunshine Gallery
85 Nichols Street; P.O. Box 153; Friday Harbor, WA 98250;
phone – (360) 378-5819

This gallery is a cooperative, representing more than 45 local artists and craftspersons. The variety of their talent is astounding; some are quite unique. I loved the gossamer silk scarves that had been dipped in marbleized dye, and arrangements of butterflies mounted in glass cases. The choices at the bright, airy gallery are limitless: oils, watercolors, sculptures, ceramics, pottery, jewelry, wearable art, baskets, limited edition prints, and fine photographs. Displays change regularly, so stop in often. Custom framing is available for your art selection.

Ten Cannery Landing

10 Cannery Landing; Friday Harbor, WA 98250; phone – (360) 378-4700

This shop on the lower level of Cannery Landing carries upscale, quality women's apparel. You'll find just the outfit for a romantic dinner out or a yacht club shindig. Great accessories, too!

The Toggery

155 Spring Street West; Friday Harbor, WA 98250; phone – (360) 378-2299

Friday Harbor doesn't lack for excellent clothing shops, and The Toggery is a dandy one, with a wide selection of apparel. It stocks a full line of clothes for both men and women, with racks full of separates, heavy on comfortable casual clothes, perfect for boat or resort. Jackets, underwear, jewelry, leather goods—you should be able to find whatever you need right here.

The Toy Box

Cannery Landing; Friday Harbor, WA 98250; phone – (360) 378-8889

Toys and games for your kids, or the kid in you. There are lots of inexpensive, educational toys to keep kids happy for long hours. A plastic folding binocular/compass/magnifying glass would be fun for a young camper.

The Toy Box also features fine wooden wind chimes, puzzles, and games. We marveled at some pick-up-sticks crafted of various hardwoods with an elegant leather pouch. Are you old enough to remember that fun game?

Waterworks Gallery

315 Spring Street at Argyle, P.O. Box 28; Friday Harbor, WA 98250;
phone – (360) 378-3060

Waterworks Gallery is one of the best places in the islands to find top drawer original paintings, etchings, lithographs, and sculpture. The artists represented by Waterworks hail from the San Juans and throughout the Northwest. The shows, which are designed to display a group of complementary works, change every five to six weeks, so be sure to stop in regularly. The gallery will also help you chose a perfect frame for your purchase.

Westcott Bay Sea Farms

4071 Westcott Drive; Friday Harbor, WA 98250; phone – (360) 378-2489;
fax – (360) 378-6388

If you feast on oysters at one of the San Juans' fine restaurants, chances are good that your appetizer or main course came from Westcott Bay Sea Farms. This company, one of the San Juan Island's major aquaculture enterprises, runs a large oyster-growing operation off the east shore of Westcott Bay, a saltwater inlet east of Roche Harbor. The water temperature in the bay is ideal for raising the two varieties of oysters and one variety of Manila clam that the venture specializes in. Because of their rich flavor, Westcott Bay oysters are highly prized by gourmands. They are shipped to markets as far away as Europe.

Although the company harvests oysters primarily for commercial sales, visitors to the operation may buy these fresh gourmet shellfish.

How to get there: The Sea Farms are at the end of Westcott Drive, off Roche Harbor Road, 1 mile east of Roche Harbor Resort.

Whalesong Gallery

20 First Street North; P.O. Box 1577; Friday Harbor, WA 98250;
phone – (360) 378-ORCA

You'll find extraordinary artwork featuring the island's beloved orca whales at this hole-in-the wall gallery. Proprietor Kelley Balcomb-Bartok is responsible for most of the terrific whale photos. Balcomb-Bartok aided film crews taking footage for the film "Free Willy" in the San Juans and British Columbia.

In addition to whale photos, there are original paintings, prints, posters, jewelry, note cards, and books featuring whales and other wildlife themes. Framing is available for the photos or posters you purchase there or those that you bring in.

Windhorse

155 Nichols Street; Friday Harbor, WA 98250; phone – (360) 378-3515

Incense, essences, and aromatherapy. Just stepping inside this bright shop makes you feel good. You'll discover crystals, music cassettes, and books that help you get in touch with your inner self.

EVENTS & ATTRACTIONS

Fourth of July Parade

I love a parade—I'll bet you do too! And small-town parades, where everyone joins in, are the best of all. Friday Harbor puts its own special touch on the traditional celebration; there're marching bands, clowns, flags, and fire trucks, of course, but have you ever seen a "pod" of dogs dressed like killer whales, or a solar-powered horse? One year a wheelchair brigade from the Islands' Convalescent Center won the drill team competition. This grand old home town fun is what America is all about! You can see nighttime fireworks in the harbor from your boat.

Annual San Juan Island Celebrity Golf Classic
San Juan Golf Club; 2261 Golf Course Road; Friday Harbor, WA 98250; phone – (360) 378-2254

San Juan Island charities benefit from this popular golf tournament held in early June at the San Juan Golf Club. Pros from clubs around the region are teamed with celebrities from professional sports teams for a day of fun and fundraising.

San Juan Island Artist's Studio Open House
When: First weekend in June
Information: (360) 378-5318

Once a year a group of professional San Juan Island artists open their studios and offer their work directly for sale to visitors. This is a terrific opportunity to talk with the artists and learn more about how their works are created. The quality of the work is uniformly outstanding. You'll be able to select from sculpture, handmade furniture, jewelry, weaving, tapestries, jewelry, stained glass serigraphs, and paintings in watercolor and oil. It's a fine way to tour the island and discover some out-of-the way spots, too. The artists are located at nine different spots around the island; by calling the above number you will receive a brochure and map showing the location of the studios of artists on the current year's tour.

San Juan Island Jazz Festival

*P.O. Box 1666; Friday Harbor, WA 98250; phone – (360) 378-4224
or (360) 378-5509; fax – (360) 378-7796*

When: *The last full weekend in July (Friday, Saturday, Sunday). 1996: July 26,
27, and 28; 1997: July 25, 26, 37*

Ragtime, New Orleans, Chicago, Two-Beat, Dixieland, Traditional—
call it what you will, this mid-summer San Juan Island festival dishes up
three days of the best live jazz you'll ever tap a toe to. More than a dozen
bands belt out the beat throughout the day and evening from Friday afternoon through Sunday night. All of the four or five different locations have
dance platforms for listeners who can't sit still while there's a great two-beat
in the air.

*Strummin' on the old banjo at the Friday Harbor Jazz Festival. Photo
courtesy of San Juan Island Jazz Festival.*

The festival kicks off on Friday with the Promenade, a real, old-time, everybody-participate parade, as is only found in small towns like Friday Harbor. On Saturday morning a special concert, "Kids Like Jazz Too," is woven with story-telling to amuse and entertain beginning jazz lovers. The Pianorama, held in the Community Theater on Saturday afternoon, features impromptu gigs and informal banter by piano players from the various bands. On Sunday morning, free Gospel Services at two locations feature a sermon by a local minister with a jazz band providing emotional, prayer-weaving rhythms. Many island churches use the program in lieu of their normal services.

There's food, too—you can eat yourself silly throughout the festival. Each site has food and beverage stands sponsored by local service clubs; other organizations have pancake breakfasts or a steak barbecue. Sidewalks en route to the venues are lined with stands of young entrepreneurs hawking lemonade, homemade brownies, ice cream bars, candies, flavored ice, you name it. You'll have to hit the dance floor to work off all those calories.

All the venues as well as downtown stores offer a wide variety of memorabilia, T-shirts, posters, pins, sweatshirts, patches, caps, visors—anything you might want to take the fun of the weekend home with you. The annual poster is always a collector's item.

Probably the biggest challenge of the festival is getting there and finding a place to stay overnight. If you're coming by ferry, the most common mode of travel, it's a good idea to park in the ferry lots at Anacortes and walk aboard. Anyone driving a vehicle can expect long waits in ferry lines. In addition to normal camping facilities on the island, the fairgrounds parking lot is opened to RVs during the festival. Many inns and B&B's are booked months in advance, although you may find space at some of the larger places. Call (800) 752-5752 for help in locating accommodations. If you're arriving by boat, the Port of Friday Harbor doesn't accept reservations for this weekend, and they encourage rafting where possible. Latecomers may find they have to anchor offshore in the harbor—but that can be fun too, as the frivolity spills over to the water.

Although the locations of the jazz performances vary from year to year, generally there are one or more sites in downtown Friday Harbor, one at the county fairgrounds (just up the hill on Argyle Avenue), one at Roche Harbor, and one at Jazz Alley, just off Spring Street. Shuttle buses deliver you to all the sites. Some of the ferry runs even have bands entertaining the riders.

Event badges for one, two, or three days serve as admission passes for any of the venues. Purchased them in advance, or at the festival office in downtown Friday Harbor. Contact the Jazz Festival office for information on the upcoming year's festivities.

San Juan County Fair
Friday Harbor Fairgrounds

When: Mid-August

Chicken and rabbit races! Oyster barbecues! Largest zucchini awards! A scarecrow contest! Grab the kids and join the fun at an old-fashioned county fair, done up San Juan style. Traditional events such as livestock judging, riding competitions, and displays of homemade goodies are always interesting, but there's lots more. The island folks really show off their talents in arts, crafts, and performances. You may see a demonstration of basket making, hear a concert on a Native American flute, or a listen to a "storytelling" of life in Alaska. The Sheep to Shawl race is always terrific. Teams race to shear wool from a sheep, card and spin it, and then weave the yarn into a shawl. Quality counts as well as speed.

But the hands-down favorites of all are the chicken and rabbit races. Never did the Kentucky Derby generate such excitement as owners wildly cheer their entries on, and the entrants—well they're usually pretty casual about it all, less concerned about crossing the finish line, and more interested in checking out the other entrants (especially in the case of the rabbits), or trying to figure out what everyone's so excited about.

The fairgrounds is on Argyle Avenue, about five blocks from the waterfront, within easy walking distance. Schedules are printed in the local newspaper, and may be posted on bulletin boards in town. Stop by—you'll remember it forever.

The Pig War Barbecue Jamboree
Friday Harbor Fairgrounds

When: Saturday in mid-June

I doubt the porker that gave up his life, thereby guaranteeing the San Juans a place in history, would appreciate having a barbecue in his honor. Be that as it may, it's a glorious event, and one you won't want to miss if you're in the San Juans the Saturday that it rolls around.

Teams from all over the region compete for "Best Barbecue in the Northwest," as judged by celebrity judges such as Jeff Smith, TV's "Frugal Gourmet," or John Hinterberger, food columnist for the *Seattle Times*. Past entrants have included Lopez Island's Beautiful Butts and Buns, El Porko Loco of Mercer Island, and Pig Al's Chicago Trickynoses.

In addition to some of the best cooking you'll ever taste, this gustatory extravaganza features parades, car exhibits, kids' games, entertainment, music, dancing, and all-round hilarity.

Faim-ous Pig War Museum
620 Guard Street; Friday Harbor, WA 98250; phone – (360) 378-6495 or (360) 378-5581

For a trip back to life on San Juan Island in the mid-1800s, don't miss the Pig War Museum in Friday Harbor. It's the labor of love for long-time San Juan resident, Emelia Bave. The museum commemorates the war that almost happened after an American farmer shot a British pig that had the fatal habit of rooting up his potato patch.

The incident triggered deployment of both British and American forces to San Juan Island with the intent of reinforcing disputed claims of sovereignty over the islands of the San Juan archipelago. The two sides maintained troops on the island for the 13 years that it took to arbitrate the dispute. Over time all hostile intents dissolved as the boredom of camp life led to friendly social exchanges between the American and British detachments, as well as with the citizens of the rough-and-tumble island communities.

In the museum, mannequins placed in period tableaus depict life on San Juan Island before, during, and after "Pig War" times. One grouping shows Indians as they lived before the coming of the settlers. In another, a prostitute plys her wares at a barroom table in Old San Juan Town; written labels describe the scenes and explain their historical context.

How to get there: The Pig War Museum is a large, tan clapboard building at the corner of Guard and Tucker, across the street from the Friday Harbor High School tennis courts. The museum is open Memorial Day through Labor Day from noon to 6:00 P.M. Closed Sundays. Call for information about special tours.

San Juan Historical Museum
405 Price Street; Friday Harbor, WA 98250; phone – (360) 378-3949

In the 1890s pioneer James King grew grain and apples and raised cattle on the outskirts of the fledging town of Friday Harbor. Today his farmhouse and the property around it are a heritage cherished as the San Juan Island Historical Museum. Most of the rooms in the old King farmhouse retain the homey mood of the original dwelling. Furniture and furnishings, all representative of early days on the island, include an old pump organ dating from the 1900s, a huge St. Clair wood range that dominates the kitchen, a beautiful old wooden hutch that protects antique china and crystal, and the earliest sewing machine used in the San Juans.

A museum room is loaded with relics from the island's past: a switchboard from the old San Juan Hotel that permitted the first telephone communications between Friday Harbor and Roche Harbor, a cannon cover from Pig War days, a family bible belonging to an American officer on duty during the Pig War. Photos record the history of old-time island residents.

Old buildings scattered about the grounds hold antique farm equipment. Two historic bells decorate the lawn. One once hung in the tower of the Methodist church (now the Grange Hall); the second was the old Friday Harbor fire bell. It is open 1:00 P.M. to 4:30 P.M., Wednesday through Saturday, May through September; Thursday and Friday in winter.

How to get there: Follow Spring Street southwest from Friday Harbor. Just past the Mullis Road Y turn right on Price Street. The museum is on the left in a short distance.

The Whale Museum

62 First Street North; P.O. Box 945; Friday Harbor, WA 98250;
(360) 378-4710; fax – (360) 378-5790; Whale Hotline (to report sightings)
(800) 562-8832, (Washington), (800) 334-8832 (BC)

Peer eyeball-to-eyeball with a model orca, gaze up and see a humpback whale soaring over your head, duck into a darkened room and listen to the strangely musical underwater whale conversation, or learn the Native American legend of how the killer whale came to be. It's all here at this unique museum in Friday Harbor.

The Whale Museum holds fascinating exhibits of whale skeletons, life-sized models of whales, murals, interpretive displays, Native American legends about whales, and an extensive collection of slides and photographs of the orca pod members. In addition, members of the Whale Museum track and maintain a history of the orca whale pods (or families) that spend time in the Washington and British Columbia waters. Whale research is conducted from a lab at Lime Kiln State Park.

The museum also offers both in-class and field courses, programs, and workshops, on marine mammals, and local ecology and natural history. College credits are offered for some of its field courses in whale biology. As a fund raising effort, its highly successful Orca Adoption Program issues

A model of an orca is suspended overhead at The Whale Museum.

certificates of adoption for individual members of the San Juan orca pods, and provides you with photos and a biography of your adopted whale.

The Whale Museum is open daily; in addition to its displays there are video programs on the orca pods of the San Juans, and a museum store that carries educational toys and games, books, orca identification guides, videos, T-shirts, artwork, and other whale-oriented merchandise.

Wolf Hollow Wildlife Rehabilitation Centre
240 Boyce Road; Friday Harbor, WA 98250; phone – (360) 378-5000

Thanks to the dedicated staff and volunteers at Wolf Hollow, orphaned or injured wild animals have a better chance at life. Located on Boyce Road, between West Valley Road and San Juan Valley Road, the center is a licensed wildlife rehabilitation center, not a zoo; its goal is to return the animals to the wild. The over 400 animals treated yearly include seal pups, otters, deer, eagles, owls, and other birds. Because Wolf Hollow is a wild animal hospital, random visitors are not permitted, and human contact with the animals must be minimized.

Although the center offers educational programs, these folks need your donations (tax deductible) far more than your visit, as the organization receives no government funding. A copy of the organization's newsletter *Wild Times*, is available upon request. Guided visits are scheduled Tuesday, Thursday, and Saturday between 11:00 A.M. and 2:00 P.M.; advance permission is required to attend.

A final note: If you should notice a seal pup on the beach, or a fawn without its mother, and believe it is orphaned or abandoned, *do not touch it*. Most likely Mom is right nearby and will reclaim her offspring once you are gone. There is a stiff fine for handling marine mammals without a permit. Call Wolf Hollow and one of the people there will determine if the animal needs help and take appropriate action.

Boaters in the San Juans often see harbor seals on offshore rocks or near reefs.

San Juan Community Theater

*100 Second Street; Friday Harbor, WA 98250; phone – (360) 378-3211;
box office: (360) 378-3210*

World-acclaimed musicians here in the San Juans? Yes, indeed! The very active San Juan Community Theater attracts celebrated musicians, vocalists, and actors. Even productions by groups such as the Straits of Juan de Fuca (the local theater group) or the local San Juan Singers draw rave reviews. There's also community fun, such as sing-a-longs, local school productions, and programs geared for kids. Check the local newspaper or community bulletin board to see what's going on. You'll find it a perfect break from an old video in the VCR.

ON-ISLAND TRANSPORTATION

Inn at Friday Harbor

410 Spring Street West; Friday Harbor, WA 98250; phone – (360) 378-4000

This company offers car rentals on San Juan Island for guests of the inn or for others who want to have their own transportation on the island.

Island Bicycles

*P.O. Box 1609; 380 Argyle Street; Friday Harbor, WA 98250;
phone – (360) 378-4941; fax – (360) 378-4706*

Leave your car at the Anacortes ferry terminal, enjoy a cheap, no-wait passenger trip to Friday Harbor, then tour San Juan Island by bicycle. Island Bicycles is three blocks from the ferry landing; it rents a complete selection of children's 1-speed, adult 5- and 10-speeds, mountain bikes, bike trailers, and baby strollers by the hour, day, or week. Rates vary by type of bicycle and duration of use; phone reservations are accepted 48 hours in advance. The shop also carries a full line of bicycles for sale, as well as parts, accessories, and repair services.

Island Carriages
P.O. Box 1579; Friday Harbor, WA 98250; phone – (360) 378-3565

Enjoy a slow, quiet, woodland ride in an elegant horse-drawn carriage. Tours may include a picnic lunch or festive bottle of champagne. For a romantic touch, depart from your wedding with panache.

M and W Auto Sales
960 Guard Street; Friday Harbor; WA 98250; phone – (800) 323-6037; or (360) 378-2794

For ferry walk-ons, this company will pick you up at the ferry landing and rent cars or mini-vans for the duration of your stay on San Juan Island.

Practical Rent-a-Car
Friday Harbor Airport; Friday Harbor; phone 293-6750; fax – (360) 378-6577

This franchised car rental agency associated with West Isle Air has vehicles available at Friday Harbor Airport. Call regarding availability and reservations.

San Juan Taxi
P.O. Box 2809, Friday Harbor, WA 98250; phone – (360) 378-3550

San Juan Taxi will pick you up and drop you off at any point on San Juan Island. The drivers can also take you on a personalized tour that includes interesting spots around the island, and provide a knowledgeable narration on the history and features of the sites. In addition to standard taxi service, the company offers a variety of delivery services.

San Juan Tours
P.O. Box 2809; Friday Harbor, WA 98250; phone – (360) 378-8887; fax – (360) 378-2377.

A two-hour bus tour of San Juan Island will take you to Friday Harbor, American Camp (Picket's Redoubt and South Beach), Cattle Point, False Bay, Lime Kiln State Park, and Roche Harbor. The driver is well versed in the history of the island, and provides an on-going narrative along the way.

San Juan Transit, Inc

P.O. Box 2809; Friday Harbor, WA 98250; phone – (360) 378-8887; fax – (360) 378-2377

This company runs a year-round scheduled bus service to major points of interest on San Juan Island. Locations served include Friday Harbor, Lakedale, Roche Harbor, San Juan National Historical Park (both English and American camps), Mitchell Bay, West Side Park, Lime Kiln Point State Park, Cattle Point, Cape San Juan, the golf course, fairgrounds, and the airport. Point-to-point fares run $3 to $4, and round trip fares are $5 to $7. Daily, two-day, and commuter passes are available. Call for latest schedules, routes, and rates.

Susie's Mopeds

Churchill Square; Friday Harbor, WA 98250; phone – (800) 532-0087 or (360) 378-5244

Leave the strenuous pedaling to someone else and enjoy a pleasant two-wheeled tour of San Juan Islands via an easily operated moped. Rent by the hour or by the day from Friday Harbor, just a hop above the ferry landing. A valid driver's license is required.

White Whale Tours

471 Short Lane; Friday Harbor, WA 98250; phone – (360) 378-6130

Tour San Juan Island in style in the White Whale, a classic 1965 Lincoln Continental convertible. Visit all of the historic, scenic, and special places such as Roche Harbor, British and American Camps, the Westcott Bay Oyster Farm, Cattle Point, Giannangelo Herb Farms, and more. Call for reservations and rates.

Zzoomers Scooter and Bike Rentals

85 Front Street; Friday Harbor, WA 98250; phone – (360) 378-8811

Rent bicycles or mopeds by the hour or the day at two locations on San Juan Island, in Friday Harbor, just across from the ferry landing, or at Roche Harbor.

BOAT & KAYAK TOURS, CRUISES & CHARTERS

Adventures Under Sail
P.O. Box 2139; Friday Harbor, WA 98250; phone – (360) 378-8330

Let your sailing dreams become reality aboard the *Martin Eden*, a 50-foot classic sloop sailing out of the Port of Friday Harbor. Captain Rick Hastie and his wife Patti will help you plan a charter just to suit your needs, whether it's just to a quiet cove for lunch or a weekend or longer adventure through the San Juans and Canadian islands. You can even take your turn at the helm to experience the thrill of handling this handsome vessel.

Alaskan Dawn
Spring Street Landing; Friday Harbor, 98250; phone – (360) 378-6773; cell phone 317-8276

Captain Don Ritter offers sightseeing, fishing, and whale watch excursions, as well as custom charters. The 37-foot Uniflite, moored at the Port of Friday Harbor, can accommodate up to six persons. Fishing gear and bait are provided.

Bon Accord Wildlife Charters
P.O. Box 472; Friday Harbor, WA 98250; phone – (360) 378-5921

Berthed in the Port of Friday Harbor Marina at slip M-8, the 30-foot *Bon Accord* can be chartered for one- to six-hour cruises for up to six guests. Have a picnic lunch ashore at one of the marine state parks, go scuba diving, search out orca whales, porpoises, seals, and eagles, or just enjoy the beautiful island scenery. In addition to a being a USCG licensed captain, the skipper is a trained naturalist.

Buffalo Works Charters
1861 A Wold Road; Friday Harbor, WA 98250; phone – (360) 378-4612; cell phone 317-7045

Whatever your marine charter-oriented requirements are, whale watching, salmon fishing, bottom fishing, boat rides, a picnic on a remote island, or marine taxi and delivery service, Buffalo Works can accommodate you. A fifth generation San Juan fisherman will take you on half or full day fishing trips or wildlife tours out of Friday Harbor. All fishing gear is provided.

Cap'n Howard's Sailing Charters

P.O. Box 2993; Friday Harbor, WA 98250; phone – (360) 378-3958
or (360) 378-3987

Charter the 35-foot sailboat Columbia for sighting trips, cruises, whale watching tours, and sailing lessons, as well as overnight lodging while at dock.

Charters Northwest

2 Spring Street; P.O. Box 915; Friday Harbor, WA 98250;
phone – (360) 378-7196; fax – (360) 378-7179; Compuserve: 70761-3434

Three-day and full-week charters on a choice from 23 power or sail yachts from 30 to 55 feet are available year-round. In addition to USCG safety equipment, all boats come with a dinghy and oars, two anchors, navigational equipment and electronics, fully-equipped galley, and miscellaneous recreational equipment. You can also rent towels, bedding, fishing gear, and outboard engines may also be rented. Lower off-season rates are available.

Crystal Seas Kayaking, Inc.

P.O. Box 3135; Friday Harbor, WA 98250; phone – (360) 378-7899

Sea kayaking is one of the most thrilling ways to observe the wildlife of the San Juans—whales, porpoises, seals, and eagles in their natural habitat. Tours are scheduled for mid-morning and mid-afternoon, and usually last about five hours. To assure a personal touch, groups are limited to six persons. No experience is needed; each tour includes a kayaking and safety lesson, and all kayaks are extremely stable two-person models. Custom tours can be arranged.

Emerald Seas Diving and Marine Center

2 Spring Street; P.O. Box 476; Friday Harbor, WA 98250;
phone – (360) 378-2772; fax – (360) 378-5549

This full-service diving center has three custom dive boats for charter, the 30-foot Emerald Diver, the 36-foot *Jersey Girl*, and the 37-foot *Malia Kai*. The center also rents, sells, and services scuba and snorkeling equipment, kayak equipment and accessories, and refills scuba tanks. Diving instruction is offered for all levels from beginning to professional. In addition, the company provides commercial diving services such as hull inspection and maintenance, search and recovery, salvage diving, and dive support.

Fairweather Water Taxi and Tours
P.O. Box 4341, Roche Harbor, WA 98250; phone – (360) 378-8029

A high-speed hydrofoil transports up to six people from wherever they are to wherever they want to go in the San Juans, Gulf Islands, or other Canadian ports. You can go to one of the marine state park islands for a weekend of camping and hiking, or captain Lisa Lamb will take you on a nature or whale watch tour. The schedule and length of the tour is tailored to your desires. The charge is by the hour, not by the person, so for a group of people this can be less expensive than other charters.

Grey Eagle Charters
P.O. Box 2627, Friday Harbor, WA 98250; phone – (360) 378-6403

This is one of the few boat charters in the San Juans that welcomes children. Come aboard a 24-foot American Eagle, with room for six, for daily whale watch tours, seasonal salmon fishing, or inter-island transportation. All bait and tackle is provided.

San Juan Excursions
Friday Harbor, WA 98250; phone – (800) 806-4253 or (360) 378-6636

This cruise company, run by Lynn Danaher, a skipper with several years experience in Alaska, has two boats. The *Malia Kai*, which can accommodate up to 29 passengers, offers travel through San Juan Channel for whale watching, wildlife cruises, dive charters, water taxi service, and private charters. It departs daily from Friday Harbor for Roche Harbor Resort, and Islander Lopez Marina Resort on Lopez Island. The second vessel, the 60-foot yacht *High Spirits* is capable of taking 49 passengers. Both boats offer trips with a choice of lunch and dinner cruises, catered by Papa Joe's, to observe islands, eagles, and whales. Tours aboard the *High Spirits* are narrated by a local naturalist. Lunch cruises depart Friday Harbor at 11:30 A.M. and return at 2:45 P.M. Dinner cruises depart at 6:30 P.M. and return at 9:30 P.M.

San Juan Boat Rentals and Tours
P.O. Box 2281; Friday Harbor, WA 98250;
phone – (800) 232-6722 or (360) 378-3499

The 30-foot cruiser *Blackfish*, based at the lower end of Spring Street in the Port of Friday Harbor docks, carries between 10 and 15 passengers for daily three- to four-hour whale watch trips during the summer. The experienced captain and on-board naturalist are quite successful in finding orcas. In addition to providing excellent photo opportunities of whales, the vessel is equipped with an underwater hydrophone so you can listen to their conversations as well. Children under six are permitted aboard only on private charter trips. Reservations are recommended.

The firm also offers a fleet of outboard equipped, 16-foot C-Dories available for rent for local fishing trips. Each boat can carry four adults, and is equipped with all USCG-required safety equipment. Fishing gear may also be rented.

San Juan Kayak Expeditions, Inc.
P.O. Box 2041; Friday Harbor, WA 98250; phone – (360) 378-4436

Two- to five-day kayak trips leave Friday Harbor to weave through the wondrous waters of the San Juan and Gulf Islands, passing through a myriad of islets en route, with opportunities for close range observation of orca whales, seals, porpoises, bald eagles, and a variety of other marine mammals and birds. No previous kayaking experience is necessary. The kayaks are extremely stable, and before the journey starts you'll receive instruction on paddling and safe handling techniques. Camping gear and meals are provided.

San Juan Safaris
P.O. Box 2749; Friday Harbor, WA, 98250; phone – (800) 451-8910, ext. 258 or (360) 378-2155

Operating out of Roche Harbor, San Juan Safaris conducts kayak treks and whale watch cruises that have easy access to the western "wild side" of San Juan Island. Guides take daily kayak parties of up to 10 persons each on three-hour nature tour, in the morning, afternoon, and evening. No prior kayaking experience is necessary; shakedown training is conducted in protected Roche Harbor, then the tours paddle past nature preserve islands in San Juan channel.

For those who prefer to be a little farther out of the water when observing nature, a daily three-hour cruise from Roche Harbor is offered aboard the 50-foot *Saratoga Passage,* which carries up to 50 passengers.

Sea Quest Kayak Expeditions
Zoetic Research, P.O. Box 2424; Friday Harbor, WA 98250;
phone – (360) 378-5767

Sea Quest Expeditions is a non-profit organization dedicated to environmental education, scientific investigation, and financial support of environmental and conservation causes. Trips are led by experienced sea kayak guides and accompanied by environmental instructors; the trip is a learning experience, not just a "look at the whales and seals" tour. No previous kayaking experience is required; brief safety and paddling instructions are provided.

Between May and October the group offers one-day tours to seek out orca whales, porpoises, seals, bald eagles, and other marine birds and mammals. Two- and three-day tours are also offered, with overnight stays at marine state parks. Special five-day research expeditions observing and photographing minke whales are part of an ongoing 10-year study of these mammals.

Trophy Charters
P.O. Box 2444; Friday Harbor, WA; phone – (360) 378-2110;
cell phone – 317-8210

Either power boat or sailboat charters are available from the main dock at the Port of Friday Harbor Marina. A fully-equipped 30-foot Trophy Sport Fisher makes skippered fishing trips, wildlife cruises, inter-island water taxi trips, or scenic tours of the San Juans, Gulf Islands, and Saanich Inlet. Minimum party size is three; six is the maximum for overnight accommodations. Longer cruises or custom charters are available by advance arrangement.

On the sailing side, a 34-foot boat with seven berths, a full galley, head, and shower is available for either bareboat or skippered charters from half to a full week. You can also schedule sailing instruction or sunset cruises.

Water Ouzel Charters
Spieden Island; cell phone – (360) 378-7587

Operating out of Roche Harbor, this charter service offers half-day, day, and two-day trips for up to six persons. Trips of a day or less are generally nature tours seeking whales, porpoises, seals, and eagles; lunch stops can be made at San Juan Islands towns or resorts. Custom charters for fishing or crabbing can be scheduled; all fishing gear, crab pots, and bait are provided. On two-day trips accommodations will be arranged at the port of your choice.

Western Prince Cruises

P.O. Box 418; Friday Harbor, WA 98250; phone – (800) 757-ORCA, (360) 378-5315

Based at the main dock in the Port of Friday Harbor, the 46-foot Western Prince offers twice-weekly, four-hour wild life cruises in the San Juans for up to 33 guests. Although orca whales are the star attractions, your boat may also be escorted by Dall's porpoises playfully diving under the hull and through the bow wave. Watch for eagles soaring above and harbor seals basking on rocky islets. An on-board naturalist will help make your trip more meaningful. The cruise price includes a free admission to the Friday Harbor Whale Museum, and reservations are strongly advised. Children under four and pets are not permitted aboard.

The boat is available for charter on non-scheduled cruise days, as is another 24-foot boat that can accommodate up to six persons.

Whale Museum Kayak Tours

62 First Street N; Friday Harbor, WA 98250; phone – (360) 378-4710

From June 1 to September 15 the Whale Museum sponsors daily four- to five-hour kayak nature tours. No prior kayaking experience is required, but the minimum age is 13. Outdoor Odysseys, of Seattle, provides the kayaks and brief training in their use.

The trips, which leave Friday Harbor in mid-morning, are accompanied by guides who are museum educators; there is one naturalist/guide for every six to nine persons on the tour. Sign up for the kayak trips at the Whale Museum, and bring a lunch to eat at a mid-day rest stop.

Wind 'n Sails Charters

P.O. Box 337; Friday Harbor, WA 98250; phone – (800) 752-4121 or (360) 378-5343

Avoid wasting precious charter time getting to and from the San Juans; instead start in their heart at Friday Harbor. A fleet of nearly new sailboats, ranging from 31 to 51 feet, is available either for bareboat or skippered charters. Charter boats by the day for scenic trips and sailing lessons, or by the week for extended cruises. The company offers a provisioning service, or groceries, supplies, and liquor are a short walk away.

MARINAS & LAUNCH RAMPS

Port of Friday Harbor
P.O. Box 889; Friday Harbor, WA 98250; phone – (360) 378-2688;
fax – (360) 378-6114; VHF channel 66A

This large port facility boasts several hundred permanent moorage slips, 130 guest slips with power and water, a fuel dock (gas, diesel, propane), pumpout station, restrooms, and showers. A US customs office is in a building near the port offices, and during summer months a customs booth is staffed on the breakwater near the seaplane float. There are several yacht charter companies and cruise boats operating from the main port float, and during the summer you can purchase fresh fish, crab, and shrimp, either raw or cooked, at "a fish deli" on the float. The port dock is just two blocks from downtown Friday Harbor, and its many stores, gift shops, and restaurants.

Roche Harbor Resort
P.O. Box 4001; Roche Harbor, WA 98250; phone – (360) 378-2155

The resort and marina are on the northwest corner of San Juan Island on the harbor of the same name. Two large guest floats, with power and water, line the waterfront below the resort, and 52 mooring buoys are laced offshore in the harbor. A water taxi waits on call to transport guests moored on buoys ashore. US Customs maintains an office on the dock during summer months. The marina facilities include a fuel dock (gas, diesel, kerosene, butane, propane, outboard mix, alcohol), restrooms, showers, and laundry. A general store at the head of the dock carries groceries, hardware, and drugs. The resort hotel, restaurants, and a lounge are among the shoreside amenities. See also Lodging.

Shipyard Cove Marina
740 Turn Point Road; Friday Harbor, WA 98250; phone – (360) 378-5101;
fax – (360) 378-3855

Shipyard Cove Marina offers permanent moorage only, no transient or guest moorage. However, there is an excellent one-lane concrete launch ramp, usable at all tide levels, available to the public. A fee is charged each

Snug Harbor Resort has moorage and small boat rentals.

way, put-in or take-out. Contact the moorage manager to find where to park trailers; don't leave them in the parking lot in front of the marina. To reach the marina, take First Street east from downtown Friday Harbor. In a few blocks First Street changes to Harrison Street for ¼ mile, then becomes Turn Point Road. Reach the road into the marina from Turn Point Road in another ½ mile.

Snug Harbor Resort

2371 Mitchell Bay Road; Friday Harbor, WA 98250; phone – (360) 378-4762

Located on Mitchell Bay on the west side of San Juan Island, the marina has 24 guest slips with power and water, a fuel dock (gas and premix), restrooms, showers, and laundry facilities. Haulouts of boats up to 26 feet and dry storage are available. The marina store stocks dive air, groceries, and bait and tackle, and offers small boat rentals. *See also* Lodging.

Jackson Beach Boat Launch Ramp

To find this public ramp, take Argyle Avenue south out of Friday Harbor, and in ¾ mile turn east onto Pear Point Road. When the road reaches a sand and gravel operation, turn downhill on Jackson Beach Road. A single-lane concrete ramp with adjoining boarding float dips into North Bay at the tip of this narrow spit.

West Side Park Boat Launch Ramp

This county park is on West Valley Road on the west shore of San Juan Island. It holds a single-lane public launch ramp that drops into Smallpox Bay, a small cove off Haro Strait.

PARKS, CAMPGROUNDS & CAMPS

Lime Kiln State Park

6158 Lighthouse Road; Friday Harbor, WA 98250; phone – (360) 378-2044

What are all those people doing standing on the bluff, staring out to sea with faces fused to binoculars? It could be that they're trying to spot whales offshore at this, the world's only park dedicated to watching for these magnificent creatures. You may spot orca, minke, and pilot whales, or their smaller relatives, harbor and Dall's porpoises. The major salmon runs heading for Frazer River spawning grounds pass through Haro Strait, along the west side of San Juan Island, attracting whales that feed on them.

A trail leads from the parking lot to the rocky shoreline south of Lime Kiln lighthouse; here interpretive panels describe the various marine mammals that might be seen. Picnic tables scattered along the beach make comfortable spots to wait for them to appear. Because their appearance is not choreographed, sighting them requires patience, time, and sharp eyes to spot a dorsal fin breaking through offshore waters. We recommend binoculars and cameras with telephoto lenses.

How to get there: Take Roche Harbor Road west from Friday Harbor 9 miles to West Valley Road. Turn south on it, and in 3¼ miles turn west on Mitchell Bay Road. In just under a mile, turn south on West Side Road, and follow it 6½ miles to the park.

Displays at Lime Kiln State Park describe the whales you may be able to see offshore.

San Juan Island National Historical Park
P.O. Box 429; Friday Harbor, WA 98250; office: 125 Spring Street;
phone – (360) 378-2240

The US and Great Britain at war? Over a pig? Yes, it nearly happened here. A visit to this fascinating national park will take you back to the mid-1800s when it all happened. For a full description, see the introduction to San Juan Island, which describes the war.

Begin your introduction to the park in Friday Harbor at the main office at 125 Spring Street. Here you'll find brochures and information about the park and a small display of historical artifacts. Mannequins are dressed in typical uniforms worn by soldiers on both sides of the conflict. Then it's on to English Camp, on Garrison Bay, where three of the original buildings have been restored. One has historical displays and a video program describing events that almost lead to the Pig War.

The most colorful building is the blockhouse, built on the beach to protect the marines (from marauding Indians, not Americans). It was later used as a guard house for miscreant troops. The formal flower garden that once graced grounds has been replanted. Interpretive displays are found above the

The blockhouse at English Camp in San Juan Island National Historical Park dates from the Pig War.

camp, where the officers' quarters were built on hillside terraces. A trail from the park leads to a small cemetery at the base of Young Hill that holds the graves of British marines who died accidentally during the long occupation.

American Camp shows historical displays in the park headquarters building; interpretive trails lead past two restored buildings and the Hudson's Bay Company farm site. Other hiking trails lead to great views from the top of 290-foot Mount Finlayson, and along several secluded lagoons on the Griffin Bay shoreline. If you've brought your picnic lunch along, there are tables with views at South Beach, fronting on the Strait of Juan de Fuca, and on the more protected shore of Griffin Bay.

How to get there: English Camp; take Roche Harbor Road west from Friday Harbor, and in 8½ miles turn south on West Valley Road. Follow it for 1½ miles to the park. American Camp; From Friday Harbor take Argyle Avenue south, then west, to Cattle Point Road. Continue south on Cattle Point Road to the park. The total distance is about 5 miles.

Lakedale Campground

2627 Roche Harbor Road; Friday Harbor, WA 98250; phone – (360) 378-2350

Facilities: 73 standard campsites, 15 waterfront sites, 10 bicycle campsites, 19 RV sites, 6 group campsites, 3 tent cabins, showers, groceries, bait and tackle, ice, wood, camping equipment, boat rentals (paddleboat, rowboat, canoe)

Here's a terrific private campground that rivals any state park. In fact, it was voted number one campground in the Northwest by *The Bicycle Paper*. You'll find it along the south side of Roche Harbor Road, just west of Egg Lake Road.

The park's acreage includes three shallow, trout- and bass-stocked lakes. Campsites are scattered about a grassy area or nestled in the woods between the lakes. A few are right on the lakeshore. Swimming is permitted in two roped off areas of the lakes, although there are no lifeguards. Because the lakes are on private property, you don't need a fishing license to try for pond fish, but Lakedale does charge a daily fee.

The general store at the entrance to the campground stocks the usual groceries, bait, ice, and wood for sale, and in addition rents fishing tackle, tents, stoves, lanterns, and sleeping bags.

How to get there: Take Roche Harbor Road west from Friday Harbor for 5 miles; just beyond Egg Lake Road, turn into the campground.

Pedal Inn Bicycle Park

1300 False Bay Drive; Friday Harbor, WA 98250; phone – (360) 378-3049

Facilities: *25 campsites, picnic tables, fire brazier, store, restrooms, showers, laundromat*

Pedal Inn is the only campground exclusively for bicyclists on San Juan Island. Its location on the south end of the island, near the maximum distance on the island from the ferry, makes it a perfect midway camp spot for a two or more day bicycle tour of the island. The campground sites scattered in a wooded setting around a good-sized pond. A small general store near the entrance, which is open in summer, has a limited supply of basics: canned soups, pasta, cereal, health bars, cheese, butter, milk, and eggs.

How to get there: *From the east:* From Friday Harbor take Argyle Avenue south for 1 mile, then turn west on Argyle Road. In ¼ mile, at a T-intersection, this road heads south, and in ¾ miles becomes Cattle Point Road. Continue south on Cattle Point Road for 2¼ miles to False Bay Road, turn west on it, and in 1 mile reach the campground.

From the west: Take Roche Harbor Road west from Friday Harbor, and in 9 miles turn south on West Valley Road. In 3 miles turn west on Mitchell Bay Road, and in 1 mile head south on West Side Road. Follow it south for 5¾ miles, past San Juan County Park and Lime Kiln State Park, where it becomes Bailer Hill Road. Continue east for 4¼ miles, then turn south on False Bay Road. Follow it 2½ miles to the campground.

Snug Harbor Marina Resort

2371 Mitchell Bay Road; Friday Harbor, WA 98250; phone – (360) 378-4762

Facilities: *16 RV and tent sites, picnic tables, fire grates, Sani-cans, groceries, boat launch ramp*

Snug Harbor Resort is one of only two places on the west side of San Juan Island that offers campsites. Its big advantage over the other, San Juan County Park, is that the resort also rents small boats for fishing trips in nearby Haro Strait. There are four RV sites in a gravel strip along the beach just inside the gate to the resort. A narrow dirt road twists up the steep wooded hillside above the beach past 12 tent campsites, each with a tight vehicle pullout and a gravel tent platform. Sani-cans and a water tap are centrally located among the sites. See also Lodging.

How to get there: Take Roche Harbor Road west from Friday Harbor, and in 9 miles turn south on West Valley Road. In 3 miles turn west on Mitchell Bay Road. Follow it west for 2 miles to the resort.

Town and Country Mobile Home Park

595 Tucker Avenue North; Friday Harbor, WA 98250; phone 3789-4717

Facilities: 26 tent and RV sites with hookups, restrooms, showers, laundromat.

Although the majority of the facilities at Town and Country are dedicated to permanent mobile home sites, the facility has about 26 transient sites along its perimeter. All have full hookups. Half-a-dozen tent sites are scattered among the trees along one side of the park. Restrooms, showers, and laundry facilities are available in the transient RV area. Because the bulk of the patrons are long-term guests, it is advisable to call in find out if there is space available.

How to get there: From Spring Street in Friday Harbor, turn northwest on Second Street, which becomes Guard Street in about four blocks. Continue on Guard for two blocks to Tucker Avenue. Head north on Tucker, then northwest on Roche Harbor Road for two blocks to the RV park.

West Side Park

380 Westside Road North; Friday Harbor, WA 98250; phone – (360) 378-2992

Facilities: 11 campsites, picnic tables, fireplaces, restrooms, groceries, boat launch ramp, group camp

Broad grassy slopes dotted with trees reach down to the edge of Haro Strait, with cross-channel views of Victoria, BC. This is the site of San Juan County Park, on the west side of San Juan Island, the only public camping facility on the island. Natural attractions, plus a boat launch ramp on Smallpox Bay and outstanding scuba diving along the shoreline and nearby Low Island, make it a popular (and crowded) site during the summer.

The San Juan County park holds only 18 campsites, plus a small group camp. A small building containing the campground office and a store that sells groceries and fishing supplies sits above the launch ramp.

How to get there: Take Roche Harbor Road west from Friday Harbor 9 miles to West Valley Road. Turn south on it, and in 3¼ miles turn west on Mitchell Bay Road. In just under a mile, turn south on West Side Road, and follow it 3¾ miles to the park.

A quiet anchorage at Patos Island Marine State Park

The Other Islands

THE FERRY-SERVED ISLANDS are well described in earlier chapters, but what about all those remaining islands? They still represent a fair amount of real estate. People cruising by admire their beauty and "ooh" and "ahh" at the snug little waterfront cabins and gracious bluff-top homes that dot their edges. These other islands fall into one of several categories: some are private residential sites; some are privately held, but are either too small or lacking in potable water to support a home; a number are marine state parks; a few choice ecological locations (entire islets as well as sections of larger islands) are held by the Nature Conservancy as preserves; and finally, the remaining number of little isles and inhospitable rocks and reefs are part of the 84 sites of the San Juan National Wildlife Refuge.

THE RESIDENTIAL ISLANDS

Nearly all the non-ferry islands that have private residences utilize private air strips to allow residents access; some private homes have docks, and a few, such as Waldron and Decatur, have private community docks. None of these docks are open for use to the general public.

Two of the larger residential islands, Blakely and Decatur, flank either side of Thatcher Pass, where the ferry usually enters the islands. Both are strictly residential islands, although Blakely, which is nearly as large as Shaw Island, is owned by a small corporation that wisely sells only a few lots a year to ensure controlled growth on the fragile site. Obstruction, another island that holds a few homes, lies north of Blakely and south of Orcas Island, in the middle of Peavine Pass and Obstruction Pass.

The ferry passes a number of small islands that lie on Harney Channel and Wasp Passage, in the heart of the islands, giving passengers *"Better Homes and Gardens"* views of picturesque property. Some islands are dotted with homes, while others host only a summer cottage each. Additional islets passed by the ferry are lacking in water or are too small to support even a cabin. These include Frost, Crane, Cliff, McConnell, Coon, Low, Bell, Reef, and Double.

Waldron, a large, mostly-flat island immediately west of Orcas Island, is a study in self-sufficiency. On the island, all power for electricity, radio-telephones, appliances, and furnaces comes from private gasoline genera-tors or propane tanks; water comes from private wells. Neighbors rely on neighbors in the tightly knit community.

The list of privately owned islands lying scattered about the edges of the San Juans includes Trump and Center islands in Lopez Sound; Canoe in Upright Channel off the southeast side of Shaw; Pearl and Henry at the

Great blue herons are one of the many marine birds you may see in the San Juan Islands.

entrance to Roche Harbor; and at the northeast corner Speiden, Satellite, Johns, and Stuart (with the exception of Stuart Island Marine State Park). Other privately owned islands include Brown (so obvious it's almost overlooked, facing on Friday Harbor) and Barnes, lying on the north side of the San Juans, parallel to Clark Island Marine State Park. Of the multitude of islands at the south end of Lopez Island, Long, Charles, and Iceberg islands are the only ones that are not designated as wildlife refuges.

A small marina and general store on the north side of Blakely Island is the only commercial development on any of these islands.

Blakely Island General Store and Marina
Blakely Island, WA 98222; phone 375-6121; fax 375-6141

A dredged channel behind a rock breakwater leads to a small marina basin that offers both permanent and guest moorages with power and water. Restrooms, showers, and laundry facilities are available. The long fuel dock (gas and diesel) fronting on Peavine Pass leads ashore to a general store that carries groceries, ice, beer, wine, and fishing and marine supplies. Customers and guests may use a picnic shelter and barbecue in the broad lawn adjacent the store.

NATURE CONSERVANCY HOLDINGS

In an entire set of islands that seem like a nature preserve in themselves, it's to be expected that forces are hard at work keeping it that way. The Nature Conservancy, one of the forerunners in the quest for environmental preservation, is a non-profit, nationwide environmental organization that uses contributed funds to purchase property of unique ecological value. They hold the land under a protected status until appropriate government agencies can muster the public support and financial resources to assure its long-term preservation. Several San Juan Island properties have been saved from private or commercial development by this organization.

The westernmost of the Wasp Islands, Yellow Island, was purchased by the Nature Conservancy in 1980 to preserve its exotic and endangered collection of plants and wildflowers. No formal boat access is provided, although visitors may land small boats ashore, providing that they restrict their travel to designated trails and don't endanger the island's unique plant and animal biosystems. Kayakers often stop on the long sandy spits on either end of the island for brief visits.

On the west side of Waldron Island, on Cowlitz Bay, a section of beach, meadow, and marshland property of unique biological value has been purchased by the Nature Conservancy. The property is open to the public, but access is discouraged to preserve the ecosystems for which it was acquired.

Sentinel Island, in Speiden Channel on the south side of Speiden Island, is a miniature version of its larger nearby companion. The Nature Conservancy purchased the island to preserve its nesting areas for bald eagles and other marine birds. Landing on the island is permitted only with prior permission from the Nature Conservancy.

PARKS, CAMPGROUNDS & CAMPS

Marine Adventure Camp (Island Institute)
P.O. Box 661; Vashon Island, WA 98070;
phone – (206) 463-6722 (463-ORCA)

Age: *Adults, families (children 6 to 8 half price, under 5 free), and youth programs*

Fees: *4-day mini-camp $375, 7-day camp $695 to $895, 11 day Project ORCA $1100. Day trips are available too*

Facilities: *Safari-style tents (cottages are available for an additional fee), main lodge, swimming pool, Jacuzzi*

Activities: *Marine science activities, whale watching, wildlife watching, hiking, sea kayaking, tidepooling, snorkeling*

Spieden, a long, slender island lying north of San Juan Island, has a unique history. During the 1970s a group attempted to create a game farm here, with exotic animals that big game hunters could pay to shoot. The idea failed, and since that time there have been various plans to create a resort on the land; however none succeeded. Since 1991 the Island Institute has offered the uninhabited 550-acre island for perhaps its finest use—a basecamp for marine adventure activities.

The Island Institute offers active learning adventures for youths, families, and adults in a natural setting. Guests stay in four- to six-person safari-style tents on platforms, or in private cottages with kitchens. All equipment is provided, other than your sleeping bag. Family-style meals are served in the dining room of the modern main lodge, where there are also hot showers, swimming pool, and Jacuzzi.

Marine science specialists take you whale watching, hiking, beach exploring, kayaking, snorkeling, and cruising among the outer islands aboard the Institute's comfortable vessel. Sessions range from one to eleven days, and you can sign up for multiple sessions; academic credit is available with some. Custom-designed programs are also available for groups. If you're looking for a greater understanding of the island environment, the Institute's staff will make sure you have a terrific time while doing it.

THE MARINE STATE PARKS

For many boaters the jewels of the San Juans are the numerous islands designated as marine state parks for recreational boating, hiking, and camping. Over the years the Washington State Parks Commission has acquired part or all of several islands in the San Juans. They are accessible only by boat, canoe, kayak, or float plane.

All (with the exception of Posey and Doe islands) have mooring buoys available for public use in their more protected bays or coves. These buoys, which are on a first-come, first-serve basis, are set in 20 to 50 feet of water at mean low tide. Some parks also have docks with floats for overnight moorage and easy access to land; however, many floats are removed in winter months to prevent storm damage. Fees are charged for moorage on buoys or floats, and any one boat's stay is limited to 36 consecutive hours.

Campsites at marine state parks are termed "primitive," which means that they consist of only a picnic table and fire ring, and a flat space to pitch a tent. Sanitary facilities are either pit, vault, or self-composting toilets. Only a few of the islands have water, and even on those the source may dry up, especially toward the end of a long dry summer. Park budgets have been pared to the bone in recent years, and most marine state parks have no garbage pick up or disposal. *Please take all garbage away with you*—and perhaps pick up any left by other less considerate visitors.

Following are brief descriptions of the parks that have developed boating and camping facilities. In addition, there are numerous undeveloped islands and strips of public access shoreland owned by state parks or the Department of Natural Resources. All are more fully described and mapped in our companion volume, *The San Juan Islands, Afoot and Afloat.* The developed park islands are listed alphabetically on the following pages.

Sandstone eroded in fantastic patterns is typical of the northern San Juan Islands.

Blind Island Marine State Park

Contact: *Lime Kiln State Park; 6158 Lighthouse Road; Friday Harbor, WA 98250; (360) 378-2044*
Facilities: *4 primitive camping/picnic sites, vault toilet, 4 mooring buoys, no water or garbage collection*

Blind Island is tiny, nearly bald, picnic platform that protects a series of mooring buoys along its south side in Blind Bay. Decorated only with tufts of grass and scruffy brush, the main attraction of this islet is its incomparable view of boat and ferry traffic plying busy Harney Channel.

How to get there: The island sits in the middle of the entrance to Blind Bay, just west of the Shaw Island ferry landing.

Clark Island Marine State Park

*Contact: Lime Kiln State Park; 6158 Lighthouse Road; Friday Harbor, WA
98250; (360) 378-2044*
*Facilities: 8 primitive campsites, 2 picnic sites, 2 fire rings, vault toilets, 9 mooring
buoys, no water or garbage collection*

Erase the visiting boats riding on buoys, or at anchor offshore, and you
almost expect to see Robinson Crusoe stroll across the broad beach to greet
you. Campsites lie hidden in a mid-island strip of trees and brush, The north
end of this long narrow island is cliff-rimmed at waterline, and covered with
a dense barely penetrable jungle inland. As a result, all recreational use (except scuba diving) is confined to the lobe at the south end of the island.
Here the center strip of woods is flanked by wide, open beaches, sandy on
the west, and cobble on the east. The Sisters, a collection of rocks, reefs,
and islets, are but a stone's throw away from a series of minuscule rocky
coves on the south end of the island. The cacophony of marine birds on
these rocks announces that they are part of the San Juan National Wildlife
Refuge.

How to get there: The island is located in the Strait of Georgia, 2¼
nautical miles north of the northeast tip of Orcas Island.

Doe Island Marine State Park

*Contact: Lime Kiln State Park; 6158 Lighthouse Road; Friday Harbor, WA
98250; (360) 378-2044*
*Facilities: 5 primitive campsites, vault toilets, dock with float, no water or garbage
collection*

This tiny, flower garden island enjoys beautiful sunrise views across
Rosario Strait to the rugged 800-foot face of Eagle Cliff on Cypress Island.
A dock and float that lie in the small protected bay between Doe Island and
Orcas Island are reserved for short term landing during daylight hours; because no mooring buoys are provided, boats planning overnight stays must
be able to be beached or ride at anchor. Primitive campsites on headlands
between its minuscule coves are favorite overnight spots for kayakers, many
who come from nearby Doe Bay Resort. A rough trail along the shoreline
overlooks nearby rocks crowded with flocks of marine birds.

How to get there: The island lies in Rosario Strait off the southeast side
of Orcas Island, ¼ nautical miles south of Doe Bay, or 2¼ nautical miles
north of Obstruction Pass.

James Island Marine State Park

Contact: Lime Kiln State Park; 6158 Lighthouse Road; Friday Harbor, WA 98250; (360) 378-2044
Facilities: 13 primitive campsites, picnic shelter, latrines, dock with float, 5 mooring buoys, 1½ miles of trail, no water or garbage collection.

This dogbone-shaped island, just off the main ferry route from Anacortes, is the easternmost doorkeeper to the San Juans. It is often used as a first stop by boaters heading into the islands, or for a wistful pause on the way home before acknowledging that an idyllic vacation is over. Steep cliffy headlands are broken by only three small coves. The cove on the west side of the island holds a dock and float; the side-by-side pair of bays on the east side share five mooring buoys. Shoreside facilities are spartan.

How to get there: The island lies in Rosario Strait off the east side of Decatur Island, south of Thatcher Pass.

Jones Island Marine State Park

Contact: Lime Kiln State Park; 6158 Lighthouse Road; Friday Harbor, WA 98250; (360) 378-2044
Facilities: 21 primitive camping/picnic sites, water, dock and float, 7 mooring buoys, hiking trails

Jones Island is the hub of boating activity in the heart of the San Juans. It is only a short cruise away from marinas and shoreside amenities at Friday Harbor or Deer Harbor, and is within an easy paddle of the myriad rock pile cluster of the Wasp Islands. Three small coves indent the shoreline of the wooded island. The larger, on the north, has a dock, float, and mooring buoys. Two smaller side-by-side coves on the south side of the island on San Juan Channel have only mooring buoys. A hiking trail across the island links the two camping areas. The park campsites were recently restored, and the park reopened after year-long cleanup of damage from a devastating windstorm that leveled huge trees all across the island.

How to get there: The island lies off the southwest tip of Orcas Island, on the west side of Spring Passage, at the junction of San Juan and President channels.

Matia Island Marine State Park

*Contact: Lime Kiln State Park; 6158 Lighthouse Road; Friday Harbor, WA
98250; (360) 378-2044*
*Facilities: 6 primitive campsites, 7 picnic tables, composting toilet, dock and float,
2 mooring buoys, 1 mile of hiking trail, no water or garbage collection*

Although most of Matia Island is a part of the San Juan Island National
Wildlife Refuge, five acres on its west tip is managed as a marine state park.
Snug little Rolfe Cove is surrounded by wave-cut sandstone cliffs on the
island itself, and a small steep-walled islet on the north side of the cove. The
gravel beach at the head of the cove holds a dock and float that access the
park's small camping and picnic area.

A crude trail seeks out other coves on the south and west end of the
island, and a long shallow indentation in its southeast shoreline. A
brushwhacked path along the top of the carved sandstone cliffs that frame
this cove leads to the east end of the island, where Mount Baker looms above
bird-refuge Puffin Island, just offshore.

How to get there: The island lies in the Strait of Georgia, 2¾ nautical
miles north of Orcas Island. The park is on the west end of the island above
Rolfe Cove.

Patos Island Marine State Park

*Contact: Lime Kiln State Park; 6158 Lighthouse Road; Friday Harbor, WA
98250; (360) 378-2044*
*Facilities: 4 primitive campsites, vault toilets, 2 mooring buoys, 1¼ miles of hik-
ing trail, no water or garbage collection*

The northernmost outpost of the San Juan Islands is Patos Island, sitting on the US/Canada border at the junction of Boundary Pass and the
Strait of Georgia. The one-time lighthouse reserve retains the Patos Island
light at the tip of Alden Point that marks the change of boat course required
to head north to Vancouver, BC. The remainder of the island is now a state
park. A primitive campground at the head of Active Cove is the starting
point of a trail around the perimeter of the island that offers access to a mile-
long hike of the island's incomparable north shore beaches.

How to get there: The island lies at the confluence of Boundary Pass
and the Strait of Georgia, 4¼ nautical miles north of Orcas Island.

Posey Island Marine State Park

Contact: Lime Kiln State Park; 6158 Lighthouse Road; Friday Harbor, WA 98250; (360) 378-2044
Facilities: 2 picnic tables, vault toilet, no water or garbage collection

This tiny, low islet barely emerges from the shallow waters over a rocky shelf just east of the entrance to Roche Harbor. The island sees few visitors, because it can be reached only by kayaks or small boats that can be beached, and its amenities are limited to a pair of weathered picnic tables. In late spring the profusion of wildflowers that intertwine with the cover of low grass and brush justify a visit for nature photography.

How to get there: The island lies in Spieden Channel, off the north side of Pearl Island at the entrance to Roche Harbor.

Stuart Island Marine State Park

Contact: Lime Kiln State Park; 6158 Lighthouse Road; Friday Harbor, WA 98250; (360) 378-2044
Facilities: 19 primitive campsites, picnic units, vault toilets, 22 mooring buoys, 2 docks with floats, 2 offshore floats, marine pumpout station, water, hiking trails

The prow of Stuart Island thrusts northwest toward the US/Canada border that runs down the centers of adjoining Haro Strait and Boundary Pass. The arrowhead-shaped island has a deep, narrow shaft-slot cut into it from the southeast by Reid Harbor, and a chip in its north side formed by companion Prevost Harbor. The state park spans the high, narrow, rocky spine between the two harbors, and laps around the broad low beach at the head of Reid. Each bay has a mooring buoys and a dock with a float; Reid also has a pair of mid-harbor floats tethered to pilings.

Campsites are scattered across the top of the narrow strip of land between the two harbors or are hidden in dense growth at the head of Reid Harbor. Hiking trails beyond the park boundary lead to island roads that can be used to reach more park-managed property at Turn Point, on the northwest tip of the island. The Coast Guard lighthouse site here presents dramatic overviews of heavy-vessel traffic in Haro Strait and Boundary Pass, and smaller craft fishing the tide rips around the point. The unmanned light is automated.

How to get there: The park straddles a narrow isthmus between Stuart Island's Prevost and Reid harbors, and wraps around the head of the latter.

Sucia Island Marine State Park

*Contact: Lime Kiln State Park; 6158 Lighthouse Road; Friday Harbor, WA
98250; (360) 378-2044*
*Facilities: 55 primitive campsites, group camps, picnic shelters, composting toilets,
docks with floats, 50 mooring buoys, 6½ miles of hiking trails, artificial underwater reef*

Among a treasure-chest of jewels, Sucia Island is the prize. Its unique
horseshoe shape gives it half-a-dozen coves offering the finest anchorages,
protected in any weather. In addition, its shape provides nearly 14 miles of
shoreline for beachcombing, picnicking, wading, sun bathing, clam digging,
or sand castle building.

Each of the bays holds numerous mooring buoys, as well as space for
additional anchorages. Fossil Bay, on the south side of the island, offers docks
and floats. Moorages range from elbow-to-elbow mooring buoys in Fossil
Bay to four tide-swept buoys in lonesome little Ewing Cove; one buoy lies

*At Sucia Island Marine State Park this rock has been eroded by wind and
water action into a mushroom shape.*

over the hulls of three sunken vessels that form an artificial reef—a prime scuba diving site.

Most of the coves are framed by fancifully shaped sandstone rocks and cliffs, sculpted and pocked by wave erosion. Trails on the long wooded fingers of the island lead to open bluffs overlooking its many picturesque bays.

How to get there: The island lies at the confluence of the Strait of Georgia and President Channel, 2½ nautical miles north of Orcas Island.

Turn Island Marine State Park

Contact: Lime Kiln State Park; 6158 Lighthouse Road; Friday Harbor, WA 98250; (360) 378-2044

Facilities: 10 primitive campsites, vault toilets, 3 mooring buoys, 3 miles of trail, no water or garbage collection

Although it is part of the San Juan Islands National Wildlife Refuge, tacit recognition of its popularity as a recreation site has led to joint management of Turn Island by the Fish and Wildlife Service and the State Parks and Recreation Commission. Primitive camping and picnicking is restricted to the low southwest corner of the island; the remainder retains its wild status and nature, except for a narrow trail around the island perimeter. The narrow channel that separates Turn from San Juan Island can be easily crossed by kayak or hand-carried boat from a public access off Turn Point Road, two miles east of Friday Harbor.

How to get there: The island lies in San Juan Channel, off the east tip of San Juan Island, 2 nautical miles east of Friday Harbor.

WILDLIFE REFUGE ISLANDS

The San Juan National Wildlife Refuge consists of 84 rocks, reefs, and islets in the San Juan Archipelago, ranging from ¼ to 140 acres in size. These are nesting and breeding grounds for sea birds such as glaucous-winged gulls, Brant's and pelagic cormorants, tufted puffins, pigeon guillemots, rhinoceros auklets, and black oystercatchers. An estimated 200 other species of birds visit the islands annually. You may sight harbor seals, porpoises, and whales in the surrounding waters, or hauled out on sunny rocks. Bald eagles use larger grassy islands for feeding areas; a few weasels and river otters are also found there.

Although this fascinating collection of marine mammals and birds is wonderful to watch and photograph, it is unlawful to go ashore on any refuge property, or to disturb the wildlife.

For Additional Information

None of the islands in the San Juans maintain a formal Chamber of Commerce office; however a phone call or letter to any of the following sources will connect you with someone who can answer your questions or point you in the right direction.

San Juan Islands Visitor Information Service
P.O. Box 65; Lopez Island, 98261; (360) 468-3663

Lopez Island Chamber of Commerce
P.O. Box 65; Lopez Island, WA 98261; (360) 468-3663

Orcas Island Chamber of Commerce
P.O. Box 252; Eastsound, WA 98245; (360) 376-2273

San Juan Island Chamber of Commerce
P.O. Box 98; Friday Harbor, WA 98250; (360) 378-5240

A phone tree offers a wealth of information about San Juan Island. By working your way through the directory you can find current information about such things as accommodations, restaurants, and activities. To reach it, call (360) 378-TREE (378-8733).

───────────●───────────

For more information on parks:

San Juan County Parks and Recreation
Friday Harbor, WA 98250; (360) 378-4953

Washington State Parks and Recreation Commission
7150 Cleanwater Lane, KY-11; Olympia, WA 98504; 753-2027

───────────●───────────

Red Tide Hotline – (800) 562-5632

Whale Hotline – (800) 562-8832

For the convenience of getting information via the Internet, the following businesses have provided their e-mail or web addresses:

Aleck Bay Inn
e-mail – abi@pacificrim.net

Bed and Breakfast Association of San Juan Island
web – http://www.pacificrim.net/~bydesign/bb.html

Brisa Charters, Ltd.
e-mail – pikenw@olympus.net

Friday's Historical Inn
web – http://www.fhsji.com/~fridays

Grand Yachts Northwest
e-mail – gynw@pacificrim.net;
web – http:/www.marinenetwork.com/.www.html

Hunter Bay House
e-mail – SWIFTINN@aol.com

The Inn at Swifts Bay
e-mail – SWIFTINN@aol.com

Panacea Bed and Breakfast
web – http://www.fhsji.com/~fridays

Shearwater Adventures, Inc.
e-mail – Paddlenw@aol.com; web – http://www.pacificrim.net/~kayak

Tower House Bed and Breakfast
e-mail – 71157.1441@compuserve.com;
web – http://ourworld.com/homepages/Joe_Luma

WindSong Bed and Breakfast
e-mail – windsong@pacificrim.net;
web – http://www.pacficws.com/orcas/windsong.html

The authors of this book, Marge and Ted Mueller, can be contacted at:
e-mail – GrMouse@aol.com

1999 LODGING UPDATES

Since the date this book was published there have been significant additions to lodging information. Many facilities now have web sites and can be contacted by e-mail. In addition, new facilities have opened, names have changed, and a few have closed. Following are changes or additions as of early 1999.

An asterisk (*) indicates a change or addition to a facility described in this book. All other changes are new lodgings that will be described in detail in this book's next edition.

If you have information that should be included in the next edition, please contact the authors by e-mail at margeted@aol.com or at the publisher's address listed in the front of this book

LOPEZ ISLAND

Aleck Bay Inn*
E-mail: abi@pacificrim.net; *web site:* www.pacificrim.net/~abi/abihome.html

Blue Fjord Cabins*
Phone: 888-633-0401

Edenwild Inn*
Fax: 360-468-4080; *e-mail:* edenwildinn@msn.com; *web site:* www.edenwildinn.com

FenWold Cottage and Gardens
Route 2, Box 3290, Lopez Island, WA 98261
Phone: 360-468-3062

Fisherman Bay Guest House
P.O. Box 6, 2612 Fisherman Bay Road, Lopez Island, WA 98261
Phone: 360-468-2884; *fax:* 360-468-2884; *e-mail:* bythebay@rockisland.com;
    web site: www.rockisland.com/~ralphndoris/fbguest.html

Inn at Swifts Bay*
856 Port Stanley Road, Box 3402, Lopez Island, WA 98261
E-mail: inn@swiftsbay.com; *web site:* www.swiftsbay.com

Lopez Farm Cottages*
Phone: 800-440-3556; *fax:* 360-468-3966

Lopez Islander Marina and Lodge*
*Name change: formerly **The Islander Lopez Marina Resort***

MacKaye Harbor Inn*
Fax: 360-468-2393; *e-mail:* mckay@pacificrim.net; *web site:* www.pacificrim.net/~mckay

Milagra Guest House
Phone: 360-468-4800

ORCAS ISLAND

The Anchorage Inn
Route 1, Box 45A, Eastsound, WA 98245
*Phone: 360-376-8288; **web site:** www.oldtroutinn.com/anchorageinn*

Black Berry Beach House
Phone: 360-376-2845

Bartwood Lodge*
Web site: www.ohwy.com/wa/b/bartwood.html

Bayside Waterfront Cottage
Star Route, Box 131, Olga, WA 98279
*Phone: 360-376-4330; **fax:** 360-376-6516; **e-mail:** jenelson@pacificrim.net;*
*   **web site:** www.pacificrim.net/~jenelson/cottage.html*

Bayview Cabin
Phone: 360-376-5901

Beach Haven Resort*
Fax: 360-376-2288

The Beach House
Eastsound, WA 98245
Phone: 360-376-6720

Buck Bay Farm B & B*
*Phone: 888-422-2825; **web site:** www.rockisland.com/~paperjam/Buck/BuckBay.html*

Buckhorn Farm Bungalow
Route 2, Box 115, Eastsound, WA 98245
*Phone: 360-376-2298; **e-mail:** buckhorn@orcasnet.com;*
*   **web site:** www.orcasisland.com/buckhorn*

Cabins-on-the-Point
Route 1, Box 70, Eastsound, WA 98245
*Phone: 360-376-4114; **web site:** www.islandcabins.com/point*

Cascade Harbor Inn*
HC One, Box 195, Eastsound, WA 98245
*Phone: 800-201-2120; **web site:** www.pacificws.com/cascade*

Cherie Lindholm Real Estate*
*Phone: 360-376-2204; **web site:** lindholm-realestate.com*

Chestnut Hill Inn*
*Fax: 360-376-5283; **e-mail:** chestnut@pacificrim.net; **web site:** www.chestnuthillinn.com*

Deer Harbor Resort*
*Phone: 888-376-4480; **e-mail:** resortinfo@deerharbor.com; **web site:** www.deerharbor.com*

Doe Bay Village Resort*
P.O. Box 437, Olga, WA 98279
***Phone:** 360-376-2291;* ***e-mail:** doebay@pacificrim.net;* ***web site:** www.orcasisle.com/doebay*

Double Mountain B & B*
***E-mail:** dblmtnbb@pacificrim.net;*
   ***web site:** www.rockisland.com/~paperjam/dblmtn/DM.html*

Eastsound Landmark Inn (formerly Landmark Inn)*
***E-mail:** landmark@pacificrim.net;* ***web site:** www.pacificrim.net/~landmark*

Foxglove Cottage
***Phone:** 360-376-4300*

Garden House
***Phone:** 360-376-4549*

Hazlewood B & B*
***Phone:** 888-**Phone:** 360-6300;* ***e-mail:** hazelwood@thesanjuans.com;*
   ***web site:** www.thesanjuans.com/hazelwood*

Heartwood House
P.O. Box 1480, Eastsound, WA 98245
***Phone:** 360-317-8220;* ***fax:** 360-376-5053;* ***e-mail:** gretchen@thesanjuans.com;*
   ***web site:** www.heartwoodconcepts.com*

Highlands House
Route 1, Box 70, Eastsound, WA 98245
***Phone:** 360-376-4114;* ***web site:** www.islandcabins.com/highlands*

Hollyhock Inn
Route 1, Box 53, Eastsound, WA 98245
***Phone:** 360-376-3745*

Kangaroo House*
***Phone:** 888-371-2175;* ***fax:** 360-376-3604;* ***e-mail:** kangaroo@thesanjuans.com;*
   ***web site:** www.pacificws.com/kangaroo*

Kingfish Inn
Crow Valley Road, Eastsound, WA 98245
***Phone:** 360-376-8882*

Lingerlonger Lodge
***Phone:** 360-376-3622;* ***e-mail:** surrender@thesanjuans.com*

Madrona House
***Phone:** 360-376-6319*

Morning by the Sea
***Phone:** 360-376-5300*

Meadowlark Guest House and Antiques
Olga, WA 98279
Phone: *360-376-3224*

Northshore Cottages*
Web site: *www.northshore4kiss.com*

Old Trout Inn*
Phone: *360-376-8282;* **web site:** *www.pacificws.com/oldtroutinn*

Orcas Hotel*
Fax: *360-376-4399*

Otters Pond B & B
6 Pond Road, P.O. Box 1540, Eastsound, WA 98245
Phone: *360-376-8844; 888-893-9680;* **fax:** *360-376-8847;* **web site:** *www.otterspond.com*

Outlook Inn*
Phone: *888-688-5665;* **web site:** *www.outlook-inn.com*

Palmer's Chart House
P.O. Box 51, Deer Harbor, WA 98243
Phone: *360-376-4231*

The Place at Cayou Cove (formerly Olympic Lodge)*
P.O. Box 361, Deer Harbor, WA 98243
Phone/Fax: *360-376-3199; 888-596-7222;* **e-mail:** *stay@cayoucove.com;*
   web site: *www.cayoucove.com*

Rosario Resort*
E-mail: *info@rosarioresort.com;* **web site:** *www.rosario-resort.com*

Sandcastle Guesthouse
Route 2, Box 1023-A, Eastsound, WA 98245
Phone: *360-376-2337;* **web site:** *www.rockisland.com/~ppicone*

Sand Dollar B & B*
P.O. Box 152, Olga, WA 98279

Small Island Farm & Inn (formerly Joy's Inn)
Fax: *360-376-4292;* **e-mail:** *smallisland@sanjuanweb.com*

Smuggler's Villa Resort*
Phone: *800-488-2097;* **e-mail:** *smuggler@pacificrim.com;* **web site:** *www.smuggler.com*

Spring Bay Inn*
Web site: *www.springbayinn.com*

Swannies
Route 1, Box 97G, Eastsound, WA 98245
Phone: *360-376-5686*

Tranquility Cottage
Phone: 360-376-2951

Truffle House B & B
Phone: 360-376-2766

Turtleback Farm Inn*
Fax: 360-376-5329; *web site:* www.turtlebackinn.com

West Beach Resort*
Phone: 877-937-8224; *e-mail:* vacation@westbeachresort.com;
    web site: www.westbeachresort.com

West Sound Cottages B & B*
Route 1, Box 71G, Eastsound, WA 98245
Phone: 360-376-5537; 800-641-2041

Windsong B & B*
Fax: 360-376-4453; *web site:* www.pacificws.com/windsong

Wonder O' the Wind
Phone: 360-376-4263

SAN JUAN ISLAND

Arbutus Lodge
1827 Westside Road N, Friday Harbor, 98250
Phone: 360-378-8840; 888-434-8840; *fax:* 360-378-8846;
    e-mail: arbutus@rockisland.com; *web site:* www.karuna.com/arbutus

Argyle House*
Phone: 800-624-3459; *e-mail:* bearli@rockisland.com;
    web site: www.pacificws.com/sj/argyle.html

Bay View B & B
2119 Cattle Point Road, Friday Harbor, WA 98250

Beaverton Valley Farmhouse B & B
3580 Beaverton Valley Road, Friday Harbor, WA 98250
Phone: 360-378-3276; *fax:* 360-378-7714

Blair House*
Phone: 800-899-3030; *fax:* 360-378-3735; *e-mail:* bobp2@webty.net;
    web site: www.karuna.com/blair

Bluebird Cottage
180 Web Street, P.O. Box 1099, Friday Harbor, WA 98250
Phone: 360-378-8488; *fax:* 360-378-8496; *e-mail:* bluebird@interisland.net;
    web site: interisland.net/bluebird

Discovery Inn (formerly Island Lodge at Friday Harbor)*
Phone: 360-378-2000; 888-999-4753; *e-mail:* d-inn@discovery-inn.com;
  web site: www.discovery-inn.com

Dreams on an Island
685 Spring Street, #143, Friday Harbor, WA 98250
Phone: 360-378-9624; *web site:* www.interisland.net/yona

Duffy House B & B*
E-mail: duffyhouse@rockisland.com

Friday Harbor House*
E-mail: fhhouse@rockisland.com; *web site:* www.karuna.com/fhhouse

Friday's Historical Inn*
E-mail: inn@friday-harbor.com; *web site:* www.friday-harbor.com/lodging.html

Gaia's Grace
P.O. Box 898, Friday Harbor, WA 98250
Phone: 360-378-3732; *web site:* www.rockisland.com/~gaiaz

Halverson House B & B
1165 Halverson Road. Friday Harbor, WA 98250
Phone: 360-378-2707; 888-238-4187; *fax:* 360-378-1693;
  e-mail: johnpatten@interisland.net; *web site:* www.karuna.com/halverson

Harbor House
1660 Wold Road, Friday Harbor, WA 98250
Phone: 800-550-3936; *web site:* www.karuna.com/harbor-house

Harrison House Suites*
Fax: 360-378-2270; *e-mail:* hhsuites@rockisland.com;
  web site: www.rockisland.com/~hhsuites

Highland Inn
P.O. Box 135, Friday Harbor, WA 98250
Phone: 360-378-9450; *fax:* 360-378-1693; *e-mail:* helen@highlandinn.com;
  web site: www.highlandinn.com

Hillside House*
E-mail: hillside@rockisland.com; *web site:* www.hillsidehouse. com

The Inns at Friday Harbor*
*Formerly **The Inn at Friday Harbor** and **The Inn at Friday Harbor Suites***
680 Spring Street, Friday Harbor, WA 98250
Phone: 360-378-3031; 800-752-5752; *fax:* 360-378-4228;
  e-mail: vonda@interisland.net; *web site:* www.pacificrim.net/~bydesign/inn.html

Jensen Bay B & B*
Web site: www.karuna.com/jensenbay

Lakedale Campground*
Phone: 800-617-2267
Fax: 360-378-3355; *e-mail:* lakedale@lakedale.com; *web site:* www.lakedale.com

The Little House on Sunshine Alley
245 Sunshine Alley, Friday Harbor, WA 98250
Phone: 360-378-3553

Long House B & B
2387 Mitchell Bay Rd, Friday Harbor, WA 98250
Phone: 360-378-2568 or 425-821-9695; *e-mail:* longhouse@rockisland.com;
   web site: www.halcyon.com//tonder/longhouse.html

Mariella Inn*
Phone: 800-700-7668; *e-mail:* mariella@rockisland.com; *web site:* www.mariella.com

Mar Vista Resort*
E-mail: richard@rockisland.com

The Meadows B & B*
E-mail: dodieburr7@rockisland.com; *web site:* www.pacificrim.net/~bydesign/
   meadpage.html

Moon & Sixpence*
Phone: 360-378-4138; *e-mail:* moon6p@rockisland.com;
   web site: www.rockisland.com/~moon6p/inn

Oak Ridge
1901 Cattle Point Road, PO Box 2083, Friday Harbor, WA 98250
Phone: 360-378-6184; *e-mail:* oakridge@rockisland.com;
   web site: www.san-juan-island.net/oakridge

Olde English Roses*
No longer a B & B

Olympic Lights B & B*
Web site: www.san-juan.net/olympiclights

The Orca Inn
770 Mullis Street, Friday Harbor, WA 98250
Phone: 360-378-2724; 888-541-6722; fax *Phone:* 360-378-7997

Panacea B & B*
595 Park Street, P.O. Box to 2983, Friday Harbor, WA 98250
Phone: 360-387-3757; 800-639-2762; *fax:* 360-378-8543;
   web site: www.karuna.com/panacea

Paradise Vacation Rentals
2959 San Juan Valley Road, Friday Harbor, WA 98250
Phone: 360-378-7259; *fax:* 360-378-7085; *e-mail:* paradise@rockisland.com;
   web site: www.san-juan.net/paradise

Roche Harbor Resort*
P.O. Box 4001, Roche Harbor, 98250
E-mail: roche@roche-harbor.com; *web site:* www.roche-harbor.com

San Juan Inn*
Fax: 360-378-6437; *e-mail:* tucker@rockisland.com; *web site:* www.san-juan.net/sjinn

Snug Harbor Resort*
Phone: 360-378-4792; *fax:* 360-378-8859; *e-mail:* sneakaway@snugresort.com; *web site:* www.snugresort.com

States Inn*
Web site: www.san-juan.net/statesinn

Tower House B & B*
Phone: 800-858-4276; *fax:* 360-378-5464; *e-mail:* chris@san-juan-island.com; *web site:* www.san-juan-island.com

Trumpeter Inn B & B*
Fax: 360-378-8235; *e-mail:* swan@rockisland.com; *web site:* www.karuna.com/trumpeter

Tucker House B & B*
E-mail: tucker@rockisland.com; *web site:* www.san-juan.net/tucker

Water's Edge Guest House
P.O. Box 2913, Friday Harbor, WA 98250
Phone: 360-378-8893; *fax:* 360-378-5803; *web site:* www.san-juan.net/waters-edge

Westwinds B & B*
No longer a B & B

Westwinds Harmony Cottage
685 Spring Street, Suite 107, Friday Harbor, WA 98250
Phone: 888-548-5662, 808-322-5103; *web site:* www.karuna.com/westwinds

Wharfside B & B - Aboard the Jacquelyn*
Port of Friday Harbor, Slip K-13
Fax: 360-378-6437; *web site:* www.san-juan-island.net/wharfside

Whitehawk B & B
2251 Bailer Hill Road, Friday Harbor, WA 98250

Wildwood Manor B & B
3021 Roche Harbor Road, P.O. Box 2255, Roche Harbor, WA 98250
Phone: 360-378-3447; *e-mail:* wildwdmanor@rockisland.com; *web site:* www.rockisland.com/~wildwdmanor

---

ADDITIONAL INFORMATION

San Juan Islands Visitor Information Service*
Web site: www.guidetosanjuans.com

Alphabetical Index

ABOUT THE AUTHORS

MARGE AND TED MUELLER are outdoor enthusiasts and environmentalists who have explored Washington State for nearly 40 years. Ted has taught classes on cruising in Northwest waters, and both Marge and Ted have instructed mountain climbing through the University of Washington. They are members of The Mountaineers, The Nature Conservancy, the Sierra Club, and the Washington Water Trails Association. They are the authors of ten guide books to the Pacific Northwest.